PRUDENS FUTURI

THE US ARMY WAR COLLEGE

1901 - 1967

"Not to promote war, but to preserve peace by intelligent and adequate preparation to repel aggression, this institution is founded."

Elihu Root

1903

Elihu Root

Secretary of War 1899 - 1904

Secretary of State 1905 - 1909

PRUDENS FUTURI

The US Army War College
1901-1967

by

George S. Pappas
COLONEL, ARTILLERY

The Alumni Association
of the
US Army War College
Carlisle Barracks, Pennsylvania

Library of Congress Catalog Number: 67-30552

1ST PRINTING 1967
2ND PRINTING 1970
3RD PRINTING 1973
4TH PRINTING 1976
5TH PRINTING 1979
6TH PRINTING 1980

Printed in U. S. A. by the Walsworth Publishing Company.

LIST OF ILLUSTRATIONS

All photographs are used through the courtesy of the US Army.

TABLE OF CONTENTS

Preface

WHEN General Salet asked me to prepare a Golden Anniversary history of the US Army War College, I had little idea of the work which lay ahead. Although I assumed that what was required was a revision and updating of previous histories, I soon learned—to my shock and dismay—that no single history of the War College had ever been prepared. What was required was, not a revision, but an entirely original work.

My research efforts, fortunately, have been aided by the assistance of the able US Army War College Library staff. Miss Joyce Eakin has been especially helpful in searching for materials in the Library files and by making a preliminary screening of many documents. Miss Carmen Clark and Mrs. Nellie E. Mitchell, whose tenure on the Library staff covers the modern era, used their personal knowledge of events of the last fifteen years to steer me to references I might otherwise have missed. Miss Mathilde Y. Carter also helped me locate source materials.

I should be much remiss if I did not pay special thanks to Mr. George Stansfield, Director of the National War College Library. Mr. Stansfield provided me with his own unpublished manuscript covering the early years of the Army War College. Far more important, however, was his guidance to original source documents in the National Archives and in the National War College Library. This not only saved me much time, it also led me to search out other documents in the Army Library and in the Army War College Library. Mr. Stansfield made available to me the complete facilities of National War College Library, assisted me in locating and interviewing civilian staff members of the pre-World War II War College, and reviewed my manuscript. His advice and assistance has been invaluable. I thank him for the many hours he has spent with me on this history.

Preface

Other individuals have contributed to this project in many ways. Brigadier General Milton O. Boone, USA, Retired, provided photographs and documents. Nils C. Noaker and Richard Nale copied many old documents and photographs for my use. Mrs. Donna H. Traxler of the US Army Photographic Library spent hours with me searching her files for photographs. Colonels John McKinney, Edward Saxby, James Ursano, and William Webb and Lieutenant Colonels Thomas Ayers and William Gordon reviewed the manuscript and made many valuable suggestions. Mrs. Toni Caserta assisted in preparation of the final draft. Mr. Daniel Bates designed the cover and dust jacket. Mr. William Monteith, representative of the Walsworth Publishing Company, provided technical assistance. Mrs. Betty Burkholder and Mrs. Darlene Stringfellow digested my draft manuscript and typed it in final form.

The Editorial Board—Colonels Paul L. Bogen, William J. Gallagher, and James G. Holland, Jr.,—reviewed the manuscript carefully. Their many comments and suggestions did much to improve my efforts. Colonel Holland has been particularly helpful during my entire study. His counsel and advice and intimate knowledge of the present day College—based upon his time as a student and two assignments to the faculty—have been invaluable. However, without the full backing of the Commandant, Major General Eugene A. Salet, and the Deputy Commandant, Brigadier General Robert B. Smith, my task would have been much more difficult. I have had their complete support in every way as well as complete academic freedom in my writing, this in the best tradition of the US Army War College.

Throughout my work, I have kept before me the statement made by General Omar Bradley in his foreword to Forrest C. Pogue's biography of General of the Army George C. Marshall:

> An historian or biographer cannot properly evaluate the trials of leadership by ignoring the personal factor, any more than he can write history by ignoring the fact that controversies did exist.

I have tried to include the personal factors behind the actual events in the history of the War College wherever possible—and I must

Preface

admit that this has been difficult at times for a piece of correspondence or an official document often belies and even disguises the personalities of the individuals involved, the reasons for, and the efforts resulting in the final piece of paper and its contents. Nor have I made any effort to ignore the controversies which have existed, for from these arguments and discussions have come a better understanding of the actions taken to develop the US Army War College into the institution it is today.

My work has been made easier by my family: Pat, Reid and Meg. The many hours I have devoted to this work over the past months could not have been taken from them without their warm understanding, complete tolerance—and even, at times, sympathy!

Carlisle Barracks, Pennsylvania   GEORGE S. PAPPAS
August 1967   Colonel, Artillery

Foreword

P ERIODICALLY, every institution—military or civilian, academic or governmental—must pause to take a detailed look at its past with a view toward improvement in the future. The United States Army War College looks at its past in this book, not content with what has been accomplished, but intent upon contined and progressive development in the years to come.

In 1964, shortly after I became the Commandant of the Army War College, I directed that a complete and comprehensive self-analysis be conducted to determine "Where are we? Where are we going? Where should we be going? How do we get there?" This analysis, the US Army War College '70 Study, has brought many evolutionary changes to the curriculum and the methodology of the War College. However, the study did not delve deeply into the earlier periods of the College. Realizing full well the lessons to be learned from an analytical study of the past, I consider this history to be another outgrowth of the Army War College '70 Study. It is fitting that this book represents the work of a member of our fiftieth anniversary Class of 1966, Colonel George S. Pappas.

More than sixty-five years have passed since Elihu Root established the Army War College, years which have seen the United States involved in two major wars as well as the armed conflicts in Korea and Vietnam. The back seat of isolationism, protected and guaranteed by the ocean barriers, has been replaced by the position of a leader of the free world. Willing or not, the United States today must face the realities, the problems, and the responsibilities inherent in world leadership.

The role of the military forces, particularly that of the Army, has changed as the position of the United States has changed in the world environment. The doctrines and the military strategies of the Army

Foreword

before 1941 were developed and constructed upon the American tradition of a small standing Army with the backup of the citizen soldier—the National Guard and the Organized Reserve. The rapid and dynamic developments of the post-World War II years, however, emphasized that this traditional concept had been outdated by the advances of science and technology, by the figurative shrinking of our ocean barriers, by the potential threats to the entire free world. These changes in the world environment forced the United States to alter its traditional military posture and to maintain relatively large forces in being, both at home and abroad.

These changes brought realization, also, that the professional soldier no longer could restrict his professional development to the study of arms and armaments, of tactics and techniques. Whereas his grandfather could be content with mastering the use of his individual weapons, learning to ride a horse, and controlling small conventional forces, today's military professional, while first and always a soldier, must also be a diplomat, an economist, a scientist, a historian, and a lawyer. The complexity of the military arts and sciences has expanded into many other disciplines and professions.

With the Army, this War College necessarily has changed to keep pace with the times. The course of study no longer is devoted only to the mechanical techniques of being a good staff officer; the curriculum is not restricted to military studies. Instead, the Army War College today presents to its students an intellectual challenge. The course includes study of the international and national environments in which a national strategy is developed as the essential background for a rational analysis of the supporting military programs which are the central focus of the curriculum.

I believe that this book will be of interest to every graduate of this War College, for it is a definitive description of the way the College has fulfilled its mission of preparing selected officers for the highest positions of command. For the young officer about to enter the College this book will provide a background of what his predecessors encountered and what he may expect.

The Army War College does not necessarily train an officer only for the assignment he goes to immediately after graduation; if this

Foreword

were the sole benefit of an officer's year at this institution, this College would not have completely achieved its assigned task. The professional military men who study here are educated to take their places as the national leaders of our Armed Forces five years, ten years hence. That the Army War College has been successful in the past can be seen in its roster of graduates: Bliss and Lejeune; Pershing and Bullard; Bradley and Eisenhower; Vandenberg and Halsey; Clark and Cates. In keeping with its motto "Prudens Futuri," the United States Army War College will continue to serve the Army and the Nation "Provident for the Future."

1 August 1967

EUGENE A. SALET
Major General, United States Army
Commandant

PRUDENS FUTURI

THE US ARMY WAR COLLEGE

1901 - 1967

PRUDENS FUTURI

IN researching the history of the US Army War College, one becomes almost immediately aware of the close relationship of the War College and the Army General Staff. The background, establishment, and earlier years of the War College are so closely interwoven with the developments leading to the establishment of the General Staff that it becomes virtually impossible to separate completely any history of either institution.

The early reform advocates — Halleck and Upton, for example — argued for reorganization of the Army with one breath; and, in the next, the necessity for postgraduate education of Army officers. Not until relatively late in the nineteenth century did other Army essayists separate their recommended reforms into staff organization and educational necessities.

Actual establishment of the Army War College by Secretary of War Elihu Root was, in itself, used to provide the Army with a General Staff rather than an educational institution. Only after Congressional and military opposition had been overcome and the General Staff authorized by Act of Congress were the first steps taken to make the War College more educational in nature. In fact, traces of General Staff characteristics were not completely eliminated from the College until the institution reopened following World War I.

In each of the three distinct periods of its history, the Army War College has reflected both the requirements of the Army and the general attitudes of the Nation and its people. Initially, the College emphasized staff procedures in training its student officers, with the primary objective of providing qualified officers for the War Department General Staff. As the reservoir of War College educated and experienced officers increased and more nearly met the needs of the

1

Army, the stress in the College curriculum turned toward overall professional requirements for the career officer.

When it appeared almost inevitable that the United States would become involved in World War I, the emphasis in the War College course of instruction turned to preparedness, mobilization, and cooperation with industry. Because the Army's small size and widely scattered units made large-scale maneuvers almost impossible, map maneuvers and wargames were developed to a high degree. The testing in World War I of the theories, concepts, and procedures taught by the War College proved the worth of the institution.

The lack of preparedness of the armed services and the Nation as a whole at the time of its entry into the war taught the Army a lesson. Planning became almost an obsession. Although the initial emphasis during the second period of the War College was preparing officers to serve with the "G" type General Staff, the curricular stress was soon changed to the overall importance of command and the necessity for planning. The focus, however, was on the Pacific rather than Europe until the late 1930's when the actions of Germany and Italy made quite apparent the new developing threat. Much time and effort were devoted to the study of mobilization of both manpower and industry and their relationship to preparedness and planning. Wargaming was again stressed as a substitute for large-scale maneuvers. The theme or keystone of the War College education of this second period may well be termed "preparation for war in time of peace," for such received prime emphasis from 1919 to 1940.

From its second testing in combat, the War College—and the armed services—learned another lesson: joint effort of all of the armed services is essential to defeat the common enemy. Again, as had happened following World War I, the lesson became almost an obsession for the Army. In giving full and wholehearted support to the joint concept, the Army completely inactivated its War College. Not until it became clearly apparent that similarly complete support was not forthcoming from the Navy and the Air Force and the shortage of Army senior service school graduates approached a critical point did the Army take steps to reinstitute its own War College.

The third and modern period of the War College began with the

Nation again in conflict, this time in Korea. Initially, the needs of the Army dictated emphasis of the War College curriculum to prepare officers almost entirely for military command and staff duty. The reactivated War College, therefore, concentrated its initial efforts on preparation for military duties. After the Korean truce had been signed, the Army found itself facing requirements never before encountered in its history. Not even the painful period of reconstruction following the Civil War had levied such widely diversified and strenuous requirements upon military officers.

In contrast to the period from 1918 to 1941 when peace brought a return to military normalcy, the 1950's brought new demands, new duties, and new technologies to the Army. Cold war, military government, occupation, foreign aid, nuclear weapons, massive deterrence, missiles, peace-keeping operations — all of these had an effect upon the Army, its doctrine, its organization, and its activities. All of these were, in turn, reflected by the War College curriculum. Emphasis moved from the stress on military duties to increased study of national and international affairs.

Not until the United States entered another conflict did the stress return to the military requirements, but the pendulum did not swing back to stress of military duties alone. Instead, a more sophisticated approach appeared: the study of the military aspects of national and international affairs with emphasis on the role of the Army in development and implementation of national security policy.

Although the primary mission of the Army War College has always been preparation of its officer students for command and high level staff duty, related requirements have been assigned the College. In the period between the two wars, for example, the War College included the Historical Division of the War Department as an integral part of its organization. In the modern era, the Institute of Advanced Studies of the US Army Combat Developments Command, which evolved from a War College faculty group, still contributes to the College in many ways. There have been other similar side-efforts and satellite activities throughout the history of the College. In this work, however, their activities and functions have not been discussed

in detail unless they were a part of or contributed directly to the
academic curriculum.

Fifty-one classes have been graduated from the Army War College. The names of some of the officer-students have since become
well known because of their later accomplishments; among them
there were many others, however, who never became known beyond
military circles. Each graduate filled his own place in the service of
his country.

Ralph Waldo Emerson said "The true test of civilization is, not
the census, nor the size of cities, nor the crops — no, but the kind of
man the country turns out." [1] The same may be said of an academic
institution: the true measure of its worth is the type of man it turns
out. This history is not intended to chronicle the accomplishments of
the graduates of the Army War College, for such would be indeed a
history of the United States Army since 1901. This is, instead, an
analysis of how the War College accomplished its assigned mission
of preparing selected officers for high command and staff duty.

II

Halleck and Upton: The Prelude

TO the student of today's Army, it is inconceivable that any military organization could have existed without its staff structure and without its educational system. Nevertheless, the Army of the United States developed for nearly 125 years, fought five major wars, explored and assisted in the settlement of the western territories, pacified the Indian tribes, mapped the coasts and rivers, and survived countless organizations and reorganizations — all without the benefit of a general staff and with a relatively elementary system of education for its personnel.

In the years immediately following the Civil War, the Army was a well-trained, hardened organization composed almost entirely of battle-tested veterans. Primarily occupied with the Indian conflicts, the Army was widely dispersed. Seldom, if ever, were more than a few companies or troops stationed at the same post.

Headquarters of the Army, headed by its Commanding General and the War Department staff under the Secretary of War, provided both support for and guidance to the units in the field. Often the Commanding General and the Secretary of War were at odds with each other. Like Winfield Scott before him, General W. T. Sherman became so disgusted with his relationships with the Secretary of War that he moved his headquarters to St. Louis. Much of the difficulty occurred because the bureau chiefs (The Adjutant General, The Inspector General, The Judge Advocate General, The Quartermaster General, The Commissary General of Subsistence, The Surgeon General, The Paymaster General, The Chief of Ordnance, The Chief of Engineers, and The Chief Signal Officer) regarded themselves as subject not to the orders of the Commanding General but directly and only to the orders of the Secretary of War. This resulted in a general

5

commanding the Army with his chief staff officers reporting to someone else.[1]   Sherman maintained that if the commanding general did not command the staff departments, he did not fully control the operations of troops of the line.

Another problem arising from this complex command and staff structure was the inability to fix the responsibility for the professional education of the officers and men of the Regular Army. Although Secretary of War John Calhoun had established the Artillery School of Practice at Fortress Monroe in 1824, it had been closed during the Jacksonian antimilitary resurgence in 1835. It was not until 1866 that advanced schools again were initiated with the establishment of the Engineer School at Willet's Point, New York. This was followed by reactivation of the Artillery School in 1868 and the organization, by General Sherman, of the School of Application for Infantry and Cavalry at Fort Leavenworth in 1881. In 1887, Congress authorized creation of a practical school for cavalry and light artillery at Fort Riley, Kansas. The Army Medical School began to train physicians for military careers in 1893. The responsibility for conduct of these institutions, however, as well as the determination of their curricula, was distributed among the arms and services concerned. Little coordination and even less centralized control could be exercised under the existing staff and command structure.

This situation was further complicated and intensified by the permanent detail of officers to the various bureaus of the War Department staff. Consequently, these officers entrenched themselves in the Washington scene, made their own contacts among the civilian members of the executive branch of the Government, and maintained close relationships with the members of the Congress. The Secretary of War could expect to receive the views of each bureau chief instead of the advice of a single representative of his military staff—and he often received as many variant views as he had bureaus.

Officers of the Army had long decried this system. Beginning with the 1840's, they discussed and debated means of improving the organization of the Army, its professional education, and the tactics with which it fought. Although few definitive volumes were published, the professional periodicals of the period—the <u>Journal of the Military</u>

Services Institution, for example—contained many essays on these subjects. An increased awareness of European armies and their educational methods resulted in many comparisons of European and United States military forces. More important, however, were the transformation of European concepts into American viewpoints.

In the 1840's Henry W. Halleck, later Commanding General of the Army during the Civil War period, stated:

> But the importance of maintaining in our military organization a suitable system of military instruction is not confined to the exigencies of our actual condition. It mainly rests upon the absolute necessity of having in the country a body of men who shall devote themselves to the cultivation of military science, so as to be able to compete with the military science of the transatlantic powers.[2]

Halleck's argument contained one sentence which is remindful of later-year arguments for preparedness:

> By perfecting ourselves in military science, paradoxical as it may seem, we are therefore assisting in the diffusion of peace, and hastening on the approach of that period when swords shall be beaten into ploughshares and spears in pruning hooks.[3]

Halleck's Elements of Military Art and Science was widely read throughout the Army. Despite the dominant Jacksonian tradition of the zealous military amateur, Halleck emphasized that the principles of military art and science constitute the body of a profession and that it makes no more sense to entrust the professional duties of a military officer to a civilian than to give the practice of medicine to a carpenter.[4] Like many other American officers of this period, Halleck was much impressed with the French military professionals, particularly Jomini. Although he termed Jomini's works as exceedingly valuable, he merely listed Clausewitz's "Vom Kriege" (On War) as one of 28 books on strategy.

The US Army did not awaken to the benefits to be derived from studying the Prussian Army's strategies and tactics until after the Civil War. There can be little doubt this awareness came as a result of Prussian victories over the Austrians and French. The seeming ease with which Prussian armies disposed of two continental powers undoubtedly created a profound impression upon the American army officer.

In 1875, Brevet Major General Emory Upton, with Major George A. Forsythe and Captain F. P. Sanger as assistants, toured the world to examine the tactics, organization, discipline, and maneuvers of armies of Asian and European nations. His instructions from the Secretary of War, William W. Belknap, added, ". . . and in Germany the special examination of the schools for the instruction of officers in strategy, grand tactics, applied tactics, and the higher arts of war . . ."[5]

Upton published the report of this trip in 1878 as The Armies of Asia and Europe. Although Upton's book provided a comprehensive analysis of the armies of the countries visited, by far the most important part to him and to his readers alike were his conclusions and recommendations. Among these recommendations can be found one for the creation of "A War Academy to educate officers in the art of war, and to prepare them for the staff and to hold high command."

Upton did not maintain any thought of completely copying the Prussian organization nor the policies of its War Academy. In a letter written at Fort Monroe in 1877 while preparing his report, Upton said:

> West Point is, in my judgment, far superior to any academy a-broad for preparatory training for officers. But, once in service, we have nothing to compare with the war academies of Europe, except the Artillery School. You know how ignorant our generals were, during the war, of all the principles of generalship. Here, I think, we can correct that defect and form a corps of officers who in any future test may form the chief reliance of the government.
> My report has yet to be written. I doubt not it will disappoint many people, as I intend to expose the vices of our system, instead of merely describing the organizations abroad. We can not Germanize, neither is it desirable, but we can apply the principles of common sense.[6]

Other officers of the same period argued for reform of the Army and for establishment of postgraduate schooling for its officers.

MAJOR GENERAL EMORY UPTON
Upton's writings urged establishment of a General Staff and a
War Academy.

Brigadier General Thomas M. Vincent published a small pamphlet "Plea for the Staff of the Army of the United States" in 1870. Lieutenant Arthur L. Wagner wrote an essay for the Journal of the Military Service Institution entitled "An American War College" in 1889. This professional journal carried many other articles for proposed reorganization, such as Captain E. L. Zalinski's "Army Organization, the Best Adapted to a Republican Form of Government, Which Will Ensure an Effective Force." Almost without exception these writings included a recommendation for establishment of a war academy, a war college, or some other form of postgraduate schooling for officers.

General Upton continued his efforts. In letters to fellow officers and to civilian friends, he continually espoused the need for reorganization and education of the Army. He not only was a strong advocate of postgraduate schooling, but also recommended establishment of a War Department bureau to supervise all education within the Army, both enlisted and officer, as well as college programs conducted by Army officers.[7] This recommendation was not completely adopted until the World War II era; approximately 60 years after General Upton's death. Upton also prepared the manuscript of his monumental Military Policy of the United States between 1877 and 1880, by which time he had covered the history of the United States from the Revolutionary War through the Civil War campaign of 1862. Although it was not published for another 20 years, this work was to give Upton status as a military strategist equal to Mahan. Moreover, it received relatively wide circulation among officers even before publication and greatly influenced the thinking of professional soldiers in the United States "even if it did not lead to reforms until after the Spanish American War."[8]

The interest in Prussian organization and systems of education continued unabated. Professional journals published articles such as Captain T. A. Bingham's "The Prussian Great General Staff and What It Contains That Is Practical from an American Standpoint." Major Theodore Schwan published his Report on the Organization of the German Army in 1894. European works such as Spencer Wilkinson's Brain of an Army, a description of the German General Staff and its War Academy, and British Lieutenant Colonel W. A. H. Hare's translation of General Von Schellendorf's The Duties of the General Staff were read widely. This interest in the German army was reflected not only in the thinking of American officers, but also in the changes in tactics advocated by Upton, and even in design of uniforms.

Reform and reoganization, however, were not to come until the War with Spain demonstrated the almost complete inefficiency of the staff organization of the Army. This conflict found the Regular Army small and unprepared for engagement with military forces of a major power. From the Civil War on, the military forces of the United States had been organized for subduing the Indians. As a result, most officers had commanded relatively small forces and, for that matter, had at most only memories of battles involving large numbers of troops.

The supply and support given the expeditionary forces best can be described as inefficient, inadequate, and unsuitable. Equipped with woolen uniforms, firing rifles and guns using old black powder, transported in civilian ships entirely unsuited as troop carriers, fed bad rations—it is a semi-miracle that the Army in Cuba was successful in its battles with the Spanish. One can only guess at the outcome, had the opponent been a first class military power; France or Germany, for example.

As a result of complaints by Volunteers and Regular Army personnel alike, President McKinley appointed Elihu Root Secretary of War to replace Alger. In preparing the Army for its duties in occupying Cuba, Puerto Rico, and the Philippines, Root recognized early the need for radical reform of the Army. However, as Major General William H. Carter emphasized

> . . . His advisors were mainly bureau chiefs, each independent in his own sphere, working under the same uncoordinated system that had been the subject of criticism for nearly a century. [9]

Carter, then a young officer in the office of the Adjutant General, once was asked by Root what was wrong with the Army. His reply included a discussion of Upton's ideas embodied in The Armies of Asia and Europe nearly a quarter century earlier. Root's interest was immediate and grew as he learned more about the proposals Upton and others had made prior to the Spanish American War.

A side benefit of Carter's discussions with the Secretary of War was the publication of Upton's Military Policy of the United States. After Upton's death, the manuscript had been entrusted to Henry Dupont, close friend and West Point classmate of Upton. Dupont was to complete the manuscript and publish it but did not. Consequently, the work lay not unknown, for it was seen and mentioned by many Army officers, but dormant. As a result of Root's interest, the manuscript was obtained from Dupont and revised by Lieutenant Colonel Joseph P. Sanger, (who had accompanied Upton on his world trip in 1875-77), Major William D. Beach, and Captain Charles D. Rhodes. It was published in 1904 with a foreword by Root paying tribute to Upton's reform concepts, including establishment of a general system of military education of which the War College was a part. The manuscript of Military Policy of the United States is now in the Army War College Library.

As a result of his study of Upton's works and influenced by the sound arguments of his young advisors—arguments which could hardly be disputed when backed by the evidence of the mismanagement inherent during the Cuban expedition—Root became convinced that reorganization of the Army was not only advisable but completely necessary. His first official statement of this opinion was made in the Annual Report of the Secretary of War for 1899. After summarizing the activities of the Army for that year, Root reviewed his concepts for improving the Army organization, emphasizing that, "It is greatly to be desired that, at the same time, while the lessons drawn from the experience of the recent war are fresh in our minds, some improvements should be made in the organization of the Army." [10]

Basing his proposed improvements on two fundamental propositions—"That the real object of having an Army is to provide for war" and "That the regular establishment in the United States will probably never be by itself the whole machine with which any war will be fought"—Root presented a strong and logical argument for establishment of a staff responsible for planning for the future and for coordination of effort during war. Other recommendations were discussed, including improved promotion policies and better militia policies. Among Root's organizational proposals was the following:

I think that the following steps may be taken to advantage:

(1) That an army war college should be established, which shall be composed of the heads of the staff departments, properly so called, and a number of the ablest and most competent officers of high rank in the Army (including, of course, the Major-General Commanding.), these officers to be detailed for service in the college for limited periods, so that while the college shall be continuous in records, character, and performance, it shall continually and gradually change its personal elements. It should be the duty of this body of officers to direct the instruction and intellectual exercises of the Army, to acquire the information, devise the plans, and study the subjects above indicated, and to advise the Commander-in-Chief upon all questions of plans, armament, transportation, mobilization, and military preparation and movement.

This college should have combined with it, reinforced and enlarged in its scope and effectiveness, the present division of military information of the Adjutant-General's Office, where its records and its conclusions should be preserved. It should not supercede, but should incorporate, continue, and bring under the same general management the present service schools, supplementing where it is necessary their courses, which now, so far as instruction is concerned, largely cover the ground. Its instruction would, at the outset and perhaps permanently, be given through these schools, but it should give unity, influence, authority, and effectiveness in military affairs to the work and the thought developed in them, aside from mere instruction, and a weight and utility to their records of efficiency and the merit of their pupils not hitherto accorded to them in proportion to the high character of the work they have done. [11]

Despite the objections of senior officers of the War Department in Washington—for once the Commanding General and the various bureau chiefs presented a united opinion and front!—Root decided to proceed with reorganization of the Army staffs and establishment of a true general staff. Realizing that Congressional action would be required for official reorganization, he took unilateral and executive action in the name of the President by establishing a War College with general staff functions and powers insofar as might be possible.[12] Therefore, by Special Order Number 42, 19 February 1900, he ordered a board of officers consisting of Brigadier General William Ludlow, Colonel Henry C. Hasbrouck, and Lieutenant Colonel William H. Carter to convene for the purpose of "considering regulations with a view to establishment of a War College for the Army." [13] Lieutenant Colonel Joseph P. Sanger—the same Sanger who accompanied Upton on his world trip—was added to the board by Special Order Number 145, 21 June 1900.

The initial step had been taken, the step which was to lead to the establishment of both the Army War College and the General Staff.

Root, Ludlow and Carter:1899-1904

THE day following appointment of the Ludlow Board, General Ludlow, as the president, was directed to take preliminary measures toward organization of a War College, including formulation of general regulations for its conduct and guidance. The letter of instruction incorporated the essential aspects of Root's 1899 report. The three major purposes in establishing the War College were to further higher instruction of Army personnel, to develop and organize existing means of education into a coherent and unified system, and to serve as a coordinating and authoritative agency through which all kinds of professional military information would be available to the War Department at any time. The general duties of the college were defined as:

1. To consider and report upon all questions affecting the welfare and efficiency of the Army, including organization, methods of administration, armament, equipment, transportation, supplies, mobilization, concentration, distribution, military preparation, plans of campaign, and other professional matters that may be referred to it.

2. To supervise and direct the conduct and methods of the several service schools in such wise as to develop to the highest degree their theoretic and practical usefulness, and, as far as practicable, to cover the entire field of military instruction.

3. To furnish means for advance and special instruction, in order that the graduates of the service schools and others found qualified, shall have the opportunity of acquiring still further professional usefulness and accomplishments.

4. To devise means for the harmonious and effective cooperation of all the military forces of the United States, to the organization of an enlisted reserve, with personnel and stations indicated in advance, in readiness for mobilization when required.

5. To devise means for full cooperation of the military and naval forces in time of war, and to that end to secure close and effective relations between the Army War College and the Naval War College, with a view to a thorough understanding and concert of action for military operations, defensive or offensive.

6. This college will have combined with it, reinforced and enlarged in its scope and effectiveness, the Division of Military Information of The Adjutant General's office, where its records and conclusions will be prepared.[1]

A careful analysis of the proposed duties indicates a concept of organization and operation far beyond that to be expected of an educational institution. In fact the first duty of the proposed War College can be defined as the multiple functions normally expected to be performed by a major staff. Organization and administration are normally functions of a G1 section; mobilization, concentration, military preparation, and plans, of a G3 section; and armament, equipment, transportation, supplies, and distribution, of a G4 section. The duties of a G2 or intelligence section are those described as the sixth duty. It would appear, therefore, that the initial concept primarily concerned the function of the War College as a general staff rather than as an educational institution.

The Board allotted various subjects to its members for special investigation and study. General Ludlow went to Europe to study the staff organization and senior schools of several nations. Colonel Carter was assigned the study of US Army service schools and a possible organization for a General Staff. General Ludlow's special report on this investigation was submitted to the Adjutant General subsequent to the final report of the Board. Apparently no other written reports were retained beyond the time during which the Ludlow Board existed.

General Ludlow's report of his European investigations far exceeded the scope of the instructions given the Board. The recommendations he submitted separately covered size of the Army, allocation of troops, consolidation of certain branches, organization of a General Staff, training and education of officers and enlisted men, qualifications of officers, and establishment of a War College.[2] His specific recommendations relating to the War College were incorporated in the final report of the Ludlow Board. Ludlow's personal

BRIGADIER GENERAL WILLIAM LUDLOW
Upton's recommendation to establish a War Academy was confirmed by Ludlow in the report of his 1900 visit to Europe.

report is of particular interest because many of its recommendations were later adopted even though for some unknown reason the report was unpublicized and remained virtually unknown to the Army and its officers.

Secretary of War Root was not idle while the Ludlow Board conducted its studies. Recognizing the continued lack of enthusiasm among the older officers in the War Department for his proposed reforms—the center of opposition being the Commanding General, Nelson Miles, and the chiefs of the various bureaus—Root conducted what today would be termed a public relations campaign. His efforts were not restricted to influencing the Army alone. Root began to send material on the Army and the War Department to the principal magazine and newspaper editors.[3]

Copies of Upton's Military Policy of the United States were sent to influential people throughout the country. In his many speeches, Root emphasized that:

> It rests with you through the Senators and Representatives in Congress whom you shall elect to determine whether the lessons of this war shall be learned and the army organization of America shall be put in the front of American progress.[4]

That Root's personal efforts were successful was evident even before the Ludlow Board completed its work. Congress, in its appropriations for the Army for the fiscal year ending 20 June 1901, authorized the expenditure of $20,000 for:

> . . . contingent expenses incident to the establishment of the Army War College, having for its object the direction and coordination of the instruction in the various service schools, extension of the opportunities for investigation and study in the Army and militia of the United States, and the collection and dissemination of military information. . . . .[5]

It is significant that the capsulized purpose of the War College cited by the Congress included the significant general duties of the institution listed in Root's letter of instruction to General Ludlow.

The Ludlow Board completed its work and submitted a report to

the Secretary of War on 31 October 1900. The Board took cognizance
of the War Department's intent to use the War College as a General
Staff by stating:

> . . . the objects had in view are to fill, as far as may be, an ex-
> isting void in our system and to constitute a body charged in
> some respects with the duties and the responsibilities imposed
> upon what is known in foreign services as the General Staff, as
> well as others in addition. [6]

The functions defined for the proposed War College included supervision of military education and information, provision for higher
and special training in command and management of troops, and conduct of military operations. An additional function of the College was
to:

> . . . constitute an authority, capable of furnishing to the War De-
> partment expert professional opinion by responsible and capable
> officers, representing all branches of the service, upon any ques-
> tion, general or technical, as to which the Secretary of War may
> desire full information and competent advice. [7]

General Ludlow and his fellow Board members were well aware
of the proposition of the proposed institution and to a General Staff.
Although it recognized the difficulties to be anticipated in introducing
such reform, the Board stated that it was not:

> . . . expedient to modify its matured views in deference alone to
> anticipated objections, or to compromise its conclusions in ad-
> vance in order to avoid personal or ex parte hostility. . . . The
> Board has preferred to commit itself to an advanced standard
> confident that, in the end this standard will be attained and con-
> firmed, provided it be definitely set in view and consistently
> striven for. [8]

It is quite evident that the Board viewed its mission objectively
and impassively. Although its recommendations would in essence provide Root with the means for establishing a War College to function

as a General Staff, the Board warned that such an institution would be
an executive creation dependent for sustenance on annual Congressional appropriations. "This financial support withheld," the report
stated, "the purposes of the College would be thwarted or seriously
impaired. Again, an executive order made by one authority may be
revoked or amended by a similar succeeding authority."

Stressing the need for continuity, if the College were to provide
"the highest order of personnel, and firmest administrative coun-
tenance and support," Ludlow and his colleagues emphasized the need
for legislative enactment rather than executive action and concluded
the report with the recommendation that:

> The Board, therefore, while convinced that the War College, if
> established and consistently sustained, can be made to effect
> valuable results, specially urges that the necessary legislative
> provision for a General Staff, on thoroughly considered and ef-
> fective lines, be recommended for incorporation in the military
> service of the United States at the earliest possible time as a
> permanent feature of the organization of the Army.[9]

A memorandum defining the organization, duties, and functions
of the War College in detail was appended to the Board's report. Although the memorandum provided for an instructional staff and student officers, the duties of the College were primarily of General
Staff nature. There can be little doubt that Root's concept of using the
War College as a General Staff had influenced the Board's recommendations, for the stress placed on the staff functions of the proposed College overshadowed its educational nature.

General Ludlow's influence on the Board's deliberations is evident, for his personal report on his European visit contained essentially identical recommendations to those made by the Board, as well
as the contents of the memorandum attached to its report. General
Ludlow died shortly after submitting his own report in 1901. However, another member of the Board, Lieutenant Colonel William H.
Carter, continued to urge implementation of the Board's recommendations at every opportunity.

Carter was in a position to influence both key members of the
War Department Staff and the Secretary of War. As Assistant Adju-

tant General, Carter had almost daily contact with Secretary Root and did not hesitate to express his own opinions to the Secretary. In a series of memoranda from early 1901 to late October of that year, Carter refined and improved the original Ludlow Board report. He was convinced that the War College could serve as a General Staff only on a temporary basis and so reported to Root in a memorandum on 14 October 1901:

> Since the adjournment of the War College board, I have devoted a great deal of time and research in the effort to reach a reasonable solution of the problem which the Secretary has in mind. The result has been to more firmly convince me that the effort to imbue the War College with General Staff functions is doomed to failure. On the other hand, the more carefully I have studied the subject the more necessary does the organization of a General Staff appear in my mind. [10]

This same memorandum included a proposed order establishing an Army system of education which provided for ". . . instruction of the Army on a progressive basis from the first entry of the young officer into the service up to as high a point as the manifestation of his abilities seem to justify the Government in carrying him" [11] With only minor modifications by Root, Carter's draft order was published as War Department General Order 155 on 27 November 1901.

Paragraph 7 of this order provided for establishment of an "advanced course of study for Army officers, to be known as the Army War College." Emphasis was on the educational character of the institution, not on its functioning as the General Staff nor as a part of such a staff. The order indicated that a course of instruction embracing the higher branches of professional study would be initiated. However, the War College was also charged with supervision of all Army service schools. The keystone of this academic system was stated thus:

> It should be kept constantly in mind that the object and ultimate aim of all this preparatory work is to train officers to command in war. Theory must not, therefore, be allowed to displace practical application. [12]

Despite the academic nature indicated for the new War College in this general order, Secretary Root did not discard his original concept of using the War College as an interim General Staff until such time as legislative authorization could be obtained for a true General Staff. In his annual report for 1901, Root stated that:

> The creation of the War College Board, and the duties which will be imposed upon it, as indicated in my report from 1899, is probably as near an approach to the establishment of a General Staff as is practicable under existing law. Consideration of the amount of work which that board ought to do, however, in the field of education alone, leads to the conclusion that it can not adequately perform all the duties of a General Staff, and that the whole subject should be treated by Congress in a broader way.

> No one can doubt that the general and field officers of our Army have been too exclusively occupied in details of administration, with inadequate opportunity and provisions for the study of great questions, the consideration and formation of plans, comprehensive forethought against future contingencies, and coordination of the various branches of the service with a view to harmonious action. A body of competent military experts should be charged with these matters of the highest importance, and to that end I strongly urge the establishment by law of a General Staff, of which the War College Board shall form a part.[13]

Not until July 1902, however, were steps taken to organize the War College. A board of officers was appointed by General Order 64, 1 July 1902, to convene at the end of the month. Members were Major General Samuel B. M. Young, President; Brigadier General William H. Carter; Brigadier General Tasker H. Bliss; Major Henry A. Greene; and Major William D. Beach. The Chief of Engineers, the Chief of Artillery, the Commandant of the General Service and Staff College, and the Superintendent of the Military Academy were added as ex officio members.

Congress had continued to provide support to Root's intent by annual appropriations for the War College. Consequently, General Young was able to organize his small staff and to prepare plans for operation of the College. The first home of the institution was a rented house at 20 Jackson Place in Washington, D.C. This building,

MAJOR GENERAL S.B.M. YOUNG
Young was president of the first War College Board which served
Elihu Root as an interim General Staff.

Prudens Futuri

proved inadequate, and the College was moved to 22 Jackson Place on 1 December 1902. The Board continued to meet in this building as did the General Staff after its authorization by Congress in 1903.

For nearly a year the War College Board functioned as directed by the Secretary of War. After Congress authorized $400,000 in June 1902 for construction of a building for the college at Washington Barracks, the Board supervised planning for its construction. Secretary of War Root noted in his 1902 annual report that:

> The Board has addressed itself especially to reinstating and regulating military instruction in the military schools and colleges of the country, which may serve as a source for future appointments of second lieutenants from civil life; to the establishment of systematic instruction of officers in the Army posts; and to organizing the General Staff and Service College at Fort Leavenworth on the foundation of the Infantry and Cavalry School which existed there before the war with Spain.[14]

Although Root did not discuss other functions of the War College Board in this annual report, he had used the Board as a general staff. In his testimony before the Senate Committee on Military Affairs on 17 December 1902—the Senate Committee was then considering Root's proposal for a General Staff—Root stated that he had been using the War College Board for general staff work to a "considerable extent." "They have not time to attend to it," he said, "but we have got to have somebody to whom I can turn for advice and information, somebody with military knowledge and experience."[15] Root cited one example of the type of information he had requested:

MEMORANDUM FOR THE WAR COLLEGE BOARD.

October 18, 1902.

> I wish to reach a definite statement of the quantities of arms, ammunition, equipments, and supplies of all kinds which it should be the aim of the War Department to provide and keep on hand for use in case of sudden and unexpected hostilities, and also to reach a definite understanding as to the domestic sources from which may be obtained in any emergency a further supply of material for arms, ammunition, equipments, and military supplies

in excess of the reserve stock kept on hand by the War Department.

For this purpose I should be glad to have your board consider and report fully upon the following questions;

(1) What quantities of arms, ammunition, equipments, transportation, engineering, ordnance, and signal corps supplies and appliances, and all other supplies and appliances of every kind and description, would be requisite to fit out an army and make it ready for the most effective service, assuming, first, an army of 150,000; second, an army of 250,000, the question being answered in each case both with reference to a campaign in a cold, northerly climate and with reference to a campaign in a hot climate?

(2) What is our present supply of each article or class of articles reported as necessary for such an emergency?

(3) What is our present capacity for the production of such articles?

(4) What are the domestic sources of supply to which we could look in an emergency for the material with which to increase, either by purchase or manufacture, our war material of all kinds, and what is the productive capacity of the establishments from which such material could be procured?

Your report will, of course, proceed upon the due proportion which should exist between the different arms of the service in armies of the numbers mentioned and the supplies which would be requisite, assuming those proportions to be observed, The terms "transportation" and "engineer supplies and appliances" are intended to include ships and vessels of all kinds for transportation and for landing. In brief, every kind of supply which an army may need is intended to be included in your consideration, so that a definite and comprehensive policy or preparation of material for war may be adopted and followed by the Department, both in manufacture and storage and in the encouragement of private manufacture, so that the requests to Congress for appropriations may be continuously and consistently guided by that policy.

I wish you also to consider and report upon the storage facilities of the Army.

(1) What are the present storage facilities of each of the supply departments and what relation do they bear to the requirements for the storage of the full stock of supplies in that department which you shall report to be requisite under the foregoing directions?

(2) Are the present places provided for storage properly located with reference to strategical requirements of possible hostili-

ties? What, if any, of the present places of storage should be enlarged? What, if any, should be abandoned? What new places, if any, should be established?

At present, subject only to the approval of a civilian Secretary of War, the Chief of Ordnance determines where powder, projectiles, and equipments shall be kept, the Quartermaster-General determines where clothing and equipage shall be kept, the Commissary-General where food shall be kept; but it is not the business of those officers to plan campaigns or determine where these things are most likely to be needed, and there is therefore no proper relation between the place where supplies are kept and the place where they will probably be needed.

The division of military information and the heads of all the administrative and supply departments will be instructed to render you every assistance in their power by way of information and the preparation of data.

ELIHU ROOT
Secretary of War.[16]

The Secretary emphasized that this was general staff work that could not be done by the heads of the supply departments, because "It requires a knowledge of military considerations which it is not their business to have." Although other concrete examples of the Board's work are not available, one can surmise that it was kept fully occupied with similar tasks.

Root's efforts culminated in the passage of "An Act to Increase the Efficiency of the Army" on 14 February 1903. Ably assisted by General Carter, the Secretary had conducted a successful campaign despite opposition from many senior officers and members of the Congress. Root recognized Carter's contribution in his annual report for 1903, saying:

Special credit is due to Brig. Gen. William H. Carter for the exceptional ability and untiring industry which he has contributed to the work of devising, bringing about, and putting into operation the general staff law. He brought thorough and patient historical research and wide experience, both in the line and the staff, to the aid of long-continued, anxious, and concentrated thought upon the problem of improving military administration, and if the new system shall prove to be an improvement the gain to the country will have been largely due to him.[17]

BRIGADIER GENERAL WILLIAM H. CARTER
Secretary of War Elihu Root praised Carter for his assistance
in establishing both the General Staff and the Army War College.

Although not specifically stated in this tribute, much credit must
be given Carter for the establishment of the Army War College. It
was Carter who first interested Root in Upton's theories and works.
It was Carter who, as the sole remaining member of the Ludlow
Board, continued to press for establishment of the College until Root
appointed the first War College Board. It was Carter who emphasized
that an effort to use the War College as a General Staff was doomed
to failure. And it was he who ably assisted Root in the final efforts
during the Congressional hearings. Thus to Carter must go the credit
for making it possible to turn the War College toward educational
functions rather than continue to use it as a provisional General Staff.

A week after the passage of the General Staff Act, the cornerstone of the War College building was laid at Washington Barracks.
It had been hoped to hold the ceremony on Washington's Birthday, but
the event was scheduled for a day earlier since February 22 occurred
on Sunday. President Theodore Roosevelt, Secretary of State John
Hay, Secretary of War Root, and many other dignitaries were present
to observe the setting of the cornerstone by the Grand Lodge of Ma-
sons, District of Columbia. The trowel used by George Washington in
laying the cornerstone of the Capitol on 18 September 1793 was used
by the Grand Master.

Although President Roosevelt addressed the audience, Elihu Root
made the primary dedicatory address. He began with a statement of
the purpose of the War College:

> Not to promote war, but to preserve peace by intelligent and ade-
> quate preparation to repel aggression, this institution is
> founded.[18]

The Secretary reviewed the evolution of the War College, paying
special tribute to Emory Upton. Were Upton alive, Root said, he would
have seen all the reforms he had advocated substantially secured, the
last being "the completion of the system of military education under
the controlling body, which will find its permanent home in the building whose cornerstone we lay today."

Secretary Root emphasized the progressive nature of Army education beginning with the post schools, the selection of the officers to

THE CORNERSTONE CEREMONY, 21 FEBRUARY 1903.
Although President Theodore Roosevelt addressed the audience, Elihu Root's remarks are best known. To Roosevelt's left are Root and Major General S.B.M. Young: to his right, representatives of the Masonic Grand Lodge of the District of Columbia.

attend the various service schools, and the designation of the "best men" from Leavenworth for the postgraduate course at the War College. From the men thus "sifted out," he said, would come the officers to be detailed to important service and promotion to high rank. Root concluded by saying:

> Many another officer has studied and striven and written and appealed in vain for improvements in the military service and has passed away, and he and his work have been forgotten. The helplessness of the single individual who seeks to improve a system has settled into hopelessness. The wisdom acquired in each officer's experience has been buried with him. Only an institution, perpetual but always changing in its individual elements, in which, by conference and discussion, a consensus of matured opinion can be reached, can perpetuate the results of individual effort, secure continuity of military policy, and command for its authorized conclusive expressions of military judgment upon military questions the respect and effectiveness to which that judgment is entitled.[19]

In the interval between passage of the Act authorizing the creation of a General Staff and the date it was to become effective, 15 August 1903, Root continued to use the War College Board for staff projects. The day after passage of the Act, Root asked the War College Board to prepare recommendations for the organization of the General Staff Corps. Its conclusions were submitted to the Secretary of War two weeks later. In addition to recommendations for organization of the General Staff and selection of officers for such duty, the Board stated that there was no necessity at the time to make any change in the status of the War College but that ". . .upon the complete establishment of the General Staff Corps many of the duties now performed by the War College Board will be performed by the General Staff Corps."[20]

The report of the Board concluded with the following statement:

> The board recommends that one of the general officers of the General Staff Corps be assigned as president of the Army War College. The employment of the officers composing the War College board will, in the future, partake of the duties of an academic faculty rather than those of a General Staff board but their

work, together with that of the classes which may from time to time be ordered to the War College, will be along lines of great advantage to the General Staff Corps, and the War College will thus become in fact, as in name, an adjunct to the General Staff Corps.[21]

The Board continued preparation of regulations for the new organization of the Army, and the incorporation of the General Staff Corps. Generals Young, Carter, and Bliss were also detailed as members of a board to select 42 officers for detail to the General Staff when it became fully active in August. These officers were directed to report to Washington as soon as possible and, upon arrival, joined the War College Board at 22 Jackson Place. By August when tentative staff organization was completed, the original members of the staff had been working together for periods of from only a few weeks to more than three months.

Its work as an interim General Staff virtually completed, the first War College Board was dissolved by General Order 2, 15 August 1903. General Young was appointed as the first Chief of Staff of the Army. General Carter departed for duty in the Philippines. By the same order, General Bliss was appointed president of the War College Board; and Colonel Alexander Mackenzie and Major William D. Beach, directors.[22]

By late October, the General Staff organization had been firmed sufficiently to enable it to operate capably under General Young. Consequently, the Chief of Staff assigned additional personnel to the College and directed its president to "immediately organize the College." Bliss was informed that the work of the College would be continuous, the college year terminating on 30 June and beginning on 1 July of each year.

It is the present intention that the theoretical instruction of classes of detailed officers shall be in connection with the practical work to be elaborated by the College as now organized.

You will therefore report to the Chief of Staff, three months prior to the close of the present college year a detailed scheme of lectures and practical work suggested by the project or projects which, it is hoped, will by that time be completed by the

FIRST HOME OF THE ARMY WAR COLLEGE
This brownstone house on Jackson Place, Washington, D.C., was occupied by the War College Board and then by the Army War College from 1902 to 1907.

College under the instructions which you have already received from the Chief of Staff.[23]

General Bliss began the task of returning the Army War College to its proper perspective as a part of the Army educational system. Eminently qualified for his mission, Bliss had already served as an instructor at the Military Academy at West Point. When the Naval War College was opened in September 1885, Bliss was designated as lecturer on the Science and Art of War, a position he held through the Naval War College's third session in 1887. During this period he was able to visit various military schools in Europe as well as learning firsthand the problems involved in the operations of the embryonic establishment. His work on the War College Board had already given him a grasp of the problems ahead.

Consequently, he was able to report to the Chief of Staff on 11 November 1903 his proposal for the operations of the Army War College. This comprehensive report covered the history of the establishment of the War College Board and its work to date. Bliss presented a thorough discussion on the philosophy of military education in which he compared the Army of the United States with those of other nations. Although viewing the training systems in some of these armies favorably, Bliss stated:

> What is especially to be noted is that these foreign systems of training are sound because they thoroughly fit the local theory of military organization. They are unsound when transplanted to a locality where this theory of military organization is quite different.[24]

He then discussed at length the value of the educational system of the United States Army, from the post schools to the service schools to the General Service and Staff College at Fort Leavenworth. Bliss concluded that it would be impossible to devise a curriculum which did not repeat at least a part of what was taught in one or more of the Army schools. This raised the question, "What is the object of the Army War College?" Bliss then referred to the annual report of the Secretary of War for 1899, citing the discussion which led Root to conclude that an Army War College should be established and that:

. . . it should be the duty of this body of officers to direct the instruction and intellectual exercise of the Army, to acquire the information, devise the plans, and study the subjects above indicated, and to advise the Commander in Chief upon all questions of plans, armament, transportation, mobilization, and military preparation and movement.

So far as regards the character of the instruction to be given at this institution his idea is contained in the following words: 'Its instruction would be at the outset and perhaps permanently be given through these service schools, but it should give unity, influence, authority, and effectiveness in military affairs to the work and the thought developed in them aside from mere instuction, etc.'

In this resume of the first and what is still the truest and soundest idea of what such an institution should be and do, the first thing that strikes us is the use of the word 'college' in its old Latin sense of collegium—that is to say, a body of men associated together by a community of interest and object for doing something rather than to learn how to do it, or, at the most, the 'learning how' is a mere incident to the 'doing.' [25]

General Bliss here stated and emphasized a principle of education which has prevailed at the Army War College through the years. He then expressed the feeling that the Army War College had been created at a time when the establishment of the General Staff could only be viewed as a hope. He clearly stated the proposition that the War College ". . . properly developed and doing the things which it should do, is more than any other institution both the creation and the creature of the General Staff." [26]

First, asking three questions: "What shall be taught? How shall it be taught? and How shall the teaching be extended to the greatest number?," Bliss then made his recommendations for the general operation of the War College. He urged that the collection of military information (intelligence) not be included as a duty of the College. This he believed to be a part of the special bureau established for that purpose as a part of the new General Staff. Because schools already existed to teach officers how to improve equipment, arms, and other materials of war, he recommended that such not be a part of the War College course of instruction. The formal study of theory of tactics and the practical application of such tactics also were not to be a part of War College instruction. This left, Bliss added, "the broad field outlined by the Secretary of War in 1899"—the study of the larger problems of military science; devising plans relating to the question of military preparation and movement in time of war. Although the ultimate responsiblity for such study was given to the General Staff, Bliss stated that the War College should be one of the General Staff's most important agencies for meeting this responsibility. The studies of the War College, in his opinion, should relate to the best application of existing material—troops and equipment—to conditions which might arise in the future.

These study projects were to be, in essence, staff studies in great detail and so complete that ". . . in case the contingency for which the study is made arises, the chief of staff should be able to formulate the daily orders governing the minutest movements during at least the early days of the operation."[27] Bliss believed improved harmony with the Navy should result because of the relations between the two war colleges.

In answer to his question of, "How shall it be taught?", Bliss expounded upon his learn-by-doing method. For the most part, the studies were to be executed as a part of a "great war game." Lectures were to be given by competent officers on each of the more important problems relating to the study. These lectures were not to be general in nature but were to be directly related to anticipated problems of the study. When questions beyond the capabilities of the faculty arose (Bliss used international law as an example) recognized authorities were to be invited to participate.

To provide for instruction for as many officers as possible, Bliss proposed that a number of officers "selected from those who are known in advance as being among the ones who will play an important part in carrying these plans into execution" should be assembled for the detailed study of the plans. At first consideration, it would appear that Bliss was merely reiterating the proposal to have a student body of selected officers. Such was not his intent, however. His reference to officers who would be among those participating in carrying out such plans was directed primarily toward officers of the General Staff. Bliss proposed that, in addition to the regular faculty and the students of the War College, officers of the General Staff participate in reviewing studies in areas of particular interest to those concerned and to the section of the General Staff to which they were assigned.

General Bliss noted that the War College had already begun work along these lines. He concluded this report with a list of regulations for operation of the College:

I. The Army War College shall be located in the city of Washington, D.C.

II. The college shall be under the direct control of the Chief of Staff.

III. Under the direction of the Chief of Staff, the management of the college shall be vested in a president and two directors, who shall be assisted by a secretary.

IV. The special duty of the college shall be to assist the Chief of Staff and the General Staff in the preparation of plans for the national defense. For this purpose such number of suitable officers as may from time to time be found to be necessary by the Chief of Staff shall be detailed from the General Staff or from officers of the line, or other staff corps and departments of the Army, and these officers shall work with and under the direction of the personnel provided in paragraph III.

V. The war college will receive from time to time instructions from the Chief of Staff as to the problems which it shall take up and the general line of investigation it shall pursue.

After the most complete study practicable a report shall be rendered to the Chief of Staff setting forth the recommendations of the college. This report will be reviewed and criticized by the Chief of Staff and such section of the General Staff as may be directed to do so by him, and if necessary will be returned to the college with these criticisms for further study and revision.

Whenever the nature of the problem is such as to require harmony of action between the two services, the report will be submitted to the joint board of army and navy officers appointed by General Order No. 107, Adjutant General's Office, 1903, and the conclusions will be further studied in light of criticisms by said board.

Upon the final acceptance of the report of the college by the Chief of Staff, the report will be filed in his office.

VI. From time to time, as may be determined by the Chief of Staff, a selected number of officers, to be taken from the Army at large, will be assembled at the war college for the minute and detailed study, under the direction of the Chief of Staff, for the projects thus formulated.

VII. The work of the college in the preparation of its reports and in the subsequent instruction based thereon shall be confidential.[28]

In organizing the work of the College, it was decided that 1 November would be a more convenient date for beginning the College year than 1 July. Therefore, the first year of systematic operation began on 1 November 1903. No student officers were detailed to attend the College during the first year of its operation. Thus, under General Bliss and his staff—Colonel Alexander Mackenzie, Major William D. Beach, directors; Colonel Charles Shaler, Major George W. Goethals, Major Montgomery M. Macomb, members of the Third Division of the General Staff; and Major Samuel Reber, secretary— the College began its functions primarily as a working adjunct of the General Staff rather than as an academic institution.

Among the problems considered by the College during the first year of its existence were:

> A plan for the withdrawal of US forces from the Philippines and the use of Philippine Scouts and Constabulary after such withdrawl.
>
> A plan for defense of the northern United States in case of war with Great Britain.
>
> A plan for operations of the Army in case of a war with Mexico.
>
> Revision of rules for joint Army and Navy maneuvers, such revision being accomplished jointly with the Naval War College.
>
> Also working jointly with the Naval War College, the preparation of a uniform system of symbols for use by the Army and Navy in preparation of war charts.
>
> Preparation of details for joint Army and Navy maneuvers in Chesapeake Bay in the summer of 1905. This plan was also a joint effort of the two war colleges.
>
> Preparation of courses of instruction and supervision of the activities of the various schools of the Army educational system [29]

It is difficult to cross the barrier of 63 years and view objectively and understandingly the actions and events involved in getting the War College—and the General Staff—underway. It is evident, for example, that the War College continued to function as a vital part of the General Staff and that its educational mission was secondary. However, the reason becomes apparent when one realizes that the previous War Department staff—if the term can be applied to the complex of independent bureaus—had little practical general staff experience. The War College Board, which by now had served Secretary of War Root as an interim general staff for nearly 4 years, embodied the only expertise available. The officers selected for detail to the General Staff had been working with and under the supervision of the War College Board since reporting for duty in Washington. Continued training and supervision of this group was essential, and the only agency capable of conducting such training and properly supervising the work of the embryonic staff was the War College. Hence, the College continued to function as an integral part and adjunct of the General Staff for the first year of its formal existence.

The new General Staff began to function more effectively by early 1904, however, enabling the War College to prepare to assume a more educational and academic aspect. General Order No. 115, issued 27 June 1904, made a clear differentiation between the permanent personnel of the College and the students detailed for a year of study. This order defined the object of the War College as ". . . not to impart academic instruction but to make a practical application of military knowledge already acquired," a rephrasing of Bliss' analysis of learning by doing.

The duties of the permanent personnel were clearly defined:

1. The preparation of projects involving the organization mobilization, and concentration of troops, general strategic plans, and preliminary operations.
2. The preparation of confidential strategical problems, involving mobilization and concentration, for officers specially designated by the Chief of Staff.
3. The preparation of tactical problems, to be solved jointly by officers of large posts, and the critical examination of the solutions of the same.
4. The preparation of tactical problems for the post-graduate course in the garrison schools.
5. The critical examination of essays, pertaining to the post-graduate course in the garrison schools, forwarded by the divi-

sion commanders in accordance with the regulations herein before prescribed.

6. The direct supervision under the Chief of Staff of the courses and methods of instruction at post, garrison, and service schools and the Staff College, including the approval of text-books when such are used.

7. The supervision of the military departments of schools and colleges at which officers of the Army are detailed as professors of military science and tactics, and for this purpose the examination of reports of inspectors at these institutions.

8. The annual classification in accordance with Paragraph XI, General Orders No. 65, War Department, April 6, 1904, of schools and colleges at which officers of the Army are detailed as professors of military science and tactics.

9. The preparation of critical analyses of foreign military systems or important parts thereof to be published from time to time as the Chief of Staff may direct.

10. The regulation and conduct of army maneuvers, and (in conjunction with naval officers) of those jointly conducted by the Army and the Navy.[30]

These duties can be summarized under four general categories: preparation of studies and plans of an operational nature for the Chief of Staff, supervision of the Army educational institutions from post and garrison schools through the Staff college at Fort Leavenworth, supervision of the instruction conducted by the various professors of military science and tactics at civilian colleges and universities, and preparation for and conduct of various maneuvers.

The course of instruction intended for student officers was also clearly defined by this General Order. The course of study to be conducted from 1 November through 31 May of the following year was to consist of:

1. The critical study of an approved plan of operations with a view to its confirmation or modification.

2. The assumption of the original conditions on which an approved plan was based, and the preparation of an independent plan, the two to be subsequently prepared and discussed.

3. In each case a minute and detailed study of a certain number of days' operations at an important period of the plan, involving the preparation of every daily order of importance to be issued

during the period, directing the position and movements of wagon trains of every kind, the tactical arrangement of marches (assignment of roads to columns, arrangement of columns on the roads, etc.), length of marches, tactical arrangement of camps and bivouacs, etc.

4. In connection with the above, the discussion of special problems encountered by the technical troops, of the tactical use of the three arms under the given conditions, the supply of ammunition, the disposition of the wounded, etc.

5. A war game, in which an actual campaign (of the Civil War, for instance) will be taken, all the initial conditions of the campaign being assumed to exist now as they actually did, except that the organization, armament, equipment, and tactical methods are those of the present day, the probable result being worked out on the map.

6. Informal lectures and general discussions of current military events and developments.[31]

This order also specified that there would be no formal opening or ending of the term of instruction and that no examinations would be given. Diplomas would not be given at the end of the course because

The course is essentially one of applied knowledge on the part of capable and qualified officers, and the announcement in orders that an officer has been selected for this course of advanced work is deemed sufficient recognition of his professional attainments.[32]

With this foundation established for the conduct of the course for the academic year beginning in November 1904, orders then were issued detailing the first student officers to the War College. The first class to enter would consist of nine officers:

Major William A. Mann, General Staff
Major Charles G. Morton, 6th Infantry
Major David DuB. Gaillard, Corps of Engineers
Captain James K. Thompson, General Staff
Captain Robert E. L. Michie, General Staff
Captain John J. Pershing, General Staff
Captain Louis C. Scherer, 4th Cavalry
Captain Ralph H. Van Deman, 21st Infantry
Captain John C. Gilmore, Jr., Artillery Corps [33]

Bliss and Wotherspoon: 1905-17

I NITIALLY, the arrival of the first class of "temporary personnel"—the students—had little effect on the activities of the War
College. Brigadier General Tasker H. Bliss, President of the War
College, had nine officers as "permanent personnel"—the faculty.
These included Colonel Arthur L. Wagner, formerly the Commandant
of the Staff College at Fort Leavenworth, and Lieutenant Colonel
William W. Wotherspoon as directors. These officers were also
members of the Third Division of the General Staff and, as such, had
general staff duties to perform. A naval representative, Commander
Sydney A. Staunton, was also a member of the permanent personnel.

The nine officers of this first class reported for duty at the end
of October 1904 and almost immediately began what can best be
termed an apprenticeship. The course established consisted of preparation of various tactical and strategic plans, special technical
studies, and a series of lectures.

For the most part, the various operational plans were prepared
under the direct supervision of the officers of the Third Division.
Although such planning was general staff work in every sense, it was
used as a teaching vehicle. Consequently, the duties of a general staff
officer were taught by the applicatory method using actual plans instead of hypothetical problems and theory. Although there was very
little, if any, purely academic instruction, the work was creative and
accomplished the prime purpose of the applicatory method of instruction so well advocated by Bliss. The student officers "learned by
doing."

Among the studies prepared by the Third Division officers and
their student assistants were plans involving prevention of the use of
Haiti-Santo Domingo as a base by a foreign maritime power at war

with the United States, an expedition against a semi-tropical country in South America by a United States force of about 12,000 men, and a series of plans involving expeditionary forces of various sizes from 5,000 to 30,000 troops. [1]

In contrast to the method used in preparation of these plans, the special studies made by the student officers represented individual work and research. For the most part, these studies were technical in nature and related to tactical or logistic problems involved in operations by one or more of the branches. For example, Major Charles G. Morton, 6th Infantry, submitted a monograph entitled "Organization, Use, and Equipment of Machine Guns." Captain James K. Thompson, formerly assigned to the General Staff, prepared his study on "Military Railroad Management." In addition, the class assisted in preparation of a problem to be solved by the Chief of Staff of the Pacific Division.

Lectures supplemented the practical instruction program. The Judge Advocate General of the Army discussed international law, and Commander Staunton lectured on "The Influence of Sea Power Upon the Movements of Armies." Much attention was given to the Russo-Japanese conflict. Five lectures were presented by US Army attaches with both sides. These talks were illustrated with "magic lantern" slides made from photographs taken by the attaches. Another first also occurred during this year: a civilian lecturer addressed the War College. James F. J. Archibald, Collier's magazine correspondent with the Russian Army, discussed his observations during the campaigns in Manchuria.

These lectures were attended by the entire War College. General Staff and other officers on duty in the Washington area also were invited. The lectures generally were an hour to an hour and a half in length, followed by a lengthy question period.

To conduct the War College course and the routine affairs of the Third Division, General Bliss organized the War College into committees. Actual preparation of the War College course was assigned as one of the duties of the Strategy Board—Bliss, Wagner, Wotherspoon, Goethals, Harrison, and Reber.[2] Permanent members of the College and the students were assigned to committees with specific areas of military interest. Wotherspoon, for example, chaired the committee on Canada; Goethals, the Philippines and the Orient. Other committees were concerned with the Caribbean area, Mexico, and joint Army-Navy maneuvers. [3]

This organization would appear to be insufficient in some respects. No committee had primary interest in Europe or even South America other than the Caribbean area. However, as Ahern states in the Army War College Chronicle, "This initial organization was adopted as suited to meet the conditions existing at the time." [4] The organization, moreover, was intended to provide the officers with the "instruction which comes from enforced and prolonged study at its broadest scope of at least one problem during the time of their detail." [5] This would indicate that the instructional functions of the College were given full consideration and that, even at this early date, they were viewed separately from General Staff creative requirements in which accurate and speedy results were highly desirable.

Bliss was well aware of possible deficiencies of the organization, for he stated:

> . . . a better organization would probably be to form a committee whose duty it should be to formulate in succession the outline of each plan and to divide the remaining personnel into committees to work under its direction upon the details, as Transportation, Equipment, Military Geography, etc. This is for future experience to decide. [6]

Realizing that the permanent staff of the War College and the Third Division lacked experience, Bliss designed the course and daily staff work to provide maximum training and educational benefits to the staff and students alike. His organizational arrangement was one means by which he hoped to attain the objective of developing staff officers; the methodology, another. Bliss commented upon this theory, thus:

> . . . The most satisfactory organization is one which will lead to its most speedy and accurate solution, in all its details, while at the same time the officers who do the work will have reasonable

BRIGADIER GENERAL TASKER H. BLISS
One of the Army's outstanding educators, Bliss greatly influenced the development of the War College as an academic institution.

opportunity for mind-broadening study, for independent and original investigation. For this purpose each officer here is a student
and all on the same plane; and each will have his opportunity to
find his level in the estimation of his fellow workers by his zeal,
his painstaking research, his soundness of judgment—in short, by
the evidence he gives of those qualities inherent and acquired
which go to make up the ideal staff officer. [7]

The War College looked forward to occupancy of the new building
under construction at Washington Barracks. Although the number of
officers in the Third Division and the War College itself was small,
the house on Jackson Place was inadequate and hampered operations
considerably. The Second Division, responsible for collecting military
information, was housed in the Lemon Building several blocks away.
The separation was obviously inefficient and undesirable, but little
change could be anticipated until the new building had been completed.

On 19 November 1904, the War College received a statue of
Frederick the Great, a personal gift from Kaiser Wilhelm of Ger-
many. The statue was a bronze replica of a marble figure in the
Siegesallee in Berlin.

The dedication of the statue at Washington Barracks was impressive. President Theodore Roosevelt and a host of governmental and
military dignitaries were present. The statue was erected on what
would be the terrace of the War College building. As conceived by the
architects, Frederick would be joined later by seven other great
military figures: Alexander, Caesar, Napoleon, Wellington, Souvaroff,
Grant, and Sherman. Although bases were provided, the remaining
statues never were erected. [8]

Few of the gala participants at the dedication envisioned the
problems to be encountered because of the statue. Less than 2 months
later an attempt was made to blow up the statue and its pedestal. The
effort failed when a workman found the satchel of explosives and
moved it away from the figure only minutes before the detonation
took place. For this action, George C. Ellis received a letter of
thanks from Secretary of War William H. Taft and an inscribed gold
watch from the Kaiser. [9]

Threats to demolish the statue and Congressional comments resulted in the removal of the figure in early 1918. It was not returned

to its pedestal until 1927. The statue again was dismounted and placed in storage during World War II, never to be returned to its original position. When the Army War College moved to Carlisle Barracks in 1951, the statue of Frederick was erected on the "Old Parade" where it stands today.

General Order 115, 27 June 1904, prohibited the award of diplomas at the end of the War College course. As stated, this restriction was made in the belief that ". . . the announcement in orders that an officer has been selected for this course of advanced work is deemed sufficient recognition of his professional attainments."[10] Designation to attend, however, did not necessarily mean completion of the course. This unforeseen situation developed when Captain John J. Pershing was relieved from the class on 27 December 1904 for special duty as military attache to Japan.

To secure appropriate recognition for the graduates of the War College, Major Charles G. Morton, a member of the first War College Class, recommended to the Secretary of the War College that a suitable entry be made in the Army Register. This request was forwarded to the Secretary of War, who approved it and directed that such a notation be made. The Chief of Staff directed that the President of the War College "report all the names of those who have completed the course for the year 1905 and that similar reports be made for each succeeding year."[11] The annotation "Army War College 1905" was entered in the 1906 edition of the Army Register after the names of the eight student officers, the President of the War College, and the faculty. These six officers had worked throughout the year with the students and were given credit for having completed the course, a precedent which has been continued to the present day.

One member of the class and one other officer of the General Staff were detailed to attend the Naval War College during the 1905 summer session. This custom was continued until War War I and did much to increase mutual understanding by providing practical knowledge of operational methods used. The exchange of officers as students and faculty members helped to bring about the "effective co-operation of the Army and Navy in the problems of National Defense"

CAPTAIN JOHN J.
PERSHING, 1905
Although a member of the
first class of the Army War
College, Pershing did not
graduate because of reas-
signment to the Far East.

cited by Elihu Root as one of the reasons for establishing the Army War College. [12]

Shortly after the completion of the first academic year, General Bliss departed for duty in the Philippines, but no general officer was designated to replace him. With the consent of the Chief of Staff, Lieutenant Colonel William W. Wotherspoon became Acting President. Wotherspoon's first duty was to submit the proposed course for the ensuing year and to recommend to the Chief of Staff the officers to attend the course. This Wotherspoon did by letter on 14 July. He proposed continuing the study of the strategic problems involving the Caribbean nations. New studies recommended included a plan involving possible war with Mexico, study of the organization of militia and volunteer forces and their effectiveness in previous conflicts, possible recruiting systems for the regular and volunteer forces, and a study of the state of preparedness of the United States. Proposed lectures were to discuss current military affairs, the operation and tactical employment of the various arms of the service, and the latest developments in war.

To prepare for the new class of seven officers, Wotherspoon had only himself, Commander Staunton, and Majors Goethals and Reber from the permanent personnel of the previous year. However, three members of the previous class had been assigned to the Third Division and, consequently, would be available as instructors. Here another precedent was established, selective retention of members of the graduating class for duty with the faculty. This precedent also has been continued usefully throughout the years.

Wotherspoon made minor changes in the internal organization of the College. The Strategy Board was redesignated as the General Board, and committee areas of interest were changed somewhat. Military resources of the United States, home defense, and South and Latin America were added to interest areas of various committees. It is significant that Europe still was considered to be of little military significance or interest since the Atlantic Ocean supposedly provided a formidable barrier to any nation unfriendly to the United States. Primary concern was given to the western hemisphere and to the island possessions of the United States in the Pacific.

To provide continuity in the studies being pursued from the previous year, Wotherspoon directed that committee chairmen be prepared to brief new committee members thoroughly on the work done during the previous session.[13] This was the first order. of business when the new class reported for duty at the end of October.

There was little change in the methods of the previous year. The various committees were in almost constant session, working on various plans and problems. The General Board met from time to time to accept or reject the work of the committees. Various problems were discussed by the entire College in a formal conference each Saturday. Plenary sessions also took place frequently to discuss the various problems undertaken by the committees.

Additional studies were undertaken. These included a joint effort with the Naval War College to devise regulations for the conduct of transports with naval convoys. Three other studies concerned the use of US troops in China, an outgrowth of the Boxer Rebellion of 1900 and other more recent unrest.

It is significant that all work undertaken was done by joint faculty-student effort or committees rather than by individuals. Committees were combined to work on larger projects, and the entire College participated in one study to prepare tables of supplies required for an individual soldier; a company, troop, or battery; a battalion or squadron; a regiment; a division; and a corps. Not all the College problems were so technical in nature nor so typical of general staff work. A series of monographs were prepared on the history, military geography, and resources of various South American and Caribbean nations. Although representing committee efforts, these studies approximate some of the research projects of today's War College classes.

Brigadier General Thomas H. Barry was appointed President of the War College in December, and Wotherspoon remained as a director. Barry cited both Wotherspoon and his fellow director, Lieutenant Colonel Smith S. Leach, for their preparation and conduct of the course, when he submitted his annual report to the Chief of Staff. Barry also evaluated the course in his report, saying:

. . . quality of the work is creditable to the industry of the personnel but its character and quality are such, while the experience and instruction which the officers gain by doing the work is very great, the immediate practical value to the service and to the government is, if possible, greater.[14]

This report also stressed the importance and value of continued cooperation with the Naval War College:

The results are already apparent in the increased interest taken by officers of each service in matter relating to the other; and by officers of both services in questions of mutual relation and cooperation in national defense.[15]

Two officers again were detailed to attend the summer session at the Naval War College.

Shortly after the Class of 1905 had left the War College for new assignments, the Secretary of War ordered the College to prepare a special study to be used as the basis for organizing an expeditionary force to Cuba. The officers of the College and the Third Division worked day and night to complete this plan. When completed, the study provided the Secretary with an operational plan for a force of 5,600 men and officers. This plan was so complete that it included draft letters to the chiefs of the supply departments informing them of the nature and strength of the expedition and detailing the requirements to be met by each department.[16] Designation of troops to participate and draft movement orders were included.

The plan was approved and adopted. Troops were assembled at Newport News, Virginia, in October 1906 and sailed for Cuba with Colonel Wotherspoon on detached duty—the equivalent of the modern temporary duty—as Chief of Staff of the expedition.

There can be little question of the general staff nature of this study and even less question of its completeness and effectiveness. The contrast between the efficiency with which the expedition was mounted and the turmoil and confusion which had existed in dispatching troops to Cuba during the War with Spain was significant proof of the value of the War College and of the General Staff as a whole. The speed with which the plan was prepared—the studies prepared by the War College committees as a part of the course of instruction were a contributory factor—and the efficiency with which the plan was placed into operation were complete vindication for the efforts a few short years before of Root, Ludlow, Carter, and the other proponents of a General Staff and a War College.

The contribution of the College to the Cuban expeditionary force did not stop with this one study. Anticipating return of the force, the College prepared a plan for its evacuation from Cuba. Primary efforts to complete this study were made by the permanent personnel during November 1906. In addition, faculty and student officers prepared a plan to reinforce the expeditionary force by 5,000 men, if required. These plans were not completed, filed and forgotten. To the contrary, the War College committees primarily responsible for their preparation made constant changes to the basic plans in an effort to keep them current with the latest developments. When required, a new basic operational plan was prepared as, for example, when the College submitted a new plan in March for the withdrawal from Cuba. [17]

Eleven officers were detailed to the War College for the 1906-07 course of instruction. They were joined by two Navy officers, Commander Harry Knapp and Lieutenant Commander Charles T. Jewell, the first students from a sister service.

Considerable change was made in the course of instruction for this class. The scope of instruction in "Applied Tactics" was expanded. Although the use of the individual arms continued to be a part of lecture and committee discussions, primary emphasis was placed on the use of combined arms; development of the joint-team concept. Cooperation with the Navy was stressed throughout the year.

For the first time, a coordinated program of lectures appears to have been considered. Seven lectures were devoted to military history and "Thoughts on War." The latest developments in industry and science were covered by discussions of "wireless telegraph" (radio) and military aeronautics. The use of the Army in civil disasters was illustrated in a report on the accomplishments of General Frederick Funston's troops after the San Francisco earthquake.

Problem assignments were divided into study areas for the

faculty and for student officers. Faculty assignments were primarily of general staff nature: the evacuation of Cuba and the suitability and value of mounted infantry, for example. Student problems involved research and original thought. Some of the topics assigned were street fighting and riot control, use of portable searchlights in the field, military instruction in civilian schools, and the history of reduction of calibers in small arms.[18] On the first day of the course, individual officers were given these assignments and instructions on methods to be used. Because it was obvious that the subjects assigned would result in studies of different lengths, and that some officers would complete their research work before others, provisions were made for additional studies as required. The importance of tactical instruction, however, was not overlooked. The instruction indicated:

> The foregoing subjects will occupy the time of the officers to which they are assigned, when not engaged in tactical subjects or special emergency work. In the preparation of the tactical problems for the use of the college, data will be given to individual officers from time to time with special instructions in each case. Tactical work when assigned will take precedence of the subject given to the officer in the foregoing list, as will also any special work of any other character which it may be necessary to assign him.[19]

The original monograph studies included 11 subjects, one for each of the student officers. Thirty-one additional problems, primarily tactical in nature, were assigned and completed during the year. Special studies were assigned to the faculty from time to time.

Tactical and strategic study became an integral part of this course. A series of related problem studies were conducted during the year. At the beginning of the course, these studies consisted of map problems and maneuvers as well as what would now be called a "staff study" on some aspect of a campaign. Each officer presented his solution to his assigned problem to the entire College and, in some cases, to visiting officers. For example, the Chief of Coast Artillery and his staff participated in the discussions which followed presentation of studies involving coastal defenses.

Presentations were made in a formal manner with the President of the War College presiding. After the officer had stated his assigned problem and given his solution, the College discussed differing opinions with him. After the discussion, nonmembers of the College were excused, and a formal vote to accept or refuse the proposed solution was taken. Modifications to the solution generally were made prior to the vote. In January 1907, the President of the War College indicated that written comments substantiating negative votes should be attached to the studies concerned.[20] The purpose of this requirement was twofold: to provide a complete written record of each study for War College files and to give the officers concerned experience in justifying nonconcurrences as a part of training for general staff duty. Formal records of each meeting included the report of the Secretary of the War College on personnel present, date and time of the session, and results of the vote. In addition, the problem and solution, justification of any negative votes, and a summary critique by a member of the faculty were included.[21]

The most significant modification of the course, however, involved actual visits to Civil War battlefields and other staff rides in the Washington area. These were not mere visits or terrain studies: they were the ultimate example of the "applicatory" method of instruction initiated by General Bliss. As part of their study of tactics, strategy, and military history, the students considered the strategic implications of various Civil War campaigns. Initially such studies involved map problems only, but by late spring when the weather had improved sufficiently to permit outdoor work, the class moved to the countryside. Short staff rides near Washington were used to instruct the students on the importance of terrain study.

In late May, the College moved to Keedysville, Maryland, for a detailed study of the Antietam campaign.[22] A field order was prepared following the general historical situation which existed in 1862, and student officers were assigned certain aspects of the problem to be studied. After a two-day inspection of the battlefield, the student officers prepared solutions to their assigned problems and presented them to the entire College in a formal session held on the battlefield.

Student solutions were not a mere review of what had actually taken place in 1862. The solution was to be based on the student's opinion and concepts of what should take place as of the date of his study using modern weapons, current Army organization, and the tactics of 1907 and justified by the individual officer's military experience and study. In other words, the intent of the historical ride and the study of the battlefield concerned was to provide the students with an actual strategic military situation on which each could base his solution of a particular military problem.

Because the experiment with the 1907 class was so highly successful, the technique was continued and expanded. This was application of knowledge to an actual situation, the study of war lacking only actual troop engagements.

General Barry was reassigned at the end of February 1907, and Colonel Wotherspoon, who had returned from Cuba, again was designated as the Acting President of the War College. At his recommendation, the course of the ensuing year was extended to a full 12 month period.[23] Wotherspoon also noted that "the most important characteristic of the system of instruction heretofore in vogue in all branches is that it provides for ready expansion . . ."[24]

The new accommodations at Washington Barracks were rapidly nearing completion, and the War College was preparing to move from its temporary Jackson Place home. Although the size of the new building would permit increasing the class to 40 or 50 officers, Wotherspoon recommended that only 16 students be scheduled for the following year. This would permit the College to "adapt itself to its new surroundings" and, in general, expand the course of instruction. Wotherspoon had already suggested detailing officers of higher rank and allocating a percentage of the student quotas to each of the arms of the service.

The College moved to Washington Barracks on 20-21 June 1907. Although the new building provided very spacious housing, some difficulty resulted because of its distance from the General Staff Second Division, the military information group, which remained in its Lemon Building location.

General Order 116 had indicated that the War College would direct and coordinate the military education conducted in Army schools and civilian colleges, but this function continued to be fulfilled by the Third Division rather than by the War College itself. However, the second object cited in that General Order was accomplished jointly by the Third Division and the War College proper: "To provide facilities for and to promote advanced study of military subjects and to formulate the opinions of the college body on the subjects studies for the information of the Chief of Staff." [25]

Although Wotherspoon had recommended 16 officers for the Class of 1907-08, it was found impractical to detail this number, and 11 officers were selected for the course. They were joined in November by Major Eli K. Cole, the first of many members of the Marine Corps to attend the Army War College. Commander W. L. Rodgers was assigned as the Naval representative on the faculty.

Wotherspoon was promoted to Brigadier General and designated as President of the War College in October 1907.[26] He thus began his fourth year with the War College, already having served as instructor, director, and acting President on two different occasions. The trends he had generated in previous years were to continue.

In general, the 1907-08 course differed little from that of the previous year. It consisted of war studies, strategic and tactical map exercises, lectures on military history and items of current importance, battlefield studies, and staff rides. The map exercises were similar to those of the previous year, but strategic exercises were expanded by adopting some of the techniques of Navy strategic games developed at the Naval War College.[27] The result was an improvement of the German "Kriegspiel" method used previously. Actual war plans prepared by the Third Division were used as the basis for these strategic exercises in an effort to test the feasibility, completeness, and effectiveness of the plans concerned.

One of the plans thus gamed was based on war with Japan. The operations involved the defense against attack in the Puget Sound and San Francisco areas; defense of the Philippines, Guam, Hawaii, and the Canal Zone; and naval actions in the Pacific. Initial assumptions were that the US fleet was in the Atlantic en route to the Pacific via Cape Horn (the Panama Canal not yet being operational); Japan had control of the Pacific until the fleet's arrival; and Japan had at-

BRIGADIER GENERAL WILLIAM W. WOTHERSPOON
The "forgotten man" of the War College, Wotherspoon with
Bliss dominated the College during its formative years.

tacked the Philippines, Guam, and Hawaii and made a successful
landing on the Pacific Coast.[28] The results of wargaming this situation caused revisions to the original plan developed by the officers
of the Third Division.

The staff historical rides were extended to include a second
visit to Antietam and a three-week trip to Wilderness, Spottsylvania,
North Anna, Totopotomoy, and Cold Harbor battlefields in Virginia.
The technique developed the previous year was used again. Each student officer developed a plan based on the historical strategic situation but modified to use modern concepts and organization. An additional feature was development of duties for maneuver directors and
umpires, since many student officers participated in the annual au-
tumn maneuvers before returning to their units.[29]

Student officers again worked on individual monographs. The
subjects assigned were diverse, varying from "The Use of Native
Troops in the Philippines" to "An Organization and Training for a
Coast Artillery Reserve." Special studies accomplished by committees were more technical in nature and included a history of night
attacks, an analysis of the value of Hawaii as a military base, and
"The Rise and Progress of Aerial Navigation as Related to the Conduct of War."

Early in the year, difficulties were encountered not only in conducting the course of instruction for the student officers, but also in
the preparation of plans by the personnel of the General Staff Third
Division. These problems resulted from the physical separation from
the military information group which had remained in its Lemon
Building quarters. After discussions with the Chief of Staff, during
which the Chief of the Second Division objected strenuously to General
Wotherspoon's recommendation that the Second Division move to the
War College building, the transfer was made in May, 1908.

This was followed by a reorganization of the General Staff in
June.[30] The division organization was abandoned and replaced by two
"sections." The old Second and Third Divisions were combined into
the Second Section which consisted of an executive staff, a Military
Information Committee, and the Army War College Committee.[31] The
primary effect of this reorganization was to provide the War College

with access to the library and files of the old Military Information Division, as well as to make available the extensive collection of maps and charts, photographic equipment, and graphic arts specialists. The additional personnel from the Military Information Division were also used as instructors. The reorganization made 16 of the 31 officers assigned to the General Staff available to the President of the War College.

Heretofore the officers of the Third Division and of the class had all been regarded as students practically on the same plane. This attitude and concept had been required initially because few, if any, of the officers of the General Staff had special training for their duties. Now, however, the small but steady output of the War College was meeting the requirements for staff officers. The experience of the 1907-08 year indicated clearly the necessity for instructors in tactical and strategic map exercises, wargaming, and the battlefield studies. The necessity for this deviation from the "applicatory method" was generated by the diversified backgrounds of the student officers. Despite the efforts of all the presidents of the War College to make graduation from the Staff College a prerequisite to War College attendance, this had proven impossible to arrange. There appeared to be little indication that the situation would improve in the future. Consequently, academic instruction had to be provided by assigning officers who were "proved experts in their line" as instructors.[32]

General Wotherspoon expressed his concern regarding the qualifications of the student officers to the Chief of Staff and recommended that officers who had not graduated from the Staff College attend a Preliminary Course prior to the beginning of the War College academic year. He also recommended additional qualification criteria for entry to the War College.[33]

As a result, the Chief of Staff, Major General John F. Bell, addressed a memorandum to the Secretary of War on this subject on 18 August 1908. The recommendations it contained were approved and placed in effect by War Department Circular 69, dated 22 August 1908. The following criteria in the memorandum continued in effect for several years:

1. Officers with over fifteen years service, upon entering the School of the Line, might be detailed to the War College regardless of class standing if recommended by the Academic Board of that school.

2. All other graduates of the School of the Line would not be permitted to enter the War College unless they had graduated from the Staff College with a recommendation from the Academic Board of that institution for instruction at the War College.

3. Officers of permanent Staff Corps might be specially selected by the Secretary of War for reasons 'dictated by the necessities of the service alone.'

4. Officers of Coast Artillery, in proportion of the strength of that arm to the overall strength of the combat arms of the service, if they were graduates of the Coast Artillery School and were recommended by the Academic Board of that school.

5. Officers with over twenty years service 'especially marked by distinguished conduct or by reputations for practical efficiency, intellectual ability, and professional zeal' provided that applications from these officers were approved by regimental and intermediate commanders.

6. Officers 'who may hereafter distinguish themselves in active operations during war, or who may hereafter become peculiarly and especially marked by distinguished conduct or by exceptional reputation for practical efficiency, intellectual ability, and professional zeal' after twenty years of service.[34]

The circular indicated that in about five years entrance to the War College might be limited to graduates of the Staff College, the second year course at the Coast Artillery School, and specially selected officers of the permanent Staff Corps. The sixth criterion permitted matriculation of selected officers who had been unable to attend either the Staff College or the Coast Artillery School, because of circumstances beyond their control.

As a result, two separate preparation or "preliminary" courses were conducted for officers, one at Leavenworth and one at the War College. Fifteen of the twenty-two officers in the Class of 1908-09 took one of these courses to study map reading, tactical and strategic map exercises, military history, wargaming, and issuing orders.

General Wotherspoon outlined the course for the year in a memorandum to War College personnel on 30 October 1908. "It is proposed to start the course at the Army War College on a higher plane than has been possible heretofore. This has been made possibly by the development of the work of the College during the past year, and particularly by the preliminary course at Fort Leavenworth and in the war college . . .'' [35]

The course outlined by Wotherspoon consisted of exercises in issuing verbal orders, conferences on tactics, tactical rides, strategic and tactical map exercises, special studies of military importance, lectures, campaign studies with accompanying staff rides, and war studies. Phonograph recordings were used in the exercises in issuing verbal orders. (One wonders if any of these old cylinder-type records still survive!) The conferences on tactics were devoted primarily to the study of the use of the various arms with practical application during the short staff rides in the Washington vicinity. Individual research efforts were devoted to special studies in the form of monographs, and the preparation of war studies continued to be a committee effort.

The lecture series included 13 discussions of the development of modern war and others on tactics, strategy, international law, logistics, naval strategy, and the Civil War. Wotherspoon also initiated a monthly conference on items of "current interest."[36] Each student officer was assigned a primary area of interest and reported on the current situation and on progress made since the previous conference. In essence, this combined a discussion of current events with an intelligence briefing.

Although the War College had occupied its new quarters for over a year, the building had not been formally dedicated. Consequently, a simple ceremony of dedication was held on 9 November 1908 as a part of the opening exercises for the new class. Elihu Root made a short address which, "though there is a rule of the college that speeches are to be received in silence, . . . evoked a burst of applause which was led by officers themselves and in which the women, of whom there were many present, joined.[37] The remarks which brought this burst of applause took the form of advice or, as Root stated, some rules by which the officers of the War College could justify its existence:

THE ARMY WAR COLLEGE, WASHINGTON BARRACKS
Designed by Stanford White, Army War College occupied this building from 1907 to 1940. It is now the home of the National War College.

Be careful not to let your attention be focused too strongly on the administration of the Army. The General Staff was created with the primary object of studying military science. You are brought together to do the thinking for the army, not the mere administration.

Settle your military questions within the limits of the military establishment. Never permit a controversy of any description to pass beyond the doors of the War Department. It is you who are brought together to settle military questions. The people are generous to the army and proud of it. Don't go to them with quarrels and expect them to settle them. Thrash these questions out and then let the proper representative of the army, the Secretary of War, go to Congress with the results.

The army should consider itself an instructor. It is the mould of form and the guide of practice for the greater army of citizens which will take up arms in case of war. Remember that when war shall come—and it is idle to disregard the possibility of its coming—it will be fought not by our little standing army, but by the militia and the volunteers. Instruction is needed to save that volunteer and militia army from paying the frightful price our armies have repeatedly paid for not learning the fundamental lessons or organization. The regular army is to officer the citizen army.

Never forget your duty of coordination with the other branches of the service—the navy, marine, and militia. This is the time to learn to serve together without friction.

Remember always that the highest duty of a soldier is self-abnegation. Campaigns have been lost for no other cause than the lack of that essential quality. Keep dissension and jealousy out of the United States army. Officers, you have no rights to rank or position incompatible with the best interests of the service.

Do not cease to be citizens of the United States. The conditions of army life are such as to narrow your views. Strive to broaden your sympathies by mingling with those outside of the service and learning from them the things they can teach you. As you are good soldiers, be good citizens. Let our army be never one of aggression, but devoted to the interests of justice and peace.[38]

The course for the year was conducted much as outlined by General Wotherspoon. Twenty-nine lectures were included, among them a discussion on Panama by Representative Edwin Daly. The purely General Staff studies were prepared by the officers of the Second

Section with members of the class assisting by preparing certain details. However, ". . . the relations of the War College committee and the class had now become more nearly that of teacher and student than ever before." [39]

Wotherspoon was reassigned on 19 June 1909, but continuity was assured, for his replacement was General Bliss, recently returned from the Philippines. [40] With five of the permanent staff and 12 student officers, Bliss participated in maneuvers held in Massachusetts in August 1909. For the first time, the War College provided the entire staff of one of the armies and most of the staff of the Chief Umpire. The improved staff work of both the maneuver army and the umpires indicated clearly the results of training under a uniform and effective system such as that conducted by the War College. [41]

The preliminary course initiated by Wotherspoon was continued. However, instead of having one group at Fort Leavenworth and another at Washington Barracks, the entire course was conducted at the War College. After two months of study, these student officers were joined by the remainder of the 20-man class on 1 November 1909. Two students were destined to serve together in France during World War I: Lieutenant Colonel Hunter Liggett and Marine Major John A. Lejeune (Lejeune commanded the Army's Second Infantry Division). Another member of the class was a future Chief of Staff, Captain Malin Craig.

For the first time, the internal organization of the Second Section assigned officers as instructors and assistant instructors of the War College. These assignments provided a decided contrast to previous years, when all officers of the section (or of the Third Division under the original General Staff Organization) were considered members of the War College permanent personnel. [42] Four instructors and two assistant instructors were assigned, five of them graduates of the War College Class of 1909.

General Bliss' second assignment as President of the War College lasted only 6 months. Once again he was succeeded by Wotherspoon. Together they dominated the early years of the War College. Their direct association with and guidance of the institution extended for a decade after its establishment. Both continued their close association with the College until World War I, and each served as Chief of Staff of the Army. The progress of the War College from an agency of the General Staff to an academic institution was due primarily to the efforts, professional ability, and guidance of these two men. Their major concepts have continued, not unchanged but progressively improved, throughout the years.

Many years later, Lejeune recalled his days as a War College student. He stated that the application and constant concentration required of the students had resulted in "quick and accurate thinking" producing an ability to form sound decisions expeditiously. He added:

> In looking back on my career, it is perfectly apparent to me that the fourteen months at the War College constituted a very marked dividing line in my professional life, and that during the years that have followed the completion of the course I have been conscious that I possessed greater mental power than I before realized, and have felt able to meet successfully any difficulty which I might find in my path.[43]

Lejeune recalled that General Wotherspoon had the "rare gift of gaining the enthusiastic cooperation of his associates without apparent effort." Lejeune noted, in a humorous way, Wotherspoon's change of locale for the tactical and strategic map exercises from France and Germany to North America, Hawaii, and the Philippines. Wotherspoon made this change because he thought it would be better to locate such exercises in "those parts of the world where it was at least possible we might someday serve." Lejeune commented on his own reaction:

> Eight years later, when in command of a division of combat troops, I stood on the very ground of the study which had been discarded and gazed at the distant spires of Metz. Farseeing man as General Wotherspoon was, it was beyond his powers or the powers of any man then living to foresee that in December, 1918, the American flag would fly over the ancient castle of Ehrebbreitstein, and that the American Army, victorious in many pitched battles on the frontiers of France, would march in triumph to the Rhine, cross that historic river where Caesar did, and occupy a bridgehead on its eastern bank.[44]

No 1 To 21 Standing

No 22 To 30 Seated

CLASS 1909-10

Left to right. Standing: Lt. Col. John A. Lejeune, USMC.; Capt. Edwin Landon, CAC.; Major Carl Reichman, 24th Inf.; Major Guy Carleton, Faculty; Major George L. Irwin, 3d FA.; Capt. Malin Craig, General Staff; Capt. William K. Naylor, 9th Inf.; Capt. Alexander Dade, 9th Cav.; Capt. Edward O. Sarratt, CAC.; Major Daniel H. Boughton, General Staff; Capt. Sherwood A. Cheney, CE.; Major William A. Brown, 3d Cav.; Capt. George H. Jamerson, 29th Inf.; Lt. Col. D.A. Frederick, Faculty; Capt. Fox Connor, General Staff; Capt. Frank Cocheu, General Staff; Capt. Gilbert A. Youngberg, CE.; Major Godfrey H. MacDonald, 13th Cav.; Major David J. Barker, Jr., 11th Inf.; Capt. Joseph D. Leitch, General Staff. Seated: Major Charles L. Beckurts, 5th Inf.; Lt. Col. John T. Knight, QMC.; Col. Robert A. Brown, 4th Cav.; Major Eben Swift, General Staff; Brigadier General W. W. Wotherspoon, President, Army War College; Lt. Col. Lyman W. V. Kennen, 14th Inf.; Lt. Col. Hunter Liggett, 15th Inf.; Lt. Col. Charles M. O'Connor, 8th Cav.; Lt. Col. John C. F. Tillson, 18th Inf.

Wotherspoon's change in locales was based on his belief that the tactical and strategic map studies would be more beneficial to the students if transferred to possible combat areas. Furthermore, the use of such locales coordinated perfectly with the use of actual war plans for wargaming. For once, he erred.

In another change, however, he moved in the right direction. Staff rides were continued with two trips scheduled: one to the Richmond area and the second to Gettysburg. Wotherspoon's innovation was the use of the class and faculty for staff officers, instructors, observers, and umpires at the Camp of Instruction for regular and militia organizations training at Gettysburg in July immediately following the War College staff ride. Wotherspoon was in command of the entire training. This experience was to serve the student officers well in the hectic period preceding and immediately following the United States entry into World War I.

Wotherspoon discussed the methodology and philosophy of the Army War College in an address to the Naval War College in August 1910. Although the entire talk is perhaps the best narrative description of the War College course in the pre-World War I period, one paragraph summarized the very essence of Wotherspoon's concept of the Army War College and its purpose:

> In arranging the regular course, the idea of preparing the officers for general staff work and high command is kept in view. To do this, we think our men should be prepared to solve rapidly and intelligently all the ordinary tactical problems which they would encounter in the field; that they should be able to estimate the value of terrain, lines of communication and rates of march in relation to ordinary military situations; should know how to work out the logistical features of a campaign, those, for instance which relate to the assembly of troops in a theater of war, their necessary equipment for a definite purpose and the difficulties which might be encountered in such operations. They should also know the value of the different arms in relation to each other and how to dispose of their troops in grand tactical movements; and, finally, how to estimate a strategical situation. All of which involves a knowledge of how to issue orders in such form as to be least susceptible to misunderstanding. . . . It has always been understood that the best method of acquiring skill and confidence in the movement and disposition of large bodies

1909 HISTORICAL RIDE TO GETTYSBURG

Historical rides to Civil War battlefields were part of the War College curriculum for many years. In the photograph above, the War College class reconnoiters Confederate positions.

The strategic military situation of Civil War campaigns provided War College classes the opportunity to develop the tactical battle plans using current tactics, weapons, and organization. In the lower photograph, Colonel Rumbough discusses Pickett's charge.

of troops was to study military history, and this is encouraged as much as possible, but, under the idea that all the military problems which the masters have encountered can be reduced to situations, we attempt to repeat those situations so frequently . . . that when a similar situation arises, the best solution may at once be apparent, as much from habit as from historical example.[45]

In his annual report to the Chief of Staff, in a memorandum dated 31 August 1910, Wotherspoon reviewed the organization of the course for the previous year, and stated the purpose of the War College in language used continuously ever since: ". . . to prepare a limited number of selected officers for the higher duties of command both in war and in peace while preparing for war." [46]

This memorandum also discussed the methods used by the College. After reviewing the purposes and benefits of the applicatory method of instruction, Wotherspoon discussed the use of the conference at the War College. The object of the conference was "to develop a school of safe leadership for officers and not to encourage unusual and extraordinary methods. We need fear little from the brilliancy of our enemies if we succeed in this."[47] He was convinced this would develop a consistent and reasonable habitual method of viewing military problems which "like the common law in jurisprudence, will guide our officers to those principles of leadership which should govern our armies." [48]

Acting upon the recommendation of Wotherspoon, the Chief of Staff directed a change to be made in the opening date of the War College academic year. The new class reported for duty on 1 September 1910 instead of in November.

The 1910-11 year differed little from the previous year. The 23 officers in the class faced 69 problems, 26 lectures, 25 map maneuvers, and completed one full war plan. Two historical trips and three staff rides provided practical application of classroom instruction.

This year is perhaps better remembered for two nonacademic events, nonacademic in that their occurrence had no direct effect on the course of instructure. The first of these was the adoption of a Coat of Arms and seal for the War College. Little if any considera-

DEVELOPMENT OF THE ARMY WAR COLLEGE
COAT OF ARMS

The original design for the War College seal, disapproved by the Secretary of War in 1907, is shown at the upper left. At the lower left is the Coat of Arms as designed by Captain George D. Moore. The first approved War College seal is at the upper right. The present Coat of Arms, last changed in 1924, is at the lower right.

tion had been given to the design of such devices until 1907. In that year, a letter from the Superintendent of the Military Academy at West Point was sent to all the service schools asking for copies of their seals for consideration as decorations on the new administration building at the Military Academy. Unfortunately, none of the schools had a Coat of Arms or seal. A flurry of activity resulted in an effort to prepare such devices and, since all the schools were under the jurisdiction of the War College, their proposals were sent to the College for approval. Only one, that of the Staff College at Fort Leavenworth, was deemed satisfactory.

The original proposal for the War College insigne consisted of the General Staff Corps star enclosed within a bordure. This was disapproved along with the proposals of all of the other service schools. Gradually, during the next three years, each school obtained approval for its own coat of arms. Finally, General Wotherspoon found a design satisfying his rigid requirements. This was approved by the Secretary of War on 3 December 1910. The Coat of Arms with some minute changes by Wotherspoon, was designed by Captain George D. Moore, 20th Infantry. Some mystery exists as to why Moore submitted his proposed design for he was stationed at Fort Shafter, Territory of Hawaii, and had had no connection whatsoever with the War College. It is evident from the language and description of the blazon and design submitted that Moore had a comprehensive knowledge of heraldry.[49] Two possibilities exist: one is that Moore was asked to provide a suggested design because he was an expert in heraldry and the other is that a competition—a popular idea during this period—was held. No correspondence has been found to indicate that Moore was contacted nor did any of the professional publications such as the Army-Navy Journal carry any mention of a competition. With some minor revisions made in 1924, the same Coat of Arms is used today.

Two weeks after the approval of the Coat of Arms for the War College, Wotherspoon submitted another request to the Secretary of War. The original order prescribing the War College course of instruction had specifically indicated that:

There will be no formal opening or ending of the term of instruction at the War College nor will there be any examinations held or diplomas given at the end of the course. The course is essentially one of applied knowledge on the part of the capable and qualified officers, and the announcement in orders that an officer has been selected for this course of advanced work is deemed sufficient recognition of his professional attainments. [50]

This provision had not been included in the new regulations prescribed in 1907.[51] Wotherspoon took advantage of this change and recommended that diplomas be awarded to officers successfully completing the course of instruction. This recommendation was also approved.

The Class of 1911 was the first to be awarded diplomas on graduation from the War College. However, the members of the previous classes, including the faculty members credited with attendance at the course, were provided with diplomas by General Wotherspoon. The Library of the US Military Academy at West Point has the diploma issued to Major George W. Goethals, one of the original "permanent personnel" of the War College.

Although the two-month preliminary course had proven satisfactory, Wotherspoon was convinced that a better means of preparing nongraduates of the Staff College for entrance into the War College could be devised. In his opinion, no substitute existed for the training received at Leavenworth. As a result of his effort, the Staff College agreed to conduct a "Field Officers Course" from January through March each year, and the course was authorized by the Chief of Staff in September 1910.

Even so, the 26 members of the class for 1911-12 were far from being a homogeneous group. Six were graduates of the Staff College; eight, including two Marines, had attended the new field officers' course; four had been graduated from the Engineer and Coast Artillery technical schools; and the remaining eight had no special qualifications other than recommendations from various commanding officers. The problem remained unsolved.

As a result, the course conducted during the month of September was largely preparatory in nature. It included 16 map problems, four

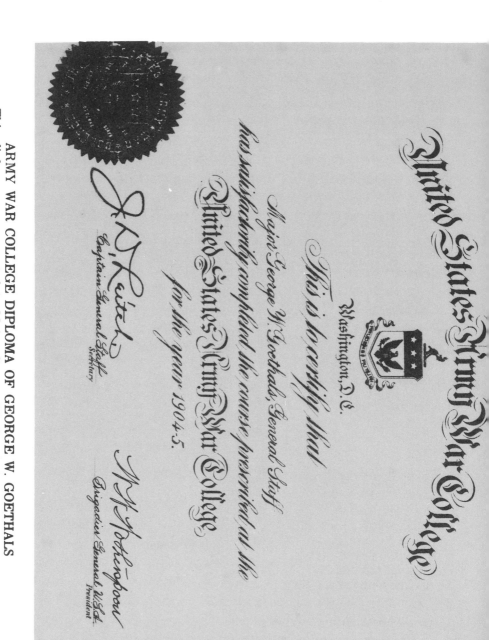

United States Army War College

Washington, D. C.

This is to certify that

Major George W. Goethals, General Staff
has satisfactorily completed the course prescribed at the
United States Army War College
for the year 1904-5.

J. W. Ruckel
Captain, General Staff
Secretary

W. W. Wotherspoon
Brigadier General U.S.A.
President

ARMY WAR COLLEGE DIPLOMA OF GEORGE W. GOETHALS

This diploma was presented to Major George W. Goethals in 1911 after the Secretary of War had approved General Wotherspoon's recommendation to award diplomas to all graduates. Goethals was a member of the faculty in 1905.

map maneuvers, four lectures, and 14 conferences on various problems. October included 13 map problems, five map maneuvers, four lectures, and 14 conferences. This was the general pattern of instructure until March, when historical studies were assigned in preparation for the rides in April and May. From January through March, committee groups also worked on a war plan to counter attacks along the northern border of the United States and upon both coasts.

General Wotherspoon was reassigned in February 1912, leaving the War College for the last time. He was replaced by Brigadier General Alfred L. Mills, a former superintendent of the Military Academy. General Mills was relieved as President of the War College on 31 August 1912, prior to entrance of the next class. He was replaced by Brigadier General William Crozier.

One of Wotherspoon's last acts was to approve placement of a plaque honoring Elihu Root in the rotunda of the College building. This large granite plaque with countersunk bronze letters cited the former Secretary of War for his efforts to obtain authorization for the building.

In the reorganization of the General Staff by General Leonard Wood in September 1910,[52] the staff was divided into four divisions: Mobile Army, Coast Artillery, Militia Affairs, and War College. The duties assigned the War College Division varied little from those of the old Second Section:

> (a) Collection and distribution of military information; War Department Library; preparation of non-technical manuals; direction and coordination of military education; plans for field maneuvers; collation and discussion of all obtainable data relating to strategical, tactical, and logistic features of future military operations and formation of complete working plans for passing from state of peace to state of war.
> (b) The Army War College.[53]

The War College thus remained under the jurisdiction of the Division but was considered a separate entity. However, the terminology "War College Division" resulted in much confusion within the Army itself and in the minds of the general public. Because of comments made in numerous speeches and in the press, the impression had been given that the War College consisted of a small group of officers taught by the comparatively large number of staff officers assigned to the War College Division. Further confusion also existed in the minds of many individuals who still considered the War College to be nothing more than a General Staff section and not an academic institution.

General Mills discussed this confusion in a memorandum to the Chief of Staff in July 1912. He pointed out that the concept of the duties of the War College Division was incorrect and that, although the conduct of the War College course was an important assignment, the Division also had many other tasks. The course of the previous year, Mills stated, had been conducted by four General Staff officers (the directors and assistant directors) aided by four officer instructors selected from previous War College classes. He also pointed out that these instructors were also the War Plans Committee of the Division with duties requiring:

> . . . the collating and discussing all obtainable data relating to the strategical, logistical, and tactical features of possible future military operations, the formation of complete working plans for passing from a state of peace to a state of war, and of submitting recommendations on the numerous subjects connected with the National Defense . . . [54]

The point emphasized by Mills was that less than 20 percent of the officers of the Division were directly connected with the course of instruction at the War College. Although no immediate action was forthcoming, General Wood included Mills' memorandum verbatim in his annual report for 1912.[55]

The class which entered the War College in September 1912 was unique in several ways. It was the first class to consist entirely of field grade officers—three colonels, five lieutenant colonels, and 14 majors. The Navy was represented by one officer; the Marine Corps, by two. Three of the group were graduates of the Staff College; two had no special schooling. All the others, however, including the two Marines, had attended the special field officers' course at Fort

Leavenworth. Commander McKean, a former member of the Naval War College faculty, had requested permission to take the entire course, although he had been assigned to represent the Navy on the War College faculty. This Class of 1913 was more homogeneous in qualification than any of those which had entered in the past.

The course of instruction for the year was almost identical in general content to that of the previous session. Indoor studies were conducted similar to those of the previous year from September through March. April was devoted to preparation for the May-June historical staff rides and to shorter trips in the Washington vicinity.

The War College group had several guests on its trips to the Civil War battlefields. Two British officers, Major General Colin Mackenzie and Colonel George Paley, visited the College sessions in early May. Harvard history professor R. M. Johnson joined the tour of the Bull Run battlefield. A short visit also was made by the Chief of Staff, General Leonard Wood.

Considerable effort was devoted to the preparation of an Army War College history of Civil War campaigns. However, this project was not completed, and Ahern stated that it "never can be until a Historical Section is established in the General Staff." [56]

Although the prestige to be gained in the eyes of the academic community from such a publication was not forthcoming, the status of the War College was recognized by the American Historical Association. The Association devoted an entire conference to a discussion of military history, the first time this had been done in any of its annual sessions. The practice was followed in succeeding years. Major James W. McAndrew, a member of the Class of 1913, represented the War College at the meeting and presented a paper on military history. [57] This is the first recorded indication of War College participation in a seminar or conference conducted by a civilian academic group.

Nevertheless, the value of historical study and research, particularly the emphasis on the Civil War, was questioned by the faculty. The student officers studied military history and did their research without expert guidance. As a result, much time was unnecessarily wasted in duplication of effort. Although the historical rides were enjoyable, their overall value was in doubt when weighed against the time required and costs involved. The shorter staff rides, on the other hand, were believed to be far more productive because of the opportunities they gave the student officers to exercise the duties of higher command.[58]

Brigadier General Hunter Liggett was assigned as President of the College in July and welcomed the new class on 1 September 1913. This group also was composed entirely of field grade officers. Only two, however, were graduates of the Staff College, and only 12 had attended the field officers' course. Major General John F. O'Ryan of New York was the first National Guard officer to attend the College. President Woodrow Wilson granted special permission for him to become a member of the 1914 class.[59]

The widely varied experience and schooling of the class caused much concern to both the President of the War College and the Chief of Staff. Discussion and study of the qualifications of this group and of previous classes resulted in a memorandum from the Chief of Staff which authorized General Liggett to relieve any officer from duty at the War College who was ". . . deemed unfitted or unworthy to continue the course . . ."[60] if so reported and recommended by the faculty. Because the regulation was not published until after the Class of 1914 had entered the College, these officers were exempted from its provisions. However, they were informed that any officer reported as unfit by the faculty would be permitted to finish the course but would not be given a certificate of graduation nor would he be reported as having satisfactorily completed the course.

The provisions of this memorandum were incorporated in new regulations published in February 1914 governing admission to the College. Although graduates of the Staff College were considered qualified for entry to the War College, other officers desiring to attend were required to take a written examination in April of each year[61] The examination prescribed for April 1914 was described in a March 1914 War Department Bulletin. Four map problems and one original study were included. One day was provided for each map problem and two for the special study. References were listed to assist officers in preparing for the map study problems, and, since the original study would be based on an assumed military situation, any references desired could be used by the officer-examinee. In other words, the study was an "open book" test in contrast to the map problems for which no references were to be used during the actual examination. The results of the new regulations were not to be known until the next class entered the College.

The proposed course for the year had followed the routine established in the previous two years, but the historical rides were cancelled by the Chief of Staff, because of "unsettled conditions on the Mexican Border." [62] US Navy forces occupied Vera Cruz in early April 1914, and Army troops under General Funston replaced them at the end of the month. As a further result of the situation, the class was graduated on 30 April and its members were directed to report to their commands as soon as possible. Three members of the class were reported as not having satisfactorily completed the course and were not awarded diplomas.

Efforts had been made to improve the course which, in its general plan, coincided closely to those of previous years. For example, the deficiencies in the study of military history were corrected to some extent by scheduling lectures by Professor R. M. Johnson, the Harvard historian who had accompanied the class on its tour of the Bull Run battlefield in 1913.

An interesting discussion of the Naval War College, published by Major George Nugent in the Artillery Journal, makes possible a comparison between the two schools. Originally, the Naval War College had conducted a one-month course. This was later increased to four months, and, attempts were made by 1912 to extend the course to a full year. Instruction prior to 1910 had consisted entirely of lectures followed by discussion periods. In that year, however,

> . . . an applicatory system of study, similar to that in use at the Army War College and at the Service Schools, was introduced. The College is endeavoring to cultivate in the minds of the officers of the Navy the habit of systematic reasoning in approaching tactical or strategic problems, such as is given by an 'Estimate of the Situation.' [63]

The changes in the Naval War College course had added "situations" which were developed in committee sessions. The solutions were discussed by the entire college, in much the same manner as the entire Army War College reviewed student solutions of various problems and exercises. A series of tactical and strategic naval exercises also were conducted, and the solutions to these were tested by wargaming.

Much emphasis was placed on the study of international law. Professor George C. Wilson of Harvard and Brown Universities had lectured at the Naval War College on this subject annually since 1902. The studies accomplished by the college were recognized nationally as outstanding in the field.

The two colleges were thus quite similar in character. Instructional methods used were almost identical, although the Naval War College scheduled more lectures. The Naval College placed greater reliance on outside expertise, including civilian academicians, although the Army War College was gradually scheduling more and more visiting lecturers. Each, moreover, emphasized the tactics and strategy of its own service. The cooperation exemplified by the exchange of instructors and students and by common solution of mutual problems was beneficial not only to the two colleges, but also to the entire Army and Navy establishments.

The Mexican problem had further effect upon the two institutions. For the first time since 1904, no member of the Army War College attended the summer session of the Naval War College. Furthermore, no Navy representative attended the 1914-15 course at Washington Barracks.

At the direction of the Chief of Staff, the War Department Library, which had been created in 1795, was moved from the War Department Building to the War College and consolidated with the College library in May 1914. More than 59,000 volumes were added to the 32,000 volumes at the War College.

Nineteen officers were in the class welcomed by the new president of the War College, Brigadier General Montgomery C. Macomb, who had replaced General Liggett in April. All the officers were of field grade. General Liggett had recommended such action in a memorandum to the Chief of Staff in February 1914 stating:

The mission of the Army War College is not to round out the education of all officers or even a large part of them, but is rather to develop those officers who have demonstrated capacity beyond their fellows for higher duties of command in war and for the duties of the General Staff in the higher grades.

Ultimately it should be the inflexible rule that all officers selected for the course at the Army War College must be graduates of the Staff College; but for the present this will not be possible without discrimination against a number of worthy and competent officers who have reached field rank without having had an opportunity of taking the course at the Service Schools.

Officers below the grade of field officer should not be considered because the actual and prospective duties of captains and lieutenants are not those involving either higher staff functions or those of command sufficiently high to necessitate or justify a course at the War College.[64]

Although General Wood, the Chief of Staff, approved and recommended action, the proposed changes were not placed in effect until November when General Wotherspoon, Wood's successor, directed their implementation. Four members of the class were graduates of the Staff College; the remaining fifteen had all passed the qualification examination.

The course for the 1915 academic year once again followed the well-established curricular line already described. Although there was little substantive change, the course was continuously modified to assure inclusion of current information from the European conflict which had begun in August. Assistant Secretary of War Henry S. Breckinridge reported his observations of the war after his return with the American Relief Expedition (conducted to evacuate US citizens from the area of conflict) in October. His detailed analysis was an amazingly comprehensive report on personnel, tactics, arms, and logistics of the Allied and German forces.[65] Even today, it must be considered as an intelligence report of outstanding character.

Professor Johnson again lectured on military history, this time in three successive sessions. His talks were attended by the entire War College Division of the General Staff and also by other officers in the Washington area. New lecture topics included the "Military Application of Graphics" and "Military Geography" delivered by

Major W. D. Connor. The war in Europe was reflected further by lectures on defensive warfare and naval engagements in European waters.

Although arrangements were made for the annual historical rides, they were cancelled by instructions from the Secretary of War in April 1915. The Secretary instructed General Macomb that nothing was to interfere with the work underway by all officers of the College, faculty and students alike, to formulate a "Proper Military Policy for the United States." [66]

Seventeen of the nineteen officers were graduated on 30 June 1915. The remaining two members of the class completed the course but were not given diplomas. Two members of the graduating class, Colonel John W. Ruckman and Lieutenant Colonel John P. Hains, were assigned to the Naval War College for the full-year course beginning in July. They were the first Army officers to attend the Naval War College "long course."

The 24 Army members of the class reporting to Washington Barracks in September 1915 were joined by one Navy officer and one Marine Corps officer. The course followed the general lines of previous years but again was modified constantly to reflect lessons reported from the European War. Lectures were given by Army observers formerly with the Austro-Hungarian and French Armies. Logistic presentations emphasized the preparations being made by the service branches for wartime needs. The Dardanelles Campaign was discussed in detail. Several General Staff war plans were analyzed by wargaming.

A number of visiting lecturers were invited to address the College. Professor George C. Wilson of Harvard discussed "The German and Other Rules for Land Warfare." "Pan-Americanism" was the subject of John Barrett, Director General of the Pan-American Union. One of very few women to lecture to the War College before World War I was Miss Mabel Boardman, who spoke on "The Organization of the American Red Cross."

One other lecture was scheduled that was so unusual in content as to warrent detailed description. This was the presentation on "The Plant, Organization, and Personnel of the American Telephone and Telegraph Company" by its chief engineer, J. J. Carty. As a part of his demonstration, Mr. Carty had installed a large number of desk telephones in the lecture room. This enabled everyone in the room to listen while he placed a call from Washington in succession to and through New York, Boston, Pittsburgh, Chicago, and finally San Francisco. Ahern notes that a phonograph record played in San Francisco could be clearly heard and that General Macomb was able to carry on a conversation with Colonel Glassford at the Presidio of San Francisco! Ahern also commented that this was ". . . a practical exhibition of the efficiency of the . . . company made under difficulties as recent storms had broken the connections in places and round-about routes had to be followed . . ." [67]

The proposed historical and staff rides again were cancelled, this time because of Pancho Villa's attack on Columbus, New Mexico, on 8-9 May. Members of the class were directed to report to their various units for duty the following day. The simple graduation ceremony planned could not be held, and the officers departed as quickly as possible for their commands.

Near disaster almost overtook both the War College and the General Staff in late 1915. President Woodrow Wilson had found an item in the Baltimore Sun which stated that the General Staff was preparing a plan in case of war with Germany. Wilson became enraged and called Acting Secretary of War Henry Breckinridge to his office and directed him to make an immediate investigation. If the charge proved true, Breckinridge was ". . . to relieve at once every officer of the General Staff and order him out of Washington"! [68] Breckinridge gave General Bliss, the Acting Chief of Staff, the responsibility for conducting the investigation. Bliss informed Breckinridge that the law creating the General Staff made it its duty "To prepare plans for the national defense" and that both the General Staff and the War College studied and revised plans over and over again. Apparently the explanation satisfied President Wilson, for no further action was directed. However, Bliss noted that "Mr. Breckinridge directed me to caution the War College to 'camouflage' its work. This resulted in practically no further official studies." [69]

Additional restrictions on the activities of the War College and its close relationship with the General Staff were included in the National Defense Act passed by Congress on 3 June 1916. This statute made the following regulations, as cited in a War Department Bulletin, mandatory:

> The War College shall remain fully subject to the supervising, coordinating, and informing powers conferred by law upon members of the General Staff Corps, and officers for duty as instructors of students in or as attaches of said college may be selected and detailed freely from among members of said corps, but any officer so selected and detailed other than one director shall thereupon cease to be a member of said corps and shall not be eligible for redetail therein so long as he shall remain on said duty; and no officer on the active list of the Army shall, for more than thirty days in any calendar year, be attached to or assigned to duty in the War College in any capacity other than that of president, director, instructor, or student, or, unless a member of the General Staff Corps, be attached to or employed in the office of the Chief of Staff.[70]

Although the primary immediate effects of this Act involved officers serving jointly on the General Staff and the War College faculty, the resultant long-reaching effects were far more serious. The title "War College Division" was dropped; a possible blessing, since it removed some of the confusion still existing regarding the work and personnel of the Division and the work and faculty of the War College in Army and public eyes alike. The law made it mandatory that the War College confine its activities to the instruction of its students. Ahern analyzed the ultimate effect to be the "complete divorce of General Staff personnel from the War College." It also placed the responsibility upon the War Department to make the War College what "the law intends it should be—an institution of military learning."[71] Henceforth, the War College could not be continued as a part of a working subdivision of the War Department General Staff nor could its faculty and students assist the General Staff in preparation of its operational plans and war studies.

Although 29 officers were selected to attend the 1916-17 course, exigencies of the service would permit actual attendance by only 19. Ten of the group were graduates of the Staff College, the largest percentage of Staff College graduates in any class to date. The remaining nine officers had passed the qualification examination. One Marine and one Navy officer were also detailed to attend the course.

The seriousness of the Mexican Border situation caused the course to start in October instead of early September. Instruction proceeded along established lines until January, with primary emphasis on preparation for war. The military forces had little doubt as to the eventual involvement of the United States in the European conflict.

The course was greatly changed in February by the tremendous amount of military information from abroad which had literally swamped the Military Information Section of the General Staff. Consequently, Brigadier General Joseph E. Kuhn, who had replaced General Macomb as President of the War College in early February, decided to substitute intensive study of the reports from Europe for the normal historical and hypothetical studies. This decision was made to provide the troops with any information that might be available and of value in training for service overseas—and despite the restrictions of the National Defense Act of 1916 prohibiting the use of War College personnel for General Staff work. Lectures and conferences were continued much as originally scheduled.

The class was divided into committees, each headed by a member of the faculty. Work proceeded on this basis until the United States declared war on Germany on 6 April 1917. The student officers were rapidly reassigned and the War College, as an academic institution, became inactive although the library, historical, and map sections continued to provide service to members of the General Staff.

The Testing of the Blade:
World War I

SIXTEEN years had passed since General S. B. M. Young and his War College Board met to formulate Elihu Root's War College. Thirteen classes had been graduated, and 254 officers had carried the teachings of the War College to the Army and its sister services.

The instruction given these officers had differed greatly and had developed slowly over the years. The first classes received very little academic teaching from the faculty, the "permanent personnel." Most of the experience gained came from actual work on General Staff problems and studies, the process of "learning by doing" so emphasized by General Tasker H. Bliss.

General Hugh L. Scott, Chief of Staff of the Army, explained the reason for this procedure in his annual report to the Secretary of War in 1917:

> It may be said that the General Staff is only just growing to man's estate. An act of Congress in 1903 created this organ in name, but the act could not endow a large body of officers with the special education and experience which are the attributes of a General Staff. This education and experience had to be created; the act merely gave the authority to undertake the task.
> The Staff College and the War College were therefore instituted, but the instructors themselves had to be evolved before these schools could turn out a useful product. Such a process is long, and it is only in the last few years that a small but steady supply of men has passed through the Staff College and the War College, and returning to their regiments, constituted a little reservoir from which could be drawn from time to time and under very strict rules officers understanding at least the theory and trained at least in the theoretical application of general-staff methods.[1]

The course of instruction during the first years was devoted not only to the study of general staff methods, but also to the actual development of staff procedures. The evolutionary development of the General Staff, as shown outwardly by reorganization and inwardly by improved and more efficient methods, was paralleled by the academic development of the War College.

From primary emphasis on staff work as "apprentice" members of the General Staff, the student officers were led to the study of tactics, strategy, and logistics necessary to qualify them for high command as well as for high level General Staff service. Much of what was taught in the War College in its first 16 years can be viewed as the equivalent of what is today taught at the Command and General Staff College at Fort Leavenworth. Terrain analysis, troop movements, estimate of the situation, tactical and strategic problems, map maneuvers and war games were adopted, used, and improved.

Lectures supplemented practical instruction throughout the period. Although primary emphasis was placed on subjects of military importance, particularly current developments at home and abroad, other areas were not ignored. International affairs, political science, geography, economics, law, and history were included. Science and technology in fields such as aeronautics, radio, transportation, and medicine were discussed.

Historical studies were gradually increased; not the study of historical examples of battles and leaders alone, but a translation of events of the past to the situation of the time to provide the students with actual strategic situations requiring command or staff action using modern equipment, tactics, organization, and knowledge. The study of historical examples was supplemented by the use of actual operational plans and war studies prepared by the General Staff. War-gaming and detailed analysis of these plans provided the students with an intimate knowledge of General Staff theories and concepts and taught staff procedures by actual example. The General Staff benefited also, for the wargaming and analysis of these studies by the students provided the basis for revision and modification.

By 1917, the War College could no longer be considered a section of the General Staff nor even an adjunct of that group. Although this severence had been required by the National Defense Act of 1916, the Act merely formalized a process that had been taking place gradually over the entire 16-year period. The War College slowly but positively had assumed the status of an academic institution and abrogated its position as a staff agency.

There is little doubt that the Army War College as originally established had been patterned after the German War Academy. However, as General Bliss had emphasized in his report of 1903,

> . . . our system of military education differs from that in the great military nations of the world in that we cannot be content merely with training a lieutenant to be a good lieutenant or a captain to be a good captain, or in training staff officers to the efficient performance of duties in peace which they will continue to perform in the same grade in time of war; but it is to train the officers who will form the leaven of a great army in time of war, so that they will be able, at a moment's notice, to perform the duties of far advanced grades and to render service in the branches of the Army, both line and staff, in which they are not commissioned in time of peace.[2]

The general system of the Prussian War Academy was modified, improved, and purified to best enable the small regular Army of the United States to qualify its officers for command and staff duty when, and if, the Army was expanded in time of crisis.

Tasker H. Bliss and William W. Wotherspoon emerge as the dominant figures in the War College of this era. Bliss laid the foundation upon which Wotherspoon developed the College into an academic institution. Together and without interruption, these two men guided the War College for more than 10 of its first 16 years. Moreover, their influence did not stop after promotion and reassignment from the College proper, for each of them served as Assistant Chief of Staff and each later became Chief of Staff.

The proof of the effectiveness of the War College came with World War I. In contrast to the muddled and confused operations to raise, equip, and transport an Army to Cuba during the war with Spain, the Army expanded quickly, efficiently, and effectively to take part in the European conflict.

At the outset of the war, the Regular Army consisted of about 133,000 officers and men. By November 1918, this force had been expanded 20 times to more than 4 million. Almost half this number were trained, equipped, armed, and transported to Europe at the rate of 10,000 a day. Two hundred days of actual combat with the enemy proved the effectiveness of this force.[3]

The figures cited are an impressive indication of the overall accomplishments of the Army. What contributions did the War College graduates make to these efforts? This can be shown by an analysis of the positions of command and high staff they held.

By the time of the Armistice, 11 November 1918, 188,434 officers were on active duty. Of the 3,885 Regular Officers, only 4.7 percent or 182, were graduates of the Army War College. By contrast, more than 30 percent of the 407 general officers serving on 11 November 1918 were graduates of the War College. More than 45 percent of division and higher command positions, including the Chief of Staff of the Army, were filled by War College graduates. Approximately 20 percent of the major unit chief of staff positions, both overseas and in the United States, also were filled by graduates. Fifty-seven percent of all War College graduates from 1905 through 1917 became general officers.[4]

Percentage and similar data do not always present the entire record, but the comments of the senior commanders supplement such information. General Hugh L. Scott, Chief of Staff of the Army in 1917, stated:

Since war was declared, the demand for officers having this [War College] education has been enormous; the supply wholly is inadequate. But these few officers have worked with a devotion and skill worthy of great praise, and it is without fear of contradiction that I record the belief that had this small category of officers educated in general-staff work never been created, the confusion, delay, and disappointments of 1898 would have been repeated and magnified in 1917.[5]

The Commander-in-Chief of the American Expeditionary Forces, General of the Army John J. Pershing—who had attended but not graduated from the War College—gave this praise to War College graduates:

> The duties of the General Staff, as well as those of the Army and Corps staffs, have been very ably performed. Especially is this true when we consider the new and difficult problems with which they have been confronted. This body of officers, both as individuals and as an organization, have, I believe, no superiors in professional ability, in efficiency, or in loyalty.[6]

McAndrew Charts a New Course: 1919-1940

AFTER the signing of the Armistice ending World War I, the War Department General Staff turned its efforts to meeting two new requirements to demobilize the huge wartime Army and prepare for peacetime operations. Although troops were returned from France and processed into civilian life quickly and efficiently, preparation for peacetime operations proved far more complicated.

The lessons learned just prior to and during the war had emphasized the need for many changes within the Army. These included tactical reorganization, restructuring the War Department General Staff, and a revision of the Army educational system. Although the war had been conducted with efficiency—particularly in comparison with the confused operations of the Spanish American War—the rapid mobilization of the nation's manpower and economic resources and the resultant inability of the War Department General Staff to cope with the greatly increased workload indicated that changes were necessary. New weapons and methods of warfare required a far greater knowledge, not only of combat principles and tactics, but also of supply procedures and means of communications at all levels. Secretary of War Newton D. Baker summed up the situation in his annual report for 1919:

> It has been made specially apparent that General Staff officers for duty with the War Department and for larger expeditionary forces should have broader knowledge, not only of their purely military duties, but also a full comprehension of all agencies, governmental as well as industrial, necessarily involved in a nation at war, to the end that coordinated effort may be secured from all these agencies, and that they may be employed economically and efficiently both in the preparation for and during war.[1]

Discussion and analysis of the many changes made within the Army during this period are not of direct importance to a study of the Army War College. The revision of the Army educational system, however, had a direct application to the War College and its position within that system.

Baker stated that the purpose in revising the Army's education of its officers and enlisted men was to modify ". . . the prewar system where the lessons learned in war indicated changes were necessary to make the system meet more modern requirements."[2] These revisions were caused, not so much by the failure of the existing system in preparing officers for wartime duties, but, rather, because the output of the schooling system had proven inadequate and duplicatory in many respects. Consequently, the entire educational program was reviewed with the objectives of improving the curriculums of the various schools to meet modern military needs, increasing the capacity of existing schools, and establishing new institutions where necessary.

Of vital importance to the Army War College was the realization that the war had demonstrated a necessity for a broader scope of education for professional officers of all grades. Changes in the missions of the General Staff School at Fort Leavenworth and the War College had a direct effect on the curricula of both institutions. The General Staff School was to concentrate on preparing selected officers for duty as General Staff officers with tactical units and for higher tactical command. The War College was to prepare officers for duty in the War Department General Staff and for higher command.[3] Furthermore, the War College was not to restrict its curriculum to subjects of purely military nature but was to include ". . . studies of an economic nature in regard to supply in general and industrial activities necessarily employed in war with a view to securing the cooperation and coordination of governmental and industrial agencies of the nation."[4]

Early in 1919, the decision was made to reinstitute courses at the War College and to have the first postwar class enter in September of that year. Major General James W. McAndrew was designated as Commandant of the College. He carefully picked his staff and

MAJOR GENERAL JAMES W. McANDREW
Appointed Commandant of the Army War College after World War I, General McAndrew convened his faculty in Germany early in 1919. The curriculum planned at that time was retained almost unchanged until 1940.

faculty and began plans for the academic year. Twenty-four officers were selected. Nineteen were in France and Germany with various units of the American Expeditionary Forces; the remainder held key assignments in the continental United States. The caliber of this group is perhaps best shown by the fact that nine of the officers held temporary general officer rank during the war, although all were reduced from one to three grades in the subsequent demobilization.

It is ironic that the first meeting of the faculty of the institution which would contribute so much toward the defeat of Germany a quarter century later was held on German soil! General McAndrew assembled many of his carefully selected staff and faculty at Treves, Germany, in May 1919.[5] The exact instructions given McAndrew are not known. However, it is quite apparent that the group was "starting out on an uncharted course."[6]

McAndrew was faced with the problem of preparing an entirely new curriculum rather than revising the course of instruction of the old Army War College. Consequently, much of the experience gained in countering the problems of the prewar institution was of little, if any, benefit and could not be used as a guide in the preparation of the new curriculum.

McAndrew based his proposed curriculum on the interpretation that the assigned mission of the War College ". . . intends training to be obtained by the actual performance of General Staff functions in the solution of practical problems in preparing for war."[7] This emphasis on staff duties was further dictated by the war experience, which had shown that "the greatest need was for trained general staff officers and officers who could handle the proposition of supply."[8] In other words, the new curriculum initially was centered on duties of the War Department General Staff officer with little emphasis on command as such.

This curriculum was not based on the existing structure of the War Department but on the staff organization of the General Headquarters of the American Expeditionary Forces. This was a farsighted decision which involved a gamble to some extent. The War Department General Staff was undergoing another of its periodic reorganizations; would this reorganization follow the AEF structure or would it be completely different? Fortunately, the National Defense Act of 1920 provided a General Staff organization which, when modified in 1921, was essentially identical to the staff structure of Pershing's headquarters.[9] With minor variations, the War Department General Staff remained unchanged until 1942, a distinct contrast to the almost annual reorganization prior to and during World War I. McAndrew's visionary decision enabled retention of the core curriculum of the Army War College basically unchanged from 1919 to 1941.

McAndrew's embryo faculty developed a curriculum emphasizing General Staff training as the basis of qualifying an officer for duty on a high-level staff or for high command or the "higher leadership."[10] McAndrew and his associates viewed the ultimate purpose of the entire military establishment of the United States as defense, in its political interpretation rather than its tactical or strategic meaning. Furthermore, the mission of the War Department General Staff was interpreted to include preparation in time of peace for defensive war as well as the conduct of war once hostilities had commenced. Preparation for war entailed not only military training but also the study of relationships with world powers and military, economic, political, and psychological analyses of those powers. The study of US resources—industry, manpower, and natural wealth—also was believed to be of prime importance.[11] All these factors were considered from the standpoint of their effect on General Staff functions.

The course of study recommended for the Army War College consisted of the "solution of one big problem, the same problem that confronts our General Staff and our military establishment, namely: preparedness of the country for war, possible if not probable."[12] The first step in solving this problem, either by the War Department or by the students, was to formulate an estimate of the situation ". . .that is, to examine the present relations of the United States to the great powers."[13] This analysis was to include a study of the military, economic, political, sociological, and geographic capabilities of the countries concerned. In the terminology of 1967, this was a strategic intelligence estimate of the national power of the various great nations.

This study was intended to provide an indication of ". . . possible enemies of the future, and the probability of war with them as indicated by our present relationships or by such future relations as can now be determined."[14] Once the hypothetical threat had been determined, the next step in staff procedure (development of war plans) became feasible. These plans were intended to provide the basis for meeting the threat of war, including mobilizing manpower and industry as well as training a military force.

After various plans had been prepared, students acting as the Operations Section of the General Staff studied the plans and prepared the staff direction necessary for the use of such forces. Close coordination was necessary with other staff sections—personnel and supply, for example—to assure proper manning, arming, supply, and transport of these forces. Supply and transport were not to be restricted to the mere study of military procedures. Instead, this portion of the War College course was to consider ". . . practically every commercial activity and line of industry . . ."[15] To aid in developing student appreciation of the civilian participation in the war effort, lecturers were to define and discuss the commercial, financial, educational, governmental, and sociological resources of the United States. This lecture program was in some ways a continuation of the lecture series begun in the pre-World War I College, a continuation much enlarged.

The curriculum plan to this point had determined ". . . the most possible war."[16] A theater of operations had been selected, based on this analysis, usually with a situation most unfavorable to the United States. The reaction of the United States had been determined up to the actual point of military contact. The "solution of the one big problem," as McAndrew viewed the work of the War Department General Staff, could not be termed completed, however, without actual conduct of the "war." This was to be accomplished by war-gaming—another carryover from the old War College—and by conducting terrain exercises. This McAndrew deemed necessary to develop leadership and ". . . to test the ability of the members of the College to perform General Staff duties under conditions closely assimilated to those of war."[17]

This, then, was the curriculum planned by the McAndrew cadre at Treves, Germany, in May 1919. The recommended course of study was sent to the Chief of Staff of the Army in June 1919, approved with minor changes, and used as the basis of study for the Class of 1919-20. With relatively minor changes, this curriculum remained the foundation of the course of study of the Army War College until its suspension just prior to the entry of the United States into World War II.

General McAndrew and his staff and faculty began to assemble in Washington shortly after their initial planning session. A number of steps taken by the War Department General Staff in connection with its preparation for peacetime operations had direct effect on the Army War College. The first of these was the announcement of selection criteria for the student officers of the Class of 1919-20.[18] Officers eligible for selection included commanders of brigades or higher units during the war, chiefs of staff of division or higher tactical units during the war, officers who had served efficiently as chiefs of General Staff sections of Corps or higher tactical units during the war, officers of the General Staff Corps, and officers who were able ". . . to establish to the satisfaction of the Commandant that their past education and service is an effective guarantee of their capacity to take this course."[19] One additional group was considered eligible for selection; graduates of the old Army Staff College, the predecessor institution of the new General Staff School at Fort Leavenworth. The qualification criteria resulted in a most unusual student body. Only two members of the class had held rank lower than colonel during the war, 44 had been colonels, and 29 had been temporary brigadier generals. Four had worn the two stars of a major general. Moreover, almost every officer in the group had been reduced from one to three grades in the subsequent demobilization of the wartime Army! Nearly three-fourths had seen service in France with the American Expeditionary Forces; the remainder either had held key positions on the War Department General Staff or had been assigned high commands elsewhere in the United States.

The close umbilical ties to the War Department began to be severed when the Commandant was relieved of his additional duty as Director of the War Plans Division, War Department General Staff.[20]

THE ARMY WAR COLLEGE CLASS OF 1920

Most of the officers in this class had served in positions of great responsibility during World War I. Thirty-three had been general officers during the war but were reduced in rank during the demobilization.

For the first time since the inception of the War College, the Commandant no longer "wore two hats" and could thus devote his entire effort to the operation of an academic institution.

A change of name for the War College was indicated in the outline of the new Army educational system which listed the "General Staff College" at the apex of that system.[21] The head of the College was to be the "commandant" rather than the "president." The Army Staff School at Fort Leavenworth also was to be redesignated as the General Staff School.[22] The similarity in the titles of the two institutions led to confusion. Consequently, the title reverted to "Army War College" less than two years later.[23] (Only "Army War College" will be used in this work to avoid confusion.)

Following the custom of the prewar College, formal opening ceremonies were held on 2 September 1919. Secretary of War Newton D. Baker and General Peyton C. March, the Chief of Staff, addressed the class and faculty. It was March who stressed the theme to be followed throughout the year with his very first words: "The opening of the General Staff College, as the logical successor of the old War College, marks the transition from the old order of things to the new."[24] This was apparent to the 76 Army and two Marine officers in the class from the outset.

The transition from the old to the new carried with it many of the methods and attitudes of the old War College. The concentration on "learning by doing," initiated so many years before by Bliss, again was a key part of the new College method. Small committee groups were continued. The use of conferences to review student solutions and to discuss items of general or wide interest was also a part of the new curriculum. The informal relationships between student and faculty, the emphasis upon academic freedom of expression, the nonattribution policy applied to lecturers—all were retained as an integral part of the method of the new College.

Here, the similarities ended. In contrast to the 21 lectures scheduled in 1916-17, more than 90 lectures were delivered during the first year of the new college, nearly one-fourth of these by nongovernmental speakers. Included were Samuel Gompers, President of the American Federation of Labor; F. M. Fling, Professor of

Government at the University of Nebraska; the former Ambassadors to Turkey and China; and an old friend of the past, R. M. Johnson, Professor of History at Harvard.

Professor Johnson remembered well his many visits to the old Army War College and his trips to the Civil War battlefields with various classes. His interest in the Army institution and his devotion to military history resulted in a proposal for joint sponsorship of "fortnightly conferences" to be held alternately at Harvard and the Army War College to discuss economic and military history.[25] These conferences were to be limited to "advanced students and outside experts." Johnson proposed that members of the Harvard group and the Army War College exchange visits, and that each conference propose topics of discussion for solution by the counterpart groups. Apparently the recommendation was not adopted by either institution. One can only speculate on the results which might have been obtained from such a bilateral cooperation between the two institutions.

In addition to the many visiting American lecturers, Colonel Jacques Adelbert de Pinston, Comte de Chambrun, of the French Army was assigned as an official observer and lecturer.[26] This is the only instance of a foreign officer being attached to the faculty. Colonel Chambrun presented several lectures during the year and served as a consultant to many of the student committees.

Habits of the past could not be completely overcome, however. The specter of the old relationship between the Army War College and the War Plans Division of the General Staff was resurrected by the Chief of that division, Major General W. G. Haan. Throughout the year, General Haan referred studies to the General Staff College for solution, a return to the concept that the College was merely an adjunct to, if not a part of, the General Staff. This situation became critical in April 1920 when General Haan asked the Commandant to initiate studies on internal subversion within the United States. Haan explained his reasoning:

There has come into being since the beginning of the World War a new enemy of organized government, who has been successful in getting control of a number of European governments and representatives of which are now attempting to get control of the United States government.[27]

Haan expressed concern over the possibility of such internal unrest, including nationwide strikes caused by subversive elements. He indicated that only military forces, with the help of the National Guard, could handle the situation. Haan considered it necessary to develop plans to meet such contingencies and bases for action against such subversion. "The present course for the General Staff College does not in my view impart the necessary instruction to meet this situation and particularly that relating to the tactical features of the problem,"[28] he informed the Commandant.

General McAndrew discussed this proposal with his faculty. The consensus was that the Haan proposal was reactionary and its acceptance would indicate a willingness to return to the prewar use of the College to conduct studies for the War Department. Only one faculty member recommended acceptance of the Haan proposal and this only because Haan was directly responsible for the entire educational system of the Army![29]

General McAndrew adopted a middle-of-the-road approach by indicating to General Haan that the curriculum of the College could not be altered to prepare studies of this nature. However, McAndrew asked Haan to provide lectures on internal subversion by members of the War Plans Division. McAndrew added:

> You understand that we stand ready and willing to give you every help in the world in this heavy problem that confronts you. I realize, and I think the others here do, how very much you are handicapped by reason of lack of officers suitable to make the study you propose, but for goodness sake do not interfere with our course here or upset the present regime until you have gone thoroughly into the work we are doing and the results at which we are aiming.[30]

The situation was further complicated by McAndrew's being senior to Haan. Neither was willing to give in and admit being in error. Haan continued to send projects to the College for solution until his reassignment in September 1921. McAndrew continued to return such requests with polite notes indicating that the College was not able. to make the desired study. Periodically, McAndrew added lectures to the curriculum to meet the suggestions proferred by Haan; e.g., he added two discussions on military geology to the 1921 course.

Haan also sent other comments to the Commandant, some of them directory in nature. A letter in March 1921 informed McAndrew that, "It is desired that the volume of matter for the next year's course be materially reduced."[31] Haan indicated that the workload assigned should necessitate no more than seven or eight hours' study daily. One letter from Haan may have enraged McAndrew so much that he crumpled and tore the paper for the copy in the Army War College files still bears signs of crumpling and badly torn edging. This letter was a general criticism of the course and stressed the necessity of emphasizing command as well as staff duty.[32]

Although the controversy ended with Haan's departure and the subsequent retirement and early death of General McAndrew, it is of particular interest because of the contrasting views of the two men. Haan had been a member of the first faculty of the War College in 1905 as a captain and had been given "constructive credit" for attending the College. McAndrew had been a member of the Class of 1913. The battle waged between the two men—and it must be considered such—was one of basic concept. Haan still considered the College to be part of the War Department General Staff; McAndrew insisted it was an academic institution with a specific mission which did not include preparation of studies for any division of the War Department. One cannot say that either Haan or McAndrew won. However, this controversy was the last visible—and vociferous—indication of any attempt to retain the College as part of the General Staff. The tie between the two may not have been broken completely, but it was so thin as to be virtually nonexistent.

In decided contrast to the controversial Haan's attitude was a suggestion made by Captain George C. Marshall. Captain Marshall was concerned about an apparent shortcoming he had noted in staff procedures in both the AEF and the War Department General Staff:

the lack of proper and sufficiently detailed instructions to action officers assigned a study project. Marshall felt that this lack resulted in unnecessary work and often produced studies of little value. He recommended that the College consider including methods for developing policy and preparing instructions to guide staff officers working on the implementation of such policy. McAndrew considered Marshall's letter so important that he provided copies to all faculty members for use in their respective parts of the course of instruction.[33]

The War College course was essentially the one developed by McAndrew and his faculty at Treves the preceding May. Detailed estimates of the major powers were made in the intelligence subcourse. The resulting analysis indicated the major threat to the United States to be Japan; the worst possible coalition, Japan and Great Britian. The operations study caused development of defensive and offensive plans of operation tied to the war plan based on the intelligence studies. Training in foreign armies was studied and compared to that of the United States Army. The recommendations were then applied to training requirements generated by the students' war plans. In the same manner, personnel and logistic studies were related to the overall student war plans.

In the spring of 1920, the class was divided for reconnaissance trips to Fort Ethan Allen, Vermont, Plattsburg Barracks, New York, and Waltervleit Arsenal, New York, to give the student officers an opportunity to conduct a War Department General Staff reconnaissance allied to war plans. This field trip was followed by a war game using the war plan and allied components developed during the year.

Although not originally planned as a part of the curriculum, the old prewar trips to Civil War battlefields were reinstituted with visits to Gettysburg and the Shenandoah Valley. These trips differed from the prewar studies in that students simply toured the battle areas without any attempt to analyze a similar campaign conducted with modern organization and equipment. An additional trip was made to Camp Meade, Maryland, to inspect the schools and shops of the Tank Corps located on that post.

All the student war plans followed the War Department procedure of referring to war plans by color names rather than by the name of the country concerned. It can be assumed that this was an outgrowth of the near-disaster which occurred when President Wilson learned of the War Department's plans for war with Germany in 1915. This practice continued throughout this period.

In March 1920, the Chief of Staff of the Army recommended to the Joint Board (Army and Navy) that the Naval and Army War Colleges use the same strategic problems. He also recommended cross assignment of officers to the faculties as well as to the student classes of the two institutions.[34] These recommendations were considered by the Joint Board, which made the following recommendations to the Secretaries of War and the Navy:

> The courses of the Army General Staff and the Naval War College shall be coordinated as far as practicable.
> If practicable, two graduates, line officers, of the Naval War College will be detailed for duty with each class at the Army General Staff College.
> If practicable, two graduates of the Army General Staff College will be detailed for duty with each alternate class at the Naval War College.
> If practicable, two Marine officers will be detailed for duty with each class at the respective colleges.[35]

These recommendations were approved by both secretaries and placed into effect the following year. As a result, the courses of study at the two institutions had many common characteristics, including a joint map maneuver, and officers of each service attended the other service's college until 1940. This resulted in close harmony within the academic framework of the curricula and in the workings of the War Department and Naval Department staffs.

In addition to the Army War College regular course of instruction designed primarily for officers of the combat arms, a special course was conducted simultaneously for 18 officers who were members of or detailed to the various services. (Non-combat arms branches such as Ordnance and Quartermaster). The decision to hold this course was based on two factors: many officers of the services were virtually eliminated from attending the regular course, because of the prerequisite for command or high level staff service during the war, and one portion of the mission of the College stated, "It will conduct such special courses for general officers and selected officers of the technical and administrative services as may be prescribed with a view of insuring harmonious cooperation throughout the services."[36]

The 18 officers in the special course were selected from the technical and administrative services. Captain P. L. Focardi of the New York National Guard also attended the course at his own expense.

The instruction given this group differed greatly from the regular curriculum. Although the special course students attended the lectures delivered to the regular student body, they did not participate in the intelligence, war plans, training, or operations parts of the curriculum. Instead, the special class was organized into committees to prepare monographs related to the roles, missions, functions, and equipment of the various services. These monographs were intended for use by the regular students working on the personnel and supply portions of the curriculum.[37] When the regular class entered these two parts of their course, the special students served as consultants and acted as the chiefs of their respective services. During the wargames conducted in the spring, the special class assisted as umpires and as special consultants to the students. These officers were not given certificates of graduation nor accorded full credit as graduates of the College.[38]

Although the student officers were not told that they would be rated on their work at the College, the faculty did prepare evaluation data for the Commandant. No numerical ratings were made; instead, each officer was recommended for specific assignments based on his demonstrated abilities for command and staff positions. The following categories were included in the final recommendations by General McAndrew:[39]

Staff assignments:
  Especially recommended for the War Department General Staff, any Division
  Recommended for the War Department General Staff, any Division

Recommended for the War Department General Staff, but only in a specified Division

Command assignments:

Recommended for high command to include divisions

Recommended for high command to include brigades

Not recommended for War Department General Staff nor high command

McAndrew also noted that "The absence of recommendations for high command in the cases of senior officers is due to a lack of initiative on their part or to temperamental characteristics which is believed disqualify. In the case of junior officers it is due to youth and inexperience."[40]

Three officers of the graduating class were included in the list as not recommended for either high command or War Department General Staff duties. In addition, ten of the original 78 did not complete the course and were not given credit for their attendance.[41] Included in this group were two officers who had held general officer rank during World War I! Following the trend established by the old Army War College in 1905, members of the faculty who were not graduates of the College also were given credit for completing the course.

Graduation exercises were held on 29 June 1920, with General John J. Pershing and Secretary of War Newton D. Baker addressing the class. Although Baker made the principal address, it was Pershing who made two statements particularly appropriate to this first postwar Class and to the philosophy on which the curriculum had been based:

> . . . It should be a fixed rule that no officer could be appointed to the grade of general officer in the future, either in the staff or line, who does not possess an intimate knowledge of the functions of the General Staff, through actual experience in war, or through the course of instruction prescribed for General Staff officers, and none without such training should ever again be entrusted with the responsibilities for high command . . .
>
> . . . The assemblage of so many officers of such large experience for military study will probably never again be possible.[42]

Even before the graduation ceremonies were completed,

McAndrew was planning revisions and improvements to the course. Well satisfied with the basic framework of the curriculum, he realized that much improvement could be accomplished without major changes. The only major change made was the addition of a subcourse on command. However, this subcourse consisted primarily of topics which had been a part of other subcourses the previous year: the historical rides, map problems, wargames, and tactical reconnaissance.

The curriculum followed the framework of the previous year. Students made a strategic intelligence estimate; developed war plans; and prepared administrative, operational, logistics, and training plans to support the war concepts. These plans were tested in detailed wargames conducted late in the spring.

The major threat again was established as coming from the Pacific, with the student efforts devoted to study of means to counter this threat, but an additional problem was used: war with Mexico. The first wargame involved testing a portion of the War Plans Division's "Green War Plan." Colonel Edward King, acting director of the G3 course, three years later informed the Commandant, Major General Hanson Ely, that:

> In 1921 the first war game was on the old Green War Plan. The game showed many weaknesses in that plan and it is a rather significant fact that the new Green Plan, while not absolutely following the war game results, took a good many features from them. War Plans Division was a little bit peeved at first at the way we shot the Green Plan to pieces, but as soon as they got over that, they took it in good part and, as I say, have I think profitted [sic] by that war game.[43]

Eighty-eight student officers, many of whom had served in France or in positions of responsibility in the United States during the war, were welcomed by the Secretary of War and the Chief of Staff on 1 September 1920. This class differed from the preceding class in several ways. Graduation from the General Staff School was almost mandatory for officers of the combat arms, although provision was made for the selection of outstanding officers over 48. Officers on the initial eligibility list of the General Staff also were considered to be qualified for selection. The major change, however, was the authorization to appoint officers from the noncombatant branches. For the first time, the services were fully represented in the regular student body,[44] and the special course no longer was necessary.

The officers of the services had performed a semi-faculty function by serving as consultants and representatives of their various branches. To fill the void created by their change to student status, McAndrew requested the Chief of Staff to have each General Staff division and each arm and service designate an official representative to advise student committees, provide current information and data to the College as a whole, and assist in the conduct of wargames. The request was approved and the practice continued until classes were suspended in 1940.[45]

In addition to lectures by military men, many distinguished civilians addressed the College. Henry Morgenthau discussed Turkey; Harvard Professor Robert H. Lord, Poland; State Department representative John Barrett, South America; and others reviewed labor, transportation, economic, and industrial matters. A number of foreign lecturers also addressed the College: Viscount Bryce of the British Embassy; Baron S. A. Kerff, former officer of the Russian Imperial Army; Dr. P. C. Chang, Chinese consul; General Ricardi, Chief of Staff of the Indian Army; and Marshall Foch of France. Over half the lectures given during the year were nonmilitary in subject and were presented by civilian or foreign speakers.

In contrast to the policy of the previous year of not informing the student officers of the basis for their academic evaluations, General McAndrew emphasized the faculty procedures in his orientation of the Class. "In all educational institutions," he said, "students wish to know, and they are entitled to know, just what is required of them and how they are to be graded or reported upon."[46] McAndrew indicated that the numerical rating of students was essential in the School of the Line, desirable at the Staff School, but "neither essential nor desirable" at the War College. "Here," he added, "you are measured but are not marked." The written work of the student officers, their oral participation, and their performance in various student staff and command assignments would form the basis for recommendations as to suitability for high command, assignment to the War Department General Staff, or to special assignments. McAndrew summed up the evaluation philosophy as a report which

> . . . will be made in no narrow spirit, but along broad lines and in a spirit of helpfulness to the War Department. This course is not conducted with a view to 'finding' [slang for failing] as many men as possible, but with a view to helping and broadening officers and adding to the list of qualified General Staff officers as many as possible without lowering the high standards of the American Army.[47]

In compliance with instructions from the War Department, the first Academic Board was established in April 1921. Its members were the Commandant, the Assistant Commandant, and the directors of the various divisions of the faculty. The major function of the Board was overall supervision and preparation of the curriculum, but it had other duties, including final approval of faculty evaluations of the students. McAndrew also used the group for doctrinal studies requested by the War Department.

Student life was not devoted entirely to academic pursuits. Following the custom of the War and Navy Departments of the time, student officers left their cards at the White House as a courtesy gesture to the Commander-in-Chief. In return, they were invited to many receptions and other social activities of the President. All officers, faculty and students alike, were required to attend the official New Year's Day reception at the White House.

Academic studies were not restricted to the College facilities. Research was conducted at the Library of Congress and in the various divisions of the General Staff. State Department assistance often was used as well as the resources of the Department of the Interior.

The historical visit to the Civil War Battlefields included Antietam and Gettysburg and tracing the route of Grant's 1864 campaign. The trips in the spring of 1921 were made in a convoy of Cadillac touring cars with four officers assigned to each car. Extra cans of oil and gasoline were carried because of the infrequency of gas stations in the areas visited. Other visits were made to Aberdeen

Proving Ground and Edgewood Arsenal, Maryland, to inspect Ordnance and Chemical Corps activities.

Eighty-one officers were graduated on 1 June 1921. After brief remarks by Senator Francis E. Warren, representing the Military Affairs Committee of the Senate, and Representative Julius Kahn, the House Committee, Assistant Secretary of War Jay M. Wainwright delivered the graduation address. Secretary Wainwright drew laughter from his audience when he expressed the regrets of Secretary of War John W. Weeks, who was unable to be present because he was attending the fortieth reunion of his own class—at the United States Naval Academy. Two points were emphasized by Wainwright, emphasis which indicated the new status of the military to the American people:

> War has become a profession in the highest sense. Science, skill, invention and all the arts must be the handmaidens of the great effort required.
> West Point, the Service Schools, and the Staff School at Leavenworth are parts of that admirably constituted university in which you gentlemen are not only the senior class, but, in a sense, represent the survival of the fittest. Considering the duties that will fall to your lot and the field laying open before you, your selection for this course of instruction confers a considerable distinction.[48]

The correlation between the Army and Naval War Colleges directed by the Joint Board had brought the two schools into a closer relationship. The Naval War College course for 1920-21 included a study of policy in relation to war, with special emphasis on the United States and Japan in a conflict situation, strategy and logistics involved in such a conflict, tactics of hypothetical battles in the Pacific area, and principles of command. In contrast to the committee-staff efforts of the Army officers, however, each Naval War College student was required to present an individual estimate of the situation in the Pacific area. Committees were used in some parts of the curriculum but not to the extent used in the Army War College system.[49] Apparently the Naval students studied in a more relaxed environment. Their afternoons were left completely free for individual reading and study, whereas the Army War College workload necessitated a full day of work at the College proper, with evening study as needed.

Brigadier General Edward F. McGlachlin, Jr., replaced McAndrew as Commandant in July 1921. In contrast to the uncharted course encountered by McAndrew in 1919, McGlachlin found the College to be a smoothly operating institution held in high esteem by the Army, civilian governmental officials, and the civilian academic community. In two short years, General McAndrew had accomplished a near miracle in creation of an academic institution unrivaled in service history.

Nevertheless, improvements still were required. Both the faculty and the students of the 1921 Class had emphasized the need for increased emphasis on command duties and responsibilities. There was little complaint about staff instruction, and few, if any, recommended reduction of the General Staff concepts included in the curriculum.

McGlachlin stressed the importance of command principles from the very outset of his tenure as Commandant. The increased emphasis insofar as the course of instruction was concerned, however, was gradual. During the 1921-22 course, 17 lectures related to command functions were given. Six conferences and four map maneuvers were complemented by three major wargames and the strategic reconnaissance. Staff work was stressed during the planning phases of the course; command, in the wargames intended to test the student war plans. Decisionmaking as a responsibility of the commander was the key of the command subcourse.

This philosophy was expressed completely and emphatically by McGlachlin in his very first official directive to the faculty:

> Instructors preferably are to be drawn from officers who are graduates of the General Staff College or the Army War College and who are also graduates of the General Staff School, the School of the Line, or the Field Officers Course. It is also desired that they be on the General Staff eligibility list because the principle object of the college is preparation for <u>high</u> <u>command</u>. [Emphasis added] [50]

MAJOR GENERAL EDWARD F. McGLACHLIN, JR.
Although McGlachlin changed curricular emphasis from staff
duty to command, many of his educational concepts were too advanced for his time.

McAndrew Charts A New Course

The confusion caused by designating the institution as the "General Staff College" was ended when it was redesignated as the Army War College in August 1921. Administrative changes were required, but few problems were encountered, for most Army and Washington references had been to the "Army War College" despite its temporary name.

General McGlachlin was keenly aware of the necessity for the nonattribution policy regarding remarks made by visiting lecturers. The relatively large number of men from all parts of the Government who lectured at the War College would have been reluctant to speak freely and candidly and to answer the questions of the students, if their remarks and answers were suddenly to appear attributed to them in print.

In the prewar institution, any Army officer on duty in the Washington area was welcome to attend these lectures. As the scope of the course increased, following the war, and more and more officials lectured on topics far from military in nature, visitors were discouraged. In reply to a request from an Assistant Chief of Staff of the Army asking that Navy supply officers be permitted to attend the lectures, McGlachlin refused permission stating that lecturers were informed that their remarks would be treated confidentially and that the audience would include only the faculty, students, and selected officers of the General Staff.[51] Consequently, McGlachlin regretted that he could not invite the Navy representatives to attend.

McGlachlin also began the practice of informing the class of the necessity for the nonattribution policy as a part of its orientation to the College. His remarks to the Class of 1922 state clearly and succinctly the policy of the Army War College toward its visiting lecturers, a policy essentially the same in 1967 as it was in 1921:

> Here it seems best to give warning that many lectures are of a highly confidential character and must not be discussed with or in the presence of other than the College and its guests of the occasion. This is so because, otherwise, the services of some lecturers could not be obtained at all, while in other instances the lecturers appearing would not be completely free and candid in their remarks. We want our field of selection to be as wide

as possible. We want the honest conclusions of our lecturers and the free and untrammeled opinions and arguments on which they are based. We will tell them so and consult them as to the limitations on their audience. We are in honor bound to observe their conditions and our promises and must emphasize this obligation.[52]

General McGlachlin reviewed carefully and in great detail the policy of evaluating students. The policy of the War Department at that time, as outlined in General Order 112, 23 September 1919, required the relief from any of the service schools of an officer who "shall be deemed unfitted for any reason to continue the course." McGlachlin took strong exception to applying this requirement to the Army War College. This directive, added to the requirement to rate the officer from unsatisfactory to superior, would, in his opinion, generate an unhealthy spirit of competition within the student class, ". . . a narrow and sometimes bitter competition between officers for marks . . ."[53]

McGlachlin believed that the highly selective process used to select an officer to the War College was the result of his total record of service as well as an indication to the caliber of his study at other service schools. Furthermore, McGlachlin maintained that it was extremely difficult to apply definitive ratings or numerical grades in a course such as that conducted by the War College. Consequently, he advocated that "There should finish the course the maximum possible number of officers, of judgement, capacity, and willingness of application," and that the overall ratings, with subsequent indication to the student officers concerned, should be restricted to either satisfactory or unsatisfactory.[54] He emphasized that officers should not be compared within the small and highly selective class of the War College but should be compared with their average contemporaries in the College and elsewhere in the service. He contended that very few officers entering the War College would turn in an unsatisfactory performance, and that none would be encountered who would not apply themselves properly. The results of his efforts were apparent in later years for, other than officers who did not complete the course because of illness, the classes were graduated in their entirety. The recommended assignments and qualifications for command and General Staff duty, however, continued to be made a part of the individual officer's record, which also contained an academic efficiency rating for his student year at the Army War College.

Although the primary mission of the College was to educate officers of the Regular Army, McGlachlin believed there was a related obligation to the officers of the National Guard and Reserve. After conducting a detailed study of possible ways to educate these officers at the War College, he recommended that the Chief of Staff authorize members of the reserve components to attend portions of the regular War College course.[55] McGlachlin emphasized that the College facilities were adequate to handle about 20 additional personnel for each subcourse and that no additional faculty members would be required. This statement made it extremely difficult to disapprove the request, particularly when the reason for the recommendation was to improve the professional education of the reserve component officers. The proposal was approved, and the first group of National Guard and Reserve officers entered the War College in the fall of 1922.[56]

In addition to these officers, McGlachlin recommended that officials of the Departments of State and Commerce be authorized to attend the G-2 subcourse. This request also was approved.[57] Consequently, the Class of 1922, composed of officers of all arms and services, had a very close association with officers of the reserve components and with representatives of the State and Commerce Departments.

McGlachlin had not restricted his recommendations to the Government personnel and reserve component officers. He had recommended that the War Department consider asking selected civilians to attend the War College, regardless of their affiliation with the Government. This part of his overall concept was not approved, because ". . . it is not desirable to request legislation authorizing selected civilians to attend the Army War College. If civilians have a desire to take these courses at the Army War College it is thought that they should seek a commission of appropriate rank in a staff corps of the Officers' Reserve Corps."[58]

This turndown did not discourage McGlachlin, who continued to press for acceptance of civilians as members of the College but with little success. This revolutionary concept and his outspoken efforts toward acceptance of other equally nonconformative ideas may have been a contributory factor to his retirement following the completion of the 1922-23 academic year. To McGlachlin, the Army War College logically should become the center of higher studies for the conduct of ". . . studies in which all departments and bureaus of the executive branch of the Government that would be vitally concerned in international policy and in the origin, prosecution, and termination of war, and in the reconstruction afterward, should participate . . ."[59]

Among the then radical concepts advocated by McGlachlin were the following:

1. That the War Department General Staff assist the College in umpiring war games to assist in determining which student officers should be detailed to the General Staff.

2. That a small number of general officers annually participate in one war game as the commanders of the opposing forces.

3. That the number of Navy officers at the Army War College be increased to twelve including two Marines and four from Navy branches other than the Line.

4. That one war game annually be scheduled using an actual War Department war plan and that the War Department General Staff function as the United States staffs and that the student officers act as the hostile commanders and staffs.[60]

To McGlachlin the horizons bounding the possible development of the Army War College had not nearly been approached and there was "free room for the imagination."[61] The imaginative steps to approach McGlachlin's horizon, however, were tempered by emphasis on logical reasoning. His interpretation of the applicatory system used in the War College almost since its inception was illustrative of this concept:

. . . It falls between learning by personal experience, which is too slow, too cumbersome, too narrow, and too expensive and teaching by rule which is too superficial and too evanescent. It is sought to develop the habit of discrimination, the faculty of analysis, the power to examine a mass of related facts concerning a particular subject, to select from among them the essential things, and to deduce the logical results flowing therefrom. The process is attentive, a concentrated study and comparison of all the elements involved, leading to a reasoned conclusion.[62]

However, McGlachlin must be remembered not for his visionary concepts nor for his minor improvement of the overall curriculum of the War College, but for his reorientation of the entire purpose of that curriculum. His insistence that preparation for war in time of peace and the actual conduct of a conflict were not the prerogatives of the military services alone but concerned equally the civilian departments of the Government and the industry of the nation gave to the course of instruction a distinct flavor of what today would be termed "international relations and political science." McGlachlin sincerely believed that:

Knowledge of the peace-time structure and of the proper means to give it military direction in war cannot be had by the study of the problem in compartments. The problem is one of the nation: of the Army, of the Navy, of the Departments of the Government and the leaders of industry and politics.

This belief he indoctrinated into his faculty and students to such a degree that his concepts were carried on long after his departure from the War College.

In addition to broadening the scope of instruction, McGlachlin reoriented the entire curriculum in an "unremitting attempt . . . to impress the College with the idea that Command is the great thing in war, the true determinant of success or failure, and that the General Staff officer, while a part of the command, is but an adviser, an agent, a subordinate coadjutor of the Commander."[63] This doctrine was in decided contrast to McAndrew's concept that General Staff service was the prime duty of the officer, and that the War College was intended to train its students by the actual performance of general staff functions.

The Command subcourse was expanded greatly during McGlachlin's tenure as Commandant. To replace the wargames, historical rides, and conferences scheduled in 1920-21, he revised the subcourse by scheduling the study of selective campaigns and operations to emphasize the principles of war; by initiating the biographical study of great military leaders, both American and foreign, to emphasize the characteristics or qualities essential in the military leader; and by stressing the importance of making decisions and the responsibilities of the commander throughout other portions of the curriculum. Subordination of the staff officer to the commander has long since become an accepted and integral part of the American military philosophy. McGlachlin's efforts and emphasis may be considered as a contribution to military science which contradicted the Prussian concept that the German General Staff, not the commander, was paramount. The test of McGlachlin's theories came in World War II in the relationships between General Marshall and his overseas commanders, Generals Eisenhower and MacArthur.

Captain Ridley McLean, Navy liaison officer to the Army War College in 1921-22, recommended to the Secretary of the Navy that seven or eight naval officers attend the College annually.[64] This letter described in great detail the course of instruction at the College and, far more important, analyzed the benefits of this course and compared it with that of the Naval War College. McLean wrote ". . . there is a prevailing impression throughout our service that the course here is similar to that at the Naval War College except that one applies to land warfare where the other applies to the sea. It therefore seems necessary to state definitely that this is not the case."[65] McLean compared the Naval War College curriculum to that of the General Staff School at Fort Leavenworth. The Army War College, he added,

> . . . goes much further. Instead of the study of assumed problems, the course here embraces the study of actual problems involved in the preparation for and the conduct of war under existing conditions . . . The idea of Command in its higher sense runs throughout the entire course. The fact is emphasized that while staff work is essential to success in any operation, the decision is the function of Command, who alone has the authority and responsibility . . . I can conceive of no better course of study for the Navy than that offered at this institution.
>   . . . The course here covers war in its broadest aspect, the

studies are national in character, all problems involve combined operations, the world rather than a limited area on land, is the theatre; naval strategy enters quite as much as land strategy. In addition, the course offers unrivalled facilities for studying the world situation as it now exists and the war-making ability in great detail of our own as well as of foreign countries. The course embraces a comprehensive series of lectures by men of preeminence, which is unrivalled in the United States. By access of the student body to the various Departments of the Government in this city, facilities are offered and training is afforded in the utilization in war plans of the vast amount of information available in their archives. It affords a unique opportunity to study in conjunction with the Army, problems which involve joint operations; it brings about close personal relations between selected officers of high rank in the two services which is in itself the best guarantee for cooperation, and it would familiarize each Service with the capabilities of the other, thus laying the foundation for cooperation in war in the fullest significance of the word.

It is therefore recommended that this be regarded as the Senior War College Course as provided for in the educational system as already approved by the Department [of the Navy] [66]

To the institution thus described came a new Commandant, Major General Hanson E. Ely, in June 1923. Ely's first year maintained the momentum begun by McGlachlin. The general organization of the course was retained, with one exception. After faculty G-2 members developed the intelligence estimate, the remainder of the course was divided into two major parts: an informative period during which the functions and methods of the various divisions of the War Department General Staff were analyzed, and a war plans period during which the students functioned as staff officers preparing war plans. Each of these two major segments of the course was subdivided into the familiar G-1, G-3, G-4, and G-5 subcourses. Throughout the year, Ely continued to stress command, as had McGlachlin.

For the first time, the class studied and devised a mobilization plan. This proved somewhat difficult, because the War Department had been working on a similar plan for a long period. Consequently, there was little direct knowledge in the College regarding what such a plan should contain or even its exact format. Students and faculty alike concentrated on the effort. They developed a mobilization plan, after lengthy discussions with personnel in the office of the Assistant Secretary of War, whose primary function was planning for mobilization of manpower and industrial resources. This study proved of direct value to the General Staff officers working on the actual plan.

Suggestions and recommendations of previous commandants and of Navy liaison officers resulted in the first joint war games with the Naval War College in the spring of 1924. Each institution had made separate strategic intelligence estimates; each had arrived at the conclusion that the most logical threat to US security would come from Japan. The wargame, therefore, centered about conflict in the western Pacific. The Naval War College charted maneuvers of the advance across the Pacific; the Army War College, a situation involving warfare in the Philippines. Jointly, the two Colleges played a map maneuver covering a hostile descent on the Philippines and operations to take the Manila Bay area. While ground actions were being gamed at Washington Barracks, bulletins were sent by the Naval War College from Newport, Rhode Island, concerning the Navy chart maneuvers at sea. These bulletins were posted and the situation kept up to date at both institutions. After the close of the school year, representatives met to discuss means of improving these games in the future.[67]

In accord with General McGlachlin's innovations, National Guard and Reserve officers continued to attend portions of the course. State Department representatives attended but were restricted to part time attendance by the press of their official duties. The Commerce Department, however, sent no representative this year nor in any future years.

Lectures were increased to 110 for the year. Included were discussions of economics, political science, psychology, and international law as well as detailed analyses of various countries. General Ely placed special emphasis on scheduling speakers with opposing views on controversial issues, to put the College in touch with the varying opinions of the outside world. More than ever, Ely emphasized the international aspects of the course of instruction and the all-inclusive characteristics of a nation's resources mobilized for defense.

General Ely gave a nostalgic farewell to his first War College Class. He had been with many of the officers in this Class for three years, two while they studied at the General Staff School at Fort Leavenworth where he had been commandant and the year at the War College. With their departure, he and his staff completed preparations for the entry of a new group.

The Class of 1925 began the year with a distinction held by no other class of the War College. It had General of the Armies John J. Pershing as a member. At the opening ceremonies for the academic year, Pershing became an honorary member of that Class. Although he had entered the old Army War College with the first group of student officers in 1904, his reassignment to duty in the Far East precluded his completing the course.

With General Ely acting as master of ceremonies, Major General James G. Harbord, who had been Chief of Staff of the American Expeditionary Forces, presented Pershing with the first diploma of the Class of 1925. Secretary of War John W. Weeks unveiled a portrait of General Pershing by Dana Pond which had been presented to the War College by the American Red Cross.

In accepting his diploma, Pershing paid tribute to the graduates of the General Staff School and the Army War College:

> . . . and I should like to make it of record that, in my opinion, had it not been for the able and loyal assistance of the officers trained at these schools, the tremendous problems of combat, supply and transportation could not have been solved.[68]

Although maintaining that the Army could not be led by "political officers," Pershing recognized the contribution of the citizen soldier in World War I. Moreover, he defined an added responsibility of the Regular Army, "In addition to the duty of educating and training our own limited personnel, we have become directly responsible for the education and training of the civilian components as well."[69] He stressed the value of this training to the Army and to the individual citizen receiving it, ". . . especially as a means of elevating the standards of citizenship."

Pershing also praised the Army officer instructors in units, at

GENERAL PERSHING RECEIVES AN HONORARY DIPLOMA

General Pershing was made an honorary member of the Class of 1925 twenty years after he entered the War College. Left to right: Major General James G. Harbord; Secretary of War, John W. Weeks; General Pershing; Chief of Staff designee John L. Hines; Commandant of the Army War College, Major General Hanson E. Ely.

reserve camps, at service schools, and at the War College. "In preparation for handling large bodies of men," he said, ". . . who could ask for a better opportunity to study the problems involved? It is my firm belief that those whose success as instructors is greatest in peace give the highest promise of leadership in War."[70]

Once again the course was conducted in two major divisions, the informative period and the war plans period. Several changes in organization were made. Instead of starting the year with the G-2 intelligence estimate, the class began its studies with the informative period of G-1, G-3, and G-4 functions and methods. A new subcourse entitled "The Assistant Secretary of War Course," concentrated on the study of economics and procurement, was added.

Following the informative period, the strategic intelligence estimate was made, much in the same manner as in previous years. This was followed by a study of the War Department General Mobilization Plan. Since the War Department had not completed the General Industrial Mobilization Plan, the class attempted to develop such a plan. Difficulties similar to those encountered the previous year in the student effort to develop a Mobilization Plan made this student-faculty effort both hard and interesting. The studies prepared were forwarded to the War Department for appropriate use in development of the actual plan.

The war plans period was pursued in the usual manner with the student war plans used as the basis for wargames in the command subcourse. The reconnaissance trips to the northeastern area were discontinued, however, and the class made its terrain survey at Camp Dix, New Jersey.

Most student work was done by small committees. Some individual research projects were assigned, however, with reports being submitted through the various committees. Normally, each committee was organized as a staff or a portion of a staff. Chairmanship of the committees rotated, with each student serving as a committee head at least once during the year. Committee reports normally were prepared as staff papers with an oral presentation being made to the entire College.

During the year, the faculty revised the Army-Navy Joint Action pamphlet at the request of the War Department. An additional request for study investigation of nine problems, ranging from antiaircraft defense of the United States to a plan for use of air forces in defense of Oahu, Hawaii, was refused for lack of time. However, the reply to the Chief of the War Plans Division of the War Department indicated that consideration would be given to adopting some of the topics for class study the following year.[71] The suggestions and request for assistance differed greatly in tone and content from the efforts made by General Haan to force topics on the War College in 1919-21.

Public and official interest in the use of airpower was widespread during this period. General William Mitchell had been primarily responsible for this awakening. Official concern was shown by a request from the Secretary of War for information regarding the amount and type of instruction given on airpower at the War College. The Commandant replied that the use of the Air Service was considered in all phases of the course of instruction, and special lectures were scheduled throughout the year. In addition, a student committee headed by Major M. F. Harmon, Jr., had, "in the absence of any authorized War Department publication on the Fundamental Principles underlying the tactics, technique, and strategy of the Air Service (or airpower)," developed a study to be used by the War College.[72] This committee study included the mission of the Air Service, doctrines and principles of operations and training, general characteristics and uses of each type of aircraft, organization and employment of the Air Service, and employment of a reduced strength Air Service. Emphasizing that the "function of the Army War College is conceived to be the formulation of ideas and policies with respect to the use of the Air Service . . . but not the initiation of doctrine based on the conclusions reached," General Ely stated that the course had been outlined in general before "the recent public agitation about the Air Service."[73]

An elaboration of the wargame concept was added to the instruction. A "field exercise" was held involving establishment of various headquarters with staffs of student officers and faculty umpires. Communications were established between the various headquarters and the exercise conducted as closely as possible to an actual operational situation. Only troops were lacking. Today, this would be called a command post exercise. It was the first conducted at the War College; and similar exercises were held annually until classes were suspended in 1940.

Field trips were conducted periodically. In 1925, the class viewed an Air Service demonstration at Bolling Field, Virginia. Aircraft from as far as Chicago were flown to the demonstration. At least one plane of each type in current use was demonstrated to the class. The students visited the Marine Corps base at Quantico, Virginia, for the first time in 1926. They were welcomed by the first Marine Corps graduate of the War College, Major General Eli K. Cole, and the Commandant of the Marine Corps, Lieutenant General John A. Lejeune of the War College Class of 1910. Command reconnaissance trips to the northeastern United States were reinstituted in 1926 and continued for several years.

In December 1927, the Adjutant General informed the Commandant of a forthcoming change in the mission of the College, to be published as War Department Regulation 350-5. Specifically, the mission was defined as:

> a. To train officers in the conduct of field operations of the Army and higher echelons; and to instruct in those political, economic, and social matters which influence the conduct of war.
> b. To instruct officers in War Department General Staff duties and those of the Office of the Assistant Secretary of War.
> c. To train officers for joint operations of the Army and the Navy.
> d. To instruct officers in the strategy, tactics, and logistics of large operations in past wars, with special reference to the World War.[74]

This change to the mission was the last to be made prior to the suspension of classes in 1940 and the subsequent deactivation of the College in 1946.

General Ely expressed concern over the qualifications of some of the officers selected to enter the College. In a letter highly reminiscent of those of Generals Wotherspoon and Bliss twenty years earlier, Ely stressed his opinion that, "A student officer of the

Army War College cannot properly undertake his duties without having the technical knowledge which is now acquired at the Command and General Staff School.''[75] Because many service branch officers had not attended the Fort Leavenworth school, Ely recommended that these noncombatant officers who were graduated from the War College be listed as "technical graduates." Although his recommendations were sound, they were not approved by the Chief of Staff who pointed out that more and more officers selected for the War College would be Leavenworth graduates as time passed.

The weighty problem of qualification of student officers to attend the War College had troubled the presidents and commandants of the War College from the time the very first class had begun its studies in 1904. All had expressed the opinion that graduation from the General Staff School at Fort Leavenworth should be a prerequisite. By Ely's time, the majority of the combat arms officers were graduates of the General Staff School, but this was not true of the officers of the various services. The disparity between background and training of the two groups was the motivation behind Ely's letter to the Chief of Staff.

Qualification criteria changed little in the next few years. Graduation from the Staff School with the Commandant's recommendation for attendance at the War College was almost a mandatory requirement for selection, although outstanding combat arms officers who had not attended the Staff School were considered and some were selected. The officers of the service branches who had attended the Army Industrial College were also deemed qualified for the War College and received priority consideration over service officers who were nongraduates of either institution. The Industrial College was considered on the same level as the Staff College and not the equivalent of the War College. This is a contrast to the present evaluation which places all war colleges and the Industrial College of the Armed Forces on an equal plane.

Officers of captain or higher grade continued to be eligible. The age limit remained 52, until 1933 when at least half of each class was required to be less than 44 years old. In 1939, the age limit was lowered one year, with the plan that the limit would be reduced one year for each entering class, until 44 would become the maximum age for the Class of 1946.[76] The system was in effect only two years when World War II caused the College to suspend its activities.

Major General William D. Connor replaced General Ely as Commandant in December 1927. In the more than four years he had served as Commandant, General Ely had guided the affairs of the War College with a firm hand. Although he had found the College a functioning academic institution on his arrival, he had improved its course of instruction by careful and logical reorganization, by stressing quality in all its operations, and by insisting that the students be presented with all sides of any controversial issue.

His replacement had been a member of the faculty before World War I. Soon after leaving the War College in 1916 to join Pershing's forces on the Mexican border, General Connor had forwarded a list of comments to the Chief of Staff relative to the course of instruction at the War College. Some of his recommendations had long since been adopted; others no longer applied. One can only wonder what Connor's reaction might have been had these recommendations been made to him as Commandant:

1. The policy of gradually increasing the requirements for entrance to the War College should be continued.
2. Qualifications for entrance should be based upon ability to pass entrance examinations and to pursue the course, and not upon any arbitrary qualification such as graduation from the Staff College.
3. Faculty members should be detailed for a period of three or four years.
4. With regard to the curriculum, the following should be done:
   a. Discontinue all efforts at historical research.
   b. Discontinue the historical rides to Civil War battlefields.
   c. Establish a thorough and comprehensive strategical and tactical study of critical areas of our own boundaries and coasts.
   d. Institute staff rides in these critical areas for the purpose of terrain analysis.
   e. Use problems involving one or more divisions operating in these same critical areas.
   f. Use general staff work and problems to test their capabili-

MARSHAL PETAIN AT THE ARMY WAR COLLEGE, 1931

Petain was one of many distinguished lecturers who came to the Army War College between the wars. Left to right: Petain; General John J. Pershing; Major General William D. Connor, Commandant of the War College.

ties and ascertain their abilities along general staff lines
of work.[77]

General Connor expressed his philosophy regarding the War
College in his welcome to his first class in September 1928:

> In a very large measure the period of your self-development be-
> gins right now for in this institution there are no marks applied
> to your daily work and there are no periodic tests or final exami-
> nations that you must undergo to show the faculty what progress
> you have made or what advantages you have accumulated during
> the year's work. From now on you become, more than ever be-
> fore, subject only to the critical judgment of your fellow
> officers.[78]

The organization of the curriculum and the conduct of the course
of instruction changed little during General Connor's years as Commandant. The course continued to be divided into two major parts;
preparation for war (equivalent to the informative period under General Ely) and conduct of war (equivalent to Ely's war plans period).
A new subcourse entitled Analytical Studies was added in 1929. The
subcourse reviewed selected campaigns, including those involving
joint Army and Navy exercises. Historical studies were a part of this
course and were intended to provide an analysis of all details of an
operation: strategic, tactical, and logistical. The length of this course
was increased annually and its coverage, consequently, extended.

Although there was little change to the curriculum during Connor's tenure, many other innovations were made. A distinctive insigne, to be worn by the officers of the College, was derived from
the War College Coat of Arms, authorized in 1910 by the Secretary
of War. The first insigne was a shield, but this was used for less than
a year. In September 1928, the distinctive insigne was changed to the
mailed fist, torch, and wreath taken from the crest of the Coat of
Arms. This was worn until the deactivation of the College in 1946 and
again from 1950 to 1951. At that time, the original shield insigne was
readopted.

General Connor also conceived the idea of a bronze plaque for
each graduating class. The plaque was to include the names of each

INSIGNIA OF THE ARMY WAR COLLEGE

Upper left: the original distinctive insigne worn in 1928. Upper right: the insigne of the War College from 1928 to 1940 and in 1950. Lower left: the insigne worn from 1950 to date. Lower right: the Faculty Identification Badge adopted in 1966.

student and faculty member. All living graduates of the War College were contacted and asked to assist in defraying the costs of the plaques. The first plaque, designed by the Federal Commission of Fine Arts, was installed in 1929. Each class has provided its own plaque since that date. Although the class plaques of the classes from 1905 through 1940 remained at the War College Building at Fort McNair when the College was deactivated in 1946, they were returned to the Army War College at Carlisle Barracks, Pennsylvania, and presented to the Commandant, Major General Eugene A. Salet, by the National War College Commandant, Vice Admiral Fitzhugh Lee, on 25 August 1965.

Major Generals George S. Simonds, Malin Craig, John L. DeWitt, and Brigadier Generals Walter S. Grant and Philip B. Peyton served as Commandant between Connor's departure on 30 April 1932 and the suspension of academic instruction after the 11 June 1940 graduation. No major changes in the curriculum occurred during this entire period, but minor variations took place from time to time.

The locale of war plans and war games changed from year to year. The Philippines, Hawaii, the Canal Zone, Puerto Rico, Mexico, the Caribbean, and Brazil were all used one or more times. The practice of using Great Britain or France as a hostile nation was discontinued in 1936, as the result of student recommendations. Japan, however, continued to be recognized as the most logical threat. In 1937, war plans included the threat of a German-Italian-Polish coalition. Little credence was given to the possibility of a German-Japanese coalition against the United States, despite the detailed strategic intelligence estimates made throughout the period and the clearly recognized Japanese threat. Furthermore, the situations developed by the student officers often showed the difficulty of adequately defending the Philippines in the initial phases of any conflict and the possibility of forced withdrawal of US forces from Hawaii.

Interest in current affairs resulted in the addition of an informal course known as "Foreign News." This was initiated by General Craig in 1935 and was monitored by the faculty G-2 division. The class was divided into five groups, each responsible for a specific area of the world. Each group reported significant developments in the particular area concerned to the entire class twice a week. Emphasis was directed toward the position of the United States in world affairs. This course continued until the last pre-World War II class was graduated in 1940.

The National Guard-Reserve course was discontinued in 1934 because of a shortage of funds. In the 12 years that these courses had been conducted, 393 officers had attended a portion of the regular instruction at the War College. Many prominent civilian officials holding reserve component commissions thus came in contact with the officers of the Regular Army. Included were men such as David Sarnoff and Robert Guggenheim.

At the request of student officers, among them Major John E. Hull, the visits to Civil War battlefields were reinstituted in 1937. Unexpected guests often turned up during these tours. In one year, traffic became so congested near a southern Virginia battlefield that state troopers were provided the following year to direct traffic and prevent vehicles from blocking the roads. One farmer indicated he had no objection to the College using his farm, if he was permitted to listen to the briefings—and if he was allowed to sell sandwiches and coffee to the students.

The report of the Inspector General for 1933 criticized the Army War College for not training officers for a "specific general staff position." The report advocated the technical preparation of officers as specialists, not education for general assignment. Major General George Simonds, the Commandant, replied tersely that the education of the officer at the War College was undertaken from "the broad viewpoint of command as distinguished from the narrower viewpoint of the specialist."[79] The Chief of Staff overruled the Inspector General, and his recommendation was disapproved.

Another recommendation had been received earlier. Colonel Troup Miller advocated establishment of a correspondence course by the War College. Miller indicated that less than half the graduates of the Command and General Staff School were selected to attend the War College. He pointed out the dissatisfaction among graduates not selected and the widespread feeling that their professional careers were "practically at an end" unless they attended the College. Miller recommended establishment of a correspondence course paralleling the actual course of instruction for officers eligible for, but not selected to attend the College. He further recommended award of a certificate of proficiency to officers who complete the course to establish their eligibility for service on the War Department General Staff.[80] The Acting Commandant, Colonel Ned B. Rehkopf, indicated the infeasibility of conducting such a course, because the regular curriculum was based on detailed analysis of materials not available in the field and because wargaming was a required part of the instruction. He added that nonselection was not limited to officers eligible for the War College, but also was true of officers eligible for attendance at other service schools. He concluded by adding, "The highly selective system of gaining eligibility for the War Department General Staff now afforded by the general service schools greatly stimulates all officers and increases the efficiency of the War Department."[81] The Secretary of War upheld Rehkopf's point of view, and Miller's recommendation was disapproved as "not being in the best interests of the service."

An unpredicted result of cancellation of the reserve component courses became apparent in 1938 and 1939. Student comments decried ignorance among General Staff officers and senior commanders of the functions, problems, and capabilities of the National Guard. Consequently, these student officers pointed out, assignment to duty with the Guard was not in high favor among active officers and was avoided whenever possible. The contacts with National Guard and Reserve officers prior to discontinuation of their attendance at the War College had done much to improve relations with and to develop understanding of the reserve components. An effort was made to alleviate the situation by committee problems and studies on the National Guard. However, the lack of direct contact with reserve component officers handicapped committee efforts.

Another student suggestion received little support. Major Frank M. S. Johnson of the Class of 1937 suggested that authority be obtained from the War Department and the Association of American Universities to confer the degree of Doctor of Philosophy in Military

Science on the graduates of the War College which would "greatly increase the prestige of the Army and the War College."[82]

Two items of historical and artistic note were presented to the College. A larger than life-size bust of Secretary of War Elihu Root was presented by the Carnegie Corporation of New York. The bust was brought to Washington by the sculptor, Earl Frazer, and placed in the rotunda of the War College building. This bust is today in the foyer of Root Hall at Carlisle Barracks.

The United Daughters of the Confederacy presented an oil portrait of Robert E. Lee by Charles Silchek, which was unveiled by Mary Lee and Hanson E. Ely, III, great-grandchildren of General Lee. The portrait today hangs in the office of the Commandant of the National War College.

With more than 110 lecturers visiting the War College annually—an average of three each week—the faculty must have anticipated problems arising from time to time. However, the problem encountered in inviting E. J. Young of the New York Times can hardly have been predicted. Young had been invited to speak to the College regarding European affairs and replied:

> Naturally I appreciate the compliment from so distinguished a source and should be glad to bring to those who have the defense of the country in charge any information I could give. There is, however, one slight complication. I am a night worker, accustomed to sleep until 11 a.m.; and I fear my mind would not function at its best at what to me is the unearthly hour of 8:45 a.m. Could the lecture be set for the afternoon? [83]

The Commandant, Major General DeWitt changed the lecture to the afternoon, but Young was not invited back the following year.

The research facilities made available to the student officers and to the faculty contributed greatly to the scope and depth of the studies made during these years. In addition to the War College Library, widely recognized as the finest military library in the United States, references in the Library of Congress, documents in the National Archives, and the files and records of Federal agencies outside the War Department were available. The Historical Section, attached to the War College since 1921, had a wealth of material on World War I which was used extensively. To this were added the reports of Historical Section officers detailed overseas and materials returned by attaches stationed throughout the world. These materials permitted the College, for instance, to study in detail in 1937-38 the causes of the Spanish Revolution, the participation of other nations therein, and the lessons to be learned from such a conflict. Translations of foreign documents for use by the G-2 Intelligence Division of the War Department also were made by the Historical Section of the War College. This made current data on the armed forces of the major powers available to the College at the earliest possible time. Thus the College had available historical, current, and intelligence information concerning the United States, its military forces, and its resources and similar data concerning many foreign nations.

The spread of war in Europe naturally occupied the interest of students and faculty alike. Student comments continually urged that more time be devoted to the European situation. As a result, the classes of 1939 and 1940 were given intensive and comprehensive briefings by G-2 personnel of the War Department General Staff. The 1940 group studied the German campaign in Poland, using special texts prepared by the Military Intelligence Division less than nine months after the German High Command declared the Polish campaign finished on 5 October 1939.[84]

The importance of the student suggestions is evidenced by the many minor changes made to the course of instruction. Although Army War College records do not indicate the exact beginnings of student critiques of the curriculum and the course in general, bound volumes of these comments date from the Class of 1937. In addition to the comments already mentioned, the following were submitted: Captain Maxwell D. Taylor commented that problems used from year to year created a tendency for students to be influenced by previous committee work. He suggested either changing the problems or withholding old reports. Captain L. L. Lemintzer recommended that the wargaming of a student war plan be done by a student group other than the officers who had prepared that particular plan, since this would result in a more valid testing of the plan. Neither of these recommendations were acted upon. Instruction at the Army War College was suspended "for the school year 1940-1941,"[85] with the graduation of the Class of 1940, and less than six months later, the United States was at war.

VII

The Second Testing: World War II

THIS entire period between two world conflicts must be viewed as an era of stability for the Army War College. The basic core curriculum conceived and developed by General McAndrew and his faculty at Treves, Germany, in 1919 was retained without major changes. Constant alterations and improvements were made within this framework to reflect corresponding requirements of the Army, the changing international situation, and the needs of the nation. Initial emphasis was placed upon the duties of the General Staff officer rather than upon the responsibilities of the commander. Such should not be surprising for the immediate interest and activity of the War Department in the early 1920's was the reorganization required by the National Defense Act of 1920 and the training of General Staff officers to meet the needs of the new "G" staff organization. The war plans and supporting operational and logistical plans emphasized in the curriculum also received the same emphasis within the General Staff. The lack of preparation and planning prior to World War I had taught the Army the need for prior planning.

The change of emphasis to command also reflected the growing awareness within the War Department that young officers progressing toward senior command status did not have an opportunity to command large units. The restrictively small size of the Army and small military budgets precluded any extensive maneuvers. Consequently, every possible means was used to provide guidance and experience in command of larger units. The War College emphasis on command throughout the course and the use of wargames and map maneuvers to develop a sense of the problems of responsibility and decision-making reflect this attitude. As a Navy liaison officer to the War College remarked in 1935:

. . . There is practically no active Army, and therefore Army officers have had no opportunity since the War to work with large forces. For this reason, they resort to a more elaborate system of schools than we have . . . Our College is supplementary to experience afloat; The Army War College, in the absence of means for large scale service in the field, tries to provide a substitute . . .[1]

McAndrew, McGlachlin, Ely, and Connor developed, improved and passed on to their successors a curriculum designed to meet the needs of the Army of their time. Intentionally or not, they gave to the course of instruction a flavor of international relations and political science far beyond the grasp of the average American of the period. The emphasis on analysis of the international and military situations, the concentration upon development of strategies for combined forces, the stress upon the mobilization of manpower and industry— all proved their worth in the conflict to come.

Over 2,000 officers had been graduated by the Army War College from 1905 to 1940. Of this number, nearly 1,800 had studied and learned from McAndrew's core curriculum. The effectiveness of McAndrew's visionary course of instruction and the many refinements made by his successors was tested in World War II conflict, a conflict far greater in magnitude than any these men could have visualized.

The Army of the United States expanded from a small force of approximately 230,000 officers and men in 1940 to a force of more than eight million in 1945.[2] The officer corps made a similar expansion from 14,000 on active duty in 1940 to more than a half-million in 1945. Less than nine percent of the regular officers on duty were graduates of the Army War College; they comprised far less than one percent of the total officer corps.

By contrast, of the more than 1,000 general officers serving in 1945, over 600 were graduates of the War College. Major command and staff positions both in the United States and overseas were occupied by graduates. Fifty-two percent of all War College graduates from 1920 to 1940 became general officers.[3] Their number included Eisenhower, Bradley, Patton, Buckner, Eichelberger, Vandenberg,

Wainwright, Somervell, Harmon, McNair, Groves, Gruenther, Smith, and Hershey of the Army; Nimitz and Halsey of the Navy; and Cates of the Marine Corps.

The role of the soldier in this conflict was not limited by the bounds of the battlefield, nor was his activity directed solely toward the sound of guns. Development of the atomic bomb, mobilization of the nation's manpower, wartime use of industry, diplomatic association with a score of allies, government of a defeated nation, rebuilding of a ravaged countryside, demobilization of a nation at war—all these became the new duties of the man in uniform.

General of the Army Dwight D. Eisenhower, reminiscing of his own time as a student at the Army War College, said,

> The War College marks a great change in the thinking or, let us say, the formal education of officers of our armed services. That formal education up until the time of the War College had been concerned with the techniques, the tactics, the logistics of battle, of campaigns; the preparation and the operation of troops. Now you are thinking about war and about victory in war, or better, about keeping us out of war. The strength of a nation can never be measured merely in guns, planes, tanks, and ships. The real influence of a nation in the world is measured by the product of its spiritual, its economic, and its military strength. And so, realizing that war involves every single facet of human existence and thinking, every asset that humans have developed, all of the resources of nature, here [at the Army War College] education deserts the formerly rather narrow business of winning a tactical victory on the battlefield; it is now concerned with the nation.[4]

An equally appropriate comment was made by Prime Minister Winston Churchill in his address to the US Army General Staff in 1946:

> . . . It remains to me a mystery as yet unexplained how the very small staffs which the United States kept during the years of peace were able not only to build up the armies and Air Force units, but also to find the leaders and vast staffs capable of handling enormous masses and of moving them faster and farther than masses have been moved in war before . . . I think it is

Prudens Futuri

a prodigy of organization, of improvisation. There have been many occasions when a powerful state has wished to raise great armies, and with time and money and discipline and loyalty that can be accomplished. Nevertheless the rate at which the small American Army of only a few hundred thousand men, not long before the war, created the mighty force of millions of soldiers is a wonder of history . . . Professional attainment, based upon prolonged study and collective study at colleges, rank by rank, age by age—those are the title needs of the commanders of future armies and the secret of future victories.[5]

The Joint Era: 1945-1950

S OME Army War College activities continued to function during the war years, even though there were no academic classes. The Historical Section and the Library continued and expanded their activities. No new commandant was designated after General Peyton departed in July 1940. Eventually, the senior officer of the post complement became the acting commandant.

Almost immediately, the physical facilities of the War College were used for other Army activities. National Headquarters of the Selective Service System occupied part of the War College building from June 1940 to February 1941. The nucleus of General Headquarters was organized and housed at the War College in August 1940. This was later designated as Headquarters, Army Ground Forces.

The expansion of this headquarters required additional space. The rotunda of the War College building was cleared of its works of Art and divided into offices. Other larger rooms were subdivided to provide a maximum amount of office space. Army Ground Forces continued to occupy the building and much of other post facilities until its move to the new Pentagon building in 1945. Its occupancy will long be remembered, however, for the post was renamed Fort Lesley J. McNair in honor of the Commanding General of the Army Ground Forces who lost his life in France in 1944.

A number of other miscellaneous activities also were conducted on the post during the war years. These included various Adjutant General Schools, a military police school, intelligence school, and the Army School of Music.

The major impact of the second World War on military education was the realization that global conflict involved political, economic, and other considerations far beyond conventional military and naval affairs. This was not a new concept, for the War College had stressed those nonmilitary factors of a nation's war potential during the entire prewar period. However, the full extent of the impact on military operations both during and following an actual conflict were not foreseen, even by the visionary McAndrew. Long before the end of the war, demands arose for competent officers capable of operating in nonmilitary fields.

Schools to train officers for military government were established by the Army, the Army Air Forces, and the Navy. All placed great emphasis on language training and area specialization studies covering the history, politics, and economics of the countries concerned. Many competent civilian specialists were commissioned specifically to fill such positions.

A second factor having important impact on the armed forces was the joint operations concept and the need for mutual understanding of the roles and functions of the various armed services. Although this need had also been recognized long before at both the Army and Naval War Colleges, all too few officers had been enabled to serve with or to study in the institutions of the opposite service. The magnitude of global conflict necessitated cooperation and coordination, particularly on the staffs of the joint commands. To meet this requirement, the Army-Navy Staff College was established by the Joint Chiefs.

Parts of the 21-week course were conducted at the Army Air Force School of Tactics at Orlando, Florida, the Army Command and General Staff School at Fort Leavenworth, Kansas, and the Naval War College at Newport, Rhode Island. Nearly two months of the course, however, were conducted in Washington in the old Army War College building. Emphasis throughout the course was given to logistics, exercise of joint command, and unified employment of military forces and arms. Twelve classes, each composed of between 30 and 40 officers of all the services, completed the course. State Department representatives also attended the last five classes.

Plans for postwar military education at all levels in the Army were a concern of the War Department and the Army Ground Forces staffs long before hostilities ceased. A 1944 study by the Army Ground Forces included proposals for reopening the Army War College with a mission similar to that of the prewar institution. The study included an alternate proposal to change its mission to preparation of officers for duty with or command of joint forces, a mission similar to that of the Army-Navy Staff College. This study did not envision a joint war college nor elimination of the Army and Naval War Colleges.

A number of unilateral studies were made in 1945 by the Army, the Army Air Forces, and the Navy with regard to their own postwar educational needs. The 1944 Army Air Forces study resulted in the 1946 organization of a single Air Corps school command incorporating advanced tactical schools, a command and staff school, a school of technology, and an "air college." This command was redesignated as the Air University in September 1946.

A Joint Chiefs study of the same period recommended permanent establishment of the Army-Navy Staff College in Washington and an expansion of its course to a full year. The curriculum recommended included subjects of broad interest—social, political, and economic affairs—as well as study of the conduct of total war and joint action. The study also recommended that any State Department college that might be established be located as near the Army-Navy State College as possible. Another recommendation was redesignation of the Army Industrial College as a joint school. All three services responded favorably to the Joint Chiefs' proposals.

This Joint Chiefs study had direct and overwhelming influence on the Gerow Board, the major Army study group concerned with postwar Army education. Lieutenant General Leonard T. Gerow, Commandant of the Command and General Staff School, and three other general officers studied the educational needs of the Army in great detail from December 1945 to February 1946. The Gerow Board recommendations were extensive, going far beyond the requirements of the Army and presenting a proposal for a coordinated educational system for all the services.

Although the Board did not review Navy school requirements in detail, it did investigate both the Army and Army Air Force needs.

The requirements for single service education were recognized by providing for basic education in Air Tactical Schools, Army Ground branch schools, and Army Service branch schools. This was to be followed by more advanced instruction at Air, Ground, and Service Colleges. This portion of the Board's concept, therefore, envisioned a three-way division of the Army educational system based on the Army Air Forces, Army Ground Forces, and Army Service Forces division of responsibility, functions, and operations.

From this point on, the Joint Chiefs' influence on the Board was clearly apparent. The Gerow Board envisioned a joint educational system far beyond the single Army-Navy College recommended by the Joint Chiefs. Gerow and his board members recommended establishment of an Armed Forces College at Fort Leavenworth to develop "commanders and staff officers qualified to plan and direct operations of Army forces and to coordinate these operations with Naval Forces."[1] This Armed Forces College was to be under Army control unless the Navy decided to participate. In that event, the school would be under the control of the Joint Chiefs.

The final level of education of officers of all services was to be provided by a National Security University. This institution was to have five separate colleges: a National War College for military personnel of all services, a State Department College, an Administrative College to train personnel for management and administration of military and civilian manpower, an Industrial College, and an Intelligence College to provide for effective overall operation of intelligence and counterintelligence efforts of the nation. The Board intended the National Security University to provide for development of officers ". . . capable of high command and staff duties in connection with prevention of war, preparation for and prosecution of war on a global scale, and the execution of the responsibilities of the Armed Forces subsequent to hostilities."[2]

The Board made another recommendation which spelled the death-knell of the old Army War College:

The former mission of the Army War College has been assigned in this proposed educational system to the Colleges of the Na-

tional Security University and the Armed Forces College. Therefore the Army War College need not be reopened. The facilities
formerly used by that institution should be made available to the
National Security University unless it is found impracticable to
establish the University under one roof.[3]

Even before the Board had concluded its deliberations and forwarded its report to the War Department, the National War College
was established by joint announcement of the War, Navy, and State
Departments on 4 February 1946. The Chief of Staff of the Army,
General Dwight D. Eisenhower, subsequently approved the Gerow
Board report with its recommendation not to reopen the Army War
College. The Army Industrial College was redesignated as the Industrial College of the Armed Forces in April 1946, thus bringing
the second college of the Gerow Board National Security University
into being. The remaining three—State, Intelligence, and Administration—never were established. Another Gerow Board recommendation
was translated into fact in August 1946 with establishment of the
Armed Forces Staff College at Norfolk, Virginia.

The Army, with the support of the Army Air Forces, urged the
authorization of the joint institutions and provided the concept and
energy to establish the joint colleges. The Navy, on the other hand,
agreed reluctantly to establishment of the National War College and
the Armed Forces Staff College. In contrast to the Army's willingness to give up its own War College, the Navy made it abundantly
clear that it had no intent of closing the Naval War College at
Newport.

At General Eisenhower's suggestion, the facilities of the Army
War College were turned over to the National War College. This was
all-inclusive, for the instructions specified that the Army War College ". . . be inactivated and that the personnel and functions assigned to the Library, Administrative, Record, Property, and Cus-
todial Sections will be transferred and consolidated with the National
War College."[4] The Historical Section had previously been absorbed
by the Historical Division Special Staff.

In its enthusiasm for the joint concept and because of its wholehearted acceptance of the Gerow Board proposals, the Army literally

burned its educational bridges. The Army sincerely believed that a single Department of Defense would be forthcoming with complete subordination of the military services to the joint agency. Such did not materialize; the hoped for joint educational system also failed to appear. This was first indicated by the Navy's lukewarm acceptance of the National War College and retention of its own War College. A further and much stronger blow came with establishment of the Air Force as a separate service.

The Air College had expanded its initial scope of instruction by 1947 to include a broader focus on nonmilitary considerations, including international relations and current world affairs. With the Air Force a separate service, the College was elevated to a higher position in its educational system and was therefore redesignated as the Air War College.

Thus the Army, because of its complete and unequivocal support of the joint concept, found it had neither a War College nor an Industrial College. Fortunately, the Command and General Staff School had not been closed, nor had its facilities been turned over to the Armed Forces Staff College, as the Gerow Board had recommended. The Army educational system had to be modified, however, and this was done in 1947. A Ground General School was established for the basic training of officers of all the arms and services. Intermediate and advanced schools were to be conducted by each branch. The Command and General Staff School was redesignated a College, with a requirement to cover both the functions of the Staff School and some activities of the old War College.

Although it supported both the Armed Forces Staff College and the National War College, the Army realized that the entire educational arrangement was unsatisfactory and that its officer corps was not being fully prepared for the duties of command and staff at the highest level.

Consequently, a board headed by Lieutenant General Wade Haislip analyzed the Army school system and Army needs in August 1947 and recommended reestablishment of the Army War College.[5] The recommendation was not adopted at this time, however. Major General H. R. Bull, made a thorough study of the situation in 1948 and found that the joint colleges were providing less than one-third of the officers the Army required. Consequently, he recommended reestablishment of the Army War College with an annual capacity of 300 students and a complete review of the Army educational system with particular emphasis on instruction at higher school levels.[6]

Bull's recommendation resulted in creation of yet another board headed by Lieutenant General Manton Eddy, Commandant of the Command and General Staff College. Instead of consisting of a few other general officers, the Eddy Board included the commandants of the principal Army schools, thus providing a study group intensely aware of the problems of Army education. The instructions to the Board were quite specific. In addition to reviewing the entire officer education system of the Army, the Board was directed to determine:

1. The adequacy of the present system to meet the educational requirement for commissioned officers.
2. The appropriateness of the scope at the various educational levels.
3. The existence of excessive overlaps or gaps in the instruction considered necessary up to the level of the National War College and Industrial College of the Armed Forces.
4. Specifically whether an Army War College (or other institution at a level comparable to the Naval and Air War Colleges) should be included in the Army School System.

It would appear that a part of the Board's conclusions were forecast, since additional direction was provided:

If the investigation of the Board indicates the need for an Army War College, the Board will
   a. Provide for an Army War College in the revised plan for the Army Educational System.
   b. Submit a plan for the establishment of the Army War College to include mission . . . scope of instruction . . . overhead requirements for staff, faculty, and students . . . estimated costs . . .[7]

After deliberation and extensive study, the Board made recommendations which covered the entire scope of its instructions. In ad-

dition to analysis of precommissioned education and military education at lower levels, the Board recommended that a ten months Advanced Course be established at the Command and General Staff College. Provisions were to be made for 100 students in the 1950-51
academic year, with an ultimate student capacity of 300 officers.
Although the final report did not so state, it is quite apparent from
the record of its detailed deliberations that the Board considered
this advanced course at Fort Leavenworth to be the nucleus for a
future Army War College. The discussion of the advanced course
content and criteria began "Advanced Course (Army War College
Course)"; and reference was made throughout to the Army War College. Furthermore, although the first year's instruction was to be
given at Leavenworth, the Board recommended that Fort Monroe
was better suited as a location than other sites. Fort Leavenworth
was considered adequate only to support the course initially.

The Eddy Board Report was studied carefully by the Department
of the Army and approved with modifications in October 1949. The
primary changes were elimination of any reference to an "advanced
course" at the Command and General Staff College and substitution
of a plan for reactivation of the Army War College as ". . . the apex
of the Army Educational system . . ." [8] Attendance at the College
was intended to represent completion of the formal educational requirement for assumption of high level positions with the Department
of Defense and other governmental agencies. Another modification
represented an almost complete reversal of the Gerow Board
concept:

> A few officers of the Army will be selected annually for attend-
> ance at the National War College and the Industrial College of the
> Armed Forces to study national and joint strategy and war plan-
> ning, and industrial mobilization. This specialized knowledge is
> required in the Department of the Army, but attendance at either
> of these two institutions ipso facto will not be given more weight
> than attendance at the Army War College . . . [9] [emphasis
> added]

Thus the Army position had changed from support of the joint
school concept with the National War College as the apex of the edu-

cational systems of the three services, to a position which placed the three service War Colleges on the same level as the joint school. The Eddy Board report and the modifications thereto do not provide the full text of the Board's deliberations and discussions nor the full reasoning behind its ultimate recommendations. A thesis study made by Lieutenant Colonel Harry L. Hillyard, an Army student at the Air War College in 1948-49, provides a list of advantages to be obtained from establishment of an Army War College.

Hillyard listed the following major advantages for the Army:

1. Educational opportunities for Army officers equal to those available to officers of the Navy and Air Force.
2. The College would provide a study group of experienced officers available to make objective studies of major problems facing the Army.
3. A tendency to eliminate branch prejudice and rivalry within the Army.
4. The ability of the Army to provide more officers with War College background for high command and staff duty.
5. Stimulation of unbiased thinking and critical appraisal of the present concepts, in the light of technological advances and the changing nature of war.
6. The Army would be insurred representation . . . on the Joint Planning Staffs with equal educational advantages comparable to the Air Force and Navy. [10]

For the Department of Defense, Hillyard listed the following advantages:

1. An approximately equal number of Army, Navy, and Air Force officers with an understanding of military problems from the National point of view.
2. Officers of approximately equal education background on the joint staffs and thus . . . insure a balanced consideration of all factors in problems involving the three services.
3. Eventually . . . facilitate the development of sound military strategy based on agreement; as opposed to the possibility of compromise strategy based upon tradition and vested interests. [11]

Comprehensive as Hillyard's study was, it neglected one important justification for reactivation of the Army War College: the increase in size of the Army in 1949 compared to the Army of 1939.

Various postwar Department of the Army studies had indicated requirements for 350 graduates from the National War College and the Industrial College of the Armed Forces to meet the needs of the greatly expanded Army structure. Instead, the annual output of Army officers from the two joint institutions was only 76 officers. By contrast, the prewar Army of 12,500 officers had available 83 graduates from the Army War College and 50 from the Army Industrial College.[12] Thus, while the size of the postwar Army was more than double that of 1939, senior school graduates had been reduced to one-half the prewar total.

Department of the Army approval of the modified Eddy Board report included a directive to reestablish the Army War College to accommodate a student body of 100 officers during the 1950-51 academic year. To implement this directive, General Eddy was named to head a new board with the specific mission of determining a location for the Army War College, the command structure for the War College and the Command and General Staff College, the curriculum for the 1950-51 academic year, the staff and faculty required; and ". . . all other details to make the Army War College operational in time for the fall 1950 class."[13]

An interim report made three weeks later made only two recommendations: that the Army War College be established initially at Fort Leavenworth; and that a command structure for an Army University, similar to the Air University at Maxwell Air Force Base, be considered.[14] The recommendation to use Fort Leavenworth was approved immediately; approval of the university concept was withheld pending receipt of the final report from the Board. Minority reports related to each of the two interim recommendations, however, indicated that the recommendations were far from being a unanimous opinion.

The President of the Board, General Eddy, objected strongly to any proposal to locate the War College anywhere but at Fort Leavenworth. His primary objection was that the concept of an Army University, would be far less feasible if the War College was not collocated with the Command and General Staff College. Eddy's justification of his minority stand was based on the cost of sustaining a separate War College rather than on a strong bid for the university concept.

The second minority report was submitted by Colonels E. M. Starr and A. D. Marston, respectively representing the Organization and Training and the Logistics Divisions of Department of the Army. They opposed the university concept and advocated that the War College be placed directly under Department of the Army control. Their argument was based on the contention that the primary purpose of the War College was to prepare officers for high level command and general staff duty and that this mission could be better accomplished under direct Department of the Army supervision without intervening administrative echelons.

Starr and Marston favored a return to the prewar relationships with the War Department; the Board majority, a new organizational structure. The controversy was settled during a discussion with the Vice Chief of Staff, General Wade Haislip, on 30 November 1949. The Army War College would be established temporarily at Fort Leavenworth, and a permanent location would be selected later. While at Leavenworth, the College would be a separate school with its own commandant. However, it would be under the general direction of the Commandant, Command and General Staff College. "In effect, this will create an Army University consisting of the Army War College and the Command and General Staff College." [15]

With the initial dispute settled by the Vice Chief of Staff, the Eddy Board resumed its deliberations. A period of several months passed before a final report was submitted. The board continued to bid for Fort Monroe as a final site for the War College, although it considered other locations ranging from Fort Winfield Scott, California, to Fort Ethan Allan, Vermont, to the Veteran's Administration Don Be-Sar Hotel at Pass-a-Grillo, Florida. [16] All of these, except Fort Leavenworth, were rejected because of the unsuitability either of the location or of the existing layout of the physical plant. [17]

Department of the Army assigned a new board headed by Colonel Marion Carson, the task of selecting a site. Colonel Carson's board concentrated on two locations after eliminating a number of other possible sites. Fort McClellan, Alabama, and Carlisle Barracks,

Pennsylvania, were studied in detail. The board considered total costs involved in occupying either site, including removing other activities, the adequacy of each physical plant, and its location. The Board forwarded its unanimous decision on 6 May 1950: Carlisle Barracks was recommended to be the location of the Army War College.

Two Department of Army orders pertaining to the College were published. General Order 4, 1 February 1950, designated the Army War College as a Class I activity to be located temporarily at Fort Leavenworth, Kansas. General Order 41, 6 June 1951, incorporating the recommendation of the Carson Board, directed the move of the War College to Carlisle Barracks, Pennsylvania, on 5 July 1951. The decision had been made; there was no longer any justification or requirement for argument or discussion.

IX

A New Era Begins, 1950-1957

E VEN before the decision to reconstitute the Army War College had been finalized, plans were being developed for the curriculum for the first year. At Fort Leavenworth, the Commandant appointed a committee to consider the mission, scope of instruction, and the curriculum for a nine month course.¹ Five senior colonels, directors of the major academic departments of the Command and General Staff College, made recommendations based on the premise that preparation for the National War College or the Industrial College of the Armed Forces should not be a primary mission of the Army War College because few of its graduates would be expected to attend either.

The committee recommended that the mission, scope of instruction, and curriculum be focused on qualifying an officer for duty in any division of the US Army General Staff and not to fill any academic gap that existed between the Command and General Staff College and the National War College. Basic emphasis was to be on the Army's role and mission in the National Military Establishment and on strategic planning and mobilization. Principles and procedures applicable to Army organization and command and staff techniques also were to be stressed.

Undoubtedly, the thinking of this committee was influenced by the final report of the Board on Army Educational System for Commissioned Officers, sponsored by the Army Field Forces,² which had surveyed the entire Army educational program. Although the Army Field Forces study had not delved into the need for a war college, it had commented most critically on the procedures used at Leavenworth:

Prudens Futuri

In examining the method of instruction and grading employed in the Command and General Staff College, one is struck by the fact that the highest form of Army education offered the officer still smacks too much of the highly competitive requiring frequent grades and tending toward a pouring in of facts and the squeezing out of the same. In short, there is no true university approach and at no time in the Army education of an officer is he given this graduate student approach. And yet, the Army officer is, in truth, a graduate student. While the Command and General Staff College has made, since the war, admirable strides in reducing the size of its classes, nevertheless the requirement for frequent grade necessitates a heavy leaning on the lecture method, and the year-long competition is not conducive toward stimulating original thinking and inviting argument and discussion. Therefore, it is felt that the Army Education System is sadly lacking in that it does not give to its graduates a true university approach.[3]

The Leavenworth committee made an effort to sponsor a university or postgraduate approach by recommending that only 50 percent of the instruction scheduled should be accomplished by conferences and lectures. The remainder of the time was to be devoted to individual and committee study under instructor guidance. The committee recommended against formal testing, stating that "it is not desirable to have examinations at a college on this level."

Despite this academic outlook, the committee emphasized that basic techniques should not be slighted. "There is a tendency," the committee report stated, "toward considering what is commonly called 'pick and shovel' staff work as being beneath the scope of a War College course. In reality most staff work is 'pick and shovel' work."[4] Consequently, the committee recommended inclusion of much instruction on the methods and techniques of proper staff functioning — a carryover from the Leavenworth methodology. One member of the committee, Colonel G. B. Barth, objected strongly to the committee proposal and advocated that "Committee participation and seminars be envisioned instead of instruction of the Command and General Staff College type."[5]

The final report of this committee, however, was very general in nature and only recommended principles to be followed in the

THE FORT LEAVENWORTH HOME OF THE ARMY WAR COLLEGE
Sherman, Grant, and Sheridan Halls, Fort Leavenworth, Kansas. During its one
year stay at Leavenworth, 1950-1951, the War College occupied academic facilities in these buildings.

final development of the course of instruction, should the War College be reestablished by the Army. Moreover, this committee did not have the advantage of using the Eddy Board report, since it was not submitted until June 1949 and was not approved by the Secretary of the Army until October of that year.

The Assistant Commandant at Leavenworth appointed another committee in September 1949 to prepare detailed plans for the "Advanced Course, Command and General Staff College (Army War College)."[6] The committee of five officers was referred to the Eddy Board report and directed to assume that this report would be approved. The committee was given far more definitive guidance than had been provided to the predecessor group. It was to plan for the organization of the faculty and student body; indicate the methods of instruction to be used and the physical facilities needed; prepare a tentative schedule and outline course directives; and estimate the number of personnel and amount of time required to prepare instructional material for the proposed course. The committee also was directed to prepare the curriculum based on the Eddy Board recommendation that an Army War College curriculum be directed toward preparation of the officer for duty with headquarters of an Army group, a theater Army, or Department of the Army General Staff.[7] To this recommendation the Assistant Commandant at Leavenworth added a requirement for review of the operations of the field Army.

In following the directed assumption that the Eddy Board report would be approved, the committee based its course of study on the Eddy concept of an Army university. As a result, the proposed curriculum was little more than an expansion of the ten week advanced course then being conducted as part of the regular course at the Command and General Staff College. The recommended curriculum included five courses: a review of Army organization down to and including division level, basic general staff subjects intended to provide the student with basic training for duty with a high level general staff, general subjects of military nature, applicatory planning exercises centered about Army plans and wargaming, and a lecture series "reserved for the Commandant for lectures and to provide flexibility in scheduling." [8] Very little coverage was provided for joint operations, national policies, or international affairs — and this was to be only lecture-type instruction. The schedule proposed included ". . . a six hour school day and four hour night study basis, while 11 weeks (58 days) will be devoted to applicatory planning exercises and a wargame involving eight hour school days with two hour night study, research or reading periods." [9]

When the newly appointed Commandant of the Army War College, Lieutenant General Joseph M. Swing, came to Leavenworth for briefings in the spring of 1950, this curriculum was proposed to him by the briefing group. General Swing would not approve the curriculum proposed nor the instructional techniques recommended and directed that a course of study of much broader scope be prepared. Furthermore, Swing insisted that the instructional methods to be used be based on an extensive lecture program and committee discussions rather than on the Leavenworth "platform presentation" method. [10]

The curriculum for the first year's course of instruction, from September 1950 to June 1951, bore little resemblance to the proposal made by the Command and General Staff College board. Divided into three major phases, the course of instruction covered the Army and its relationship to national security, current Army problems, and war planning.[11] Phase I was intended to broaden the student officer's knowledge of US organization for national security, with emphasis on the organization of the Department of the Army, through study of national policies, plans, and objectives, particularly the international aspects of national policies. This phase was to increase each student's ability to cope with problems involving national security by prescribing a series of problems involving national policy or the functions of the Department of Defense and the Joint Chiefs of Staff.

Phase II, Current Army Problems, had two objectives: familiarization with current Army programs, problems, policies, and operations, and development of the student's ability to analyze current Army problems and his capability to propose and present solutions to these problems. The third phase, War Planning, was intended to increase the student's knowledge of the techniques of war planning and his ability to solve the military problems inherent in such planning.

To support this curriculum, 195 lectures were scheduled. They covered a wide spectrum of subjects and varied in content from a discussion of "Labor as a Factor in the Formulation of National Policy" to an explanation of the Army supply distribution system. The content of these two lectures may be viewed as indicative of the wide spread to be found in the 1950-51 curriculum: a spread which oscillated from the academic and broad discussion of labor's role in national policy formulation to the technical aspects of the Army supply distribution system.

Supplementing the lecture program were the problems assigned to the student committees. Each phase required committee analysis, solution, and presentation — either oral, written, or both — of an assigned problem. Here too can be found the same wide spectrum of coverage as in the lectures: from a requirement to "Analyze critically the organization of the Joint Chiefs of Staff" to an assignment to make a strategic assessment of the Far East.[12]

Individual studies also were required. Ten major study areas were selected by the faculty and a number of subject topics listed within each area. The majority of the study areas and subtopics had been suggested by the Department of the Army or Headquarters, Army Field Forces. As a result, all study areas were military in nature with a strong emphasis on Army requirements. Each student was permitted to select three topics, listing these by preference. The faculty then assigned a topic to each student — his first choice, if possible. Four months were allocated for research and preparation of the study. Any logical method of presentation, such as the monograph or a staff study, was acceptable, but the length was limited to approximately 4,000 to 6,000 words. Oral presentation of the completed study also was required.

Although strongly oriented toward Army requirements, problems, and policies, the curriculum for the first year of the reconstituted War College can be viewed today as having a curious mix of the academic and the military. The academic environment was characterized by lecturers such as Dean Rusk, then Assistant Secretary of State for Far Eastern Affairs, and Professor Edward M. Earle from Princeton University, and by the stress placed on committee seminar-type discussions. The military training holdover can be seen, however, in the scope and nature of the individual study requirements, the project of developing theater campaign plans, and problem assignments, such as "Analyze current US doctrines and techniques of defense against air and airborne operations in order to determine their adequacy and effectiveness."

The 1950-51 curriculum included study of historical examples, the use of current problems, and the study of future needs. Such must be viewed as being on the credit side, however, for it is indicative of a desire to learn from historical example, recognition of the current situation, and an effort to project into the future. The historical comparison was drawn in studies such as the analysis of 1950 US doctrine on the organization, functions, and operations of the Army group compared to the German doctrine of World War II. Another study made a similar comparison with Russian doctrine. Current problem study was exemplified by a committee requirement to analyze Army Mobilization Training doctrines and techniques. Special problems related to future warfare included a requirement for studying current US doctrine and techniques governing organization, control, and employment of partisan forces in support of strategic and tactical operations. This study included historical perspective — the study of World War II partisan activities; current analysis — partisan activities in Asia and southern Europe; and projection into the future — determination of potentially friendly and hostile manpower resources within areas likely to be overrun by Communist forces. One wonders if Vietnam was one of the areas studied, and whether faculty member Lieutenant Colonel William C. Westmoreland was concerned with that part of Southeast Asia.

The 99 students represented a cross section of the Army and averaged 18 years of commissioned service. Less than one third were lieutenant colonels; the remainder, colonels. Although the faculty included representatives of the Navy and Air Force, only the

Marine Corps sent student officers to the first year's course. Ten percent of the students had no college degree, seventy-five percent had commanded battalion or larger size units, and nearly half had served on high level staffs.

General Swing was the only faculty member who had attended the Army War College before World War II, graduating with the Class of 1935. At his request, the Secretary of the Army approved continuation of the policy established so long before by General Tasker H. Bliss in 1905: faculty members were awarded diplomas to indicate they had completed the War College course. This action was essential, for the graduates of 1940 and previous years who were still on active duty had become far too senior to be considered for faculty positions. A number of years were to pass before a sufficient reservoir of Army War College graduates would become available for faculty assignment. This same situation — the shortage of War College educated officers — applied throughout the Army and was particularly critical in the Department of the Army headquarters and the Joint Chiefs of Staff organization.

The problems which faced General Swing and his deputy, Brigadier General Arthur Trudeau, were substantial. Swing had insisted that the faculty not assume an active teaching role, in the traditional Army service school concept, but instead adopt graduate level academic professorial techniques. This insistence may have been dictated by the fact that his first faculty included no graduates of the old War College. Despite individual professional qualifications — Swing had personally selected the best qualified of the Leavenworth faculty — the initial faculty group can be considered in the terminology of Bliss' War College of 1903:

> . . . 'college' in its old Latin sense of collegium — that is to say, a body of men associated together by a community of interest and object for doing something rather than to learn how to do it, or, at the most, the 'learning how' is a mere incident to the doing.[13]

Many of the very basic procedural concepts instituted by General Swing established a pattern still used. The small committee groups of less than 20 student officers, small group discussions with a visiting lecturer following his formal presentation, student research projects, committee problems, faculty-led seminars, academic freedom of discussion, the non-attribution policy applied to lectures — all these were reinstated by General Swing. In addition, Swing insisted on a postgraduate approach rather than the military instruction techniques used in other Army schools. Many procedures he instituted, however, can be traced to the techniques used in the War College between the wars. The informal student-faculty relationships were rekindled, developed, and stressed in an effort to achieve a mutual education through the exchange of concepts and thoughts based on individual development and experience. Swing also revived other material traces of the old War College. For example, he obtained approval for wear of the distinctive War College insigne, the mailed fist and torch. After the move to Carlisle Barracks, the insigne was changed to the shield that was originally adopted in 1928.

After graduation of the Class of 1951 on June 29, the War College moved to Carlisle Barracks, Pennsylvania, one of the oldest posts in the Army, during July. August was devoted to final preparation for receiving the new class early in September.

Although Carlisle Barracks had been the home of other Army schools for a number of years — the Medical Field Service, Adjutant General, Chaplain, and Information Schools, for example — much work was required to prepare the physical plant for War College use. Committee rooms, faculty offices, the auditorium, and a library had to be readied for the influx of the 152 students due in September. Not to be ignored was the requirement for family housing in the surrounding communities, for the post did not have sufficient family quarters to house the students and faculty.

One of the biggest problems facing the faculty was the need to develop an adequate library to support not only the curriculum, but also student and faculty research. The magnificent library assembled by the old War College over a period of 40 years, as well as the volumes from the original Army Library, had been turned over to the National War College in 1946. A small nucleus of rare books and old War College archives had been returned to the Army War

UPTON HALL, CARLISLE BARRACKS

Formerly Root Hall, this building housed the academic facilities of the Army War College from 1951 to 1967. It is now used for the US Army Military History Research Collection, Post Headquarters, and the Department of Non-Resident Instruction of the War College.

College in its first year at Fort Leavenworth. To this had been added only a comparatively small number of volumes and documents in 1950-51. This is understandable, for the War College then had complete access to the fine Command and General Staff College library.

Now a new library had to be developed, a slow process at best. By every means available — purchase, support from other Army libraries, aid from other governmental institutions — the Army War College Library was developed until, in 1966, it contains over 300,000 cataloged items. During the first few years, however, it was pitifully inadequate. During this period, students and faculty alike used the Dickinson College Library in Carlisle to supplement the material available in the developing War College collection.

Despite the difficulties of moving from the midwest to the east and settling into a new home, the College was ready to begin instruction when the new class arrived in September. The basic core curriculum remained almost unchanged. Swing and his faculty had adopted an evolutionary improvement technique to better the basic course rather than to change it completely in one year.

General Swing was replaced by Lieutenant General Edward M. Almond in August 1951. He found the curriculum plan prepared and the College an operating institution. The three phase concept of the previous year had been abandoned. Five subcourses were dropped or consolidated with other parts of the curriculum. National policy and national security organizations were reviewed at the outset of the year, followed by a study of Army operations, training, logistics, and manpower. Emphasis on war planning continued, however. After completing a strategic intelligence estimate, the students were exposed to Joint and Army planning techniques. The final subcourse was devoted to theater planning and included a review of World War II theater activities as well as a comprehensive study of the existing theaters. Throughout the course, particularly in the problem assignments in the various subcourses, more emphasis was placed on future requirements. For example, student committees surveyed Army mobilization requirements of a future war, prepared Joint plans for a future war, and discussed proposed US strategy with respect to

South Asia. Historical review continued with much stress on the campaigns of World War II. To keep students and faculty conversant with the status of the conflict in Korea, a war room was established in which troop dispositions and the combat situation were posted from intelligence information provided by Department of the Army.

The most significant change in this second year was a gradual increase in the study of international affairs. This change is most obvious in the subject areas for student research. In contrast to the completely military topics of previous years, the students were offered a wide range of subjects from "The Command Structure of the Department of Defense" to "The Soviet Economy" and "Communism in Latin America."[14] However, the primary direction of the curriculum was still military in nature.

Classwork requirements were decreased. The number of lectures was reduced approximately 15 percent, with no more than one being scheduled on any one day. As many as three lectures had been scheduled on the same day during the previous year. The number of problems assigned the student committees was also reduced. These reductions were not made to lessen the overall workload of the individual student but to provide him with more time for discussion with his fellow students, research and individual effort, and contemplative thinking.

The faculty was joined by a representative of the Department of State, and the Joint Advisory Group now included the Navy, the Air Force, and the State Department. The student body also included multiservice representation. The one Navy and two Marine officers were joined by three from the Air Force — the first to attend the Army War College — and by a member of the State Department. For the first time since the early days of the College prior to World War I, officers of the National Guard and Officers Reserve Corps were enrolled in the regular course of instruction. Representation from the other services, the various Federal departments, and the reserve components gradually increased and today approximately 20 percent of each class is composed of non-Army students.

One procedure General Almond instituted has been used periodically since. He invited a Civilian Advisory Group to visit the College, analyze its mission and objectives, review the current curriculum and activities, and recommend means of improving the overall course of instruction. The first group consisted of eight men. Among them were Professor Royden Dangerfield of the University of Illinois; retired Lieutenant General Troy H. Middleton, president of Louisiana State University; and Julius Ochs Adler, publisher of The New York Times. The other members were either distinguished educators or former Government officials.

Although the group visited Carlisle Barracks for only three days, its report was comprehensive and deeply searching in its analysis. The group began by stating that ". . . duplication in the programs of the Army War College and the National War College is not necessarily an evil; it may, on the contrary, be a positive good since few officers will attend both schools."[15] Although the Group was impressed by the breadth and variety of subject matter in the curriculum, it indicated that some change or shift in emphasis might be desirable.

Much stress was placed on a recommendation to extend the amount of time devoted to nonmilitary subjects. Specifically, the War College was urged to ". . . find room for a careful analysis not merely of the power aspects of friendly countries but of the objectives and mentality of our major allies in Europe and Asia." It recommended that more attention be devoted, through lectures or committee work or assigned reading, to ". . . the whole complex of problems that bear upon the relationship between the armed services and the civilian population both at home and abroad." Coverage was urged for the basic factors ". . . affecting international politics, the workings, and character of the American system of government, the position of the United States in world affairs, and the major problems confronting American foreign policy." The effect of the Korean conflict on the American citizen was cited and the suggestion made to include instruction which would develop ". . . an understanding of the potential stresses and strains involved in partial mobilization and preparedness in peacetime for a possible protracted period of stalemate." The Group noted that the impact of the military budget on the national economy was obvious, and that study of national economics would be desirable.

The procedures used by the College were noted favorably but with a note of caution: the three well-established pedagogical methods of instruction — lecture and discussion, committee problem solving, and individual studies —" require constant attention to make certain that proper emphasis is placed upon each . . . ." The lecture program of the War College was examined critically, and the Group noted the almost unanimous comments of students that too many lectures were scheduled. It indicated that the backgrounds of the lecturers were not being fully exploited and recommended prior reading assignments, smaller group discussions following the lecture, and longer-than-one-day visits by the lecturers. Better scheduling sequence also was recommended.

Criticism of the committee problem method indicated that too many were required. The Group recommended that a total of no more than six problems be required of each student during the entire year, and that they be phrased in such a way as to give the students "opportunity to challenge old doctrine and to try to develop new doctrine."

More student freedom in selection of topics for individual research projects was recommended. It noted that " the 'interest' factor could be tapped to a greater extent than seems to be the case . . ." with appropriate faculty monitoring. Topics already used were considered too broad for a short paper of the type required. The Group recommended breaking topics of wide scope into narrower segments which could be worked on by a number of students. The need for research time was discussed, and the Civilian Advisory Group recommended allocating ". . . some time each week for individual study, even at the expense of committee work or lecture time . . ." or setting aside an unbroken period for research.

After noting the relative inadequacy of the library and its major objectives for improvement, the Group pointed out that the most serious deficiency of the student research projects was the difficulty of providing the student with constructive criticism of his efforts. Joint discussion in student groups was deemed entirely inadequate, and the Group recommended that some method be found ". . . for detailing faculty members to the task of assisting students with regard to research methods and preparation of papers and of providing critical appraisal of student papers."

Further faculty criticism emphasized the need for additional faculty members, because ". . . the faculty appears overburdened as it is and this somewhat widened conception of its duties would call for some enlargement of the staff." The Group appreciated the military qualifications of the faculty but decried its academic shortcomings in nonmilitary fields. To supplement the military faculty, the Group recommended adding permanent civilian academicians or, if this did not prove feasible, obtaining civilian professional assistance for the nonmilitary portion of the curriculum.

Insofar as the student body was concerned, the Group advocated holding its total to no more than 200, since that number would completely utilize all existing facilities. More important, a larger student body would require an even larger augmentation of the already overburdened faculty and would result in a direct lessening of the intimate contacts currently possible between student and faculty member. The Group also advocated increasing representation of the Navy, Marine Corps, and Air Force to as much as 12 percent of the total number of students.

Although the Civilian Advisory Group commended the College on the accomplishment of its assigned mission, it noted that clarification of the mission might avoid future confusion " . . . that may result from overlapping missions of the Army War College, National War College and the Armed Forces Staff College."[16] The Group indicated that, while the differences had been clearly explained, it doubted that the differences were adequately expressed in the official missions of the College.

General Almond and the members of his faculty carefully considered the recommendations of the Advisory Group and initiated action to put many of their recommendations into effect. Some could be accomplished internally by the College without approval of higher headquarters. Others, however, required approval by Army Field Forces or by Department of the Army.

At General Almond's request, the mission of the Army War College was redefined. When finally approved and published, the mission assigned the College differed from the initial requirement to prepare officers for command and staff duty with units from Army group to Department of the Army. Instead, the War College was ". . . to prepare selected Army officers for duty as commanders and as general staff officers at the highest US Army levels . . ."[17] The Civilian Advisory Group's concern regarding confusion of the Army War College mission with the missions of the joint colleges resulted in publication of a regulation which indicated that "The National War College and the Industrial College of the Armed Forces being of coordinate level, a graduate of one college will not be considered for selection to another college . . . ."[18]

The concern of Army officers regarding attendance at one of the other senior colleges was noted by the Army Chief of Staff, for many officers had "an impression that, even though having graduated from the Army War College, they must attend the National War College or the Industrial College of the Armed Forces in order to gain maximum recognition in the Army."[19] The Chief of Staff, General J. Lawton Collins, made the very clear and emphatic statement that ". . . so far as the Department of the Army is concerned, graduates of the National War College, the Industrial College of the Armed Forces, and the Army War College will receive equal consideration for high command and staff positions."[20] Furthermore, he specifically directed that the contents of his instructions be brought to the attention of all general and field grade officers "as soon as practicable."

Some recommendations submitted by Almond, however, were not approved including his request for civilian faculty members. The immediate effect may have been negligible, but the primary and most serious result of this denial was establishment of a precedent which was to nullify similar efforts for the next 15 years.

Another suggestion which was disapproved related to establishment of an Army War College periodical. This action also established another precedent which blocked efforts for War College sponsorship of a publication for many years.

Many other recommendations of the Civilian Advisory Group were considered and adopted by the College for the 1952-53 year. Some were placed in effect almost immediately. For example, prior reading requirements were assigned students for lectures. The group discussions with a visiting lecturer, following his formal presentation, were made more intimate and beneficial by dropping the number of student participants from nearly half the class to not more than two committees — about 30 students as a maximum. Faculty members began to monitor student committee discussions and seminars. Other changes could not be started before the end of the academic year, because the course of instruction was too near completion for any major changes to be made in the curriculum.

A new format was prescribed for the course directives and curriculum pamphlet. Instead of merely listing lectures and problems by title, Almond instituted the practice of including the overall purpose of the course, a description of how it would be conducted, committee assignments for both students and faculty, background reading assignments and other reference materials, an explanation of student problem requirements, and a course calendar. The course directive pamphlets were supplemented by a Guide For Preparation of Student Papers which standardized format for all student papers, both individual and committee.

The comments of one course director resulted in another change which was not enthusiastically received by his contemporaries. The faculty director of Course 4, Operations and Training, did not follow the established precedent of merely assembling all published materials and student papers for a "final report." He prepared a detailed analysis of the conduct of his course, including an evaluation based on student comments and faculty discussions, and his conclusions and recommendations for improving the overall conduct of the course. His cover letter included this forthright justification for his unorthodox final report:

> Although my predecessor made valiant effort to completely familiarize me with all the intricacies and byways of this course, there simply was not sufficient time to do so before he left the College. Further information relating to the Course (and

to last year's comparable course) was filed in various and astonishing places, if indeed it was not filed only in someone's head.

This is an attempt, therefore, to record the story of Course 4, not from its conception because that is shrouded in the mysterious past; but this does record its birth, its all too short and crowded life which was subjected to many sudden vicissitudes, and its spasmodic twitchings (represented by lectures presented in later courses) long after it had received decent burial.[21]

Almond considered this report and made submission of similar reports a requirement for future course-end analyses. As a result, a valuable reference file has been established which permits far more accurate and detailed study of the courses conducted over the years.

Although approval was not forthcoming for a War College publication for general distribution, Almond did publish a mimeograph document called "Army War College Views." Short-lived — only one edition was issued — the pamphlet presented student and faculty opinions on current Army doctrine.[22] Distribution was restricted to members of the college.

Almond also encountered difficulties in other efforts. In response to his proposal to increase the coverage given to national and international affairs, the Commanding General of the Army Field Forces replied:

> The Course at the Army War College must provide for the indoctrination of the students in problems of International, National, and Defense Department scope to the extent that these problems affect United States Army policy, planning, and doctrine. However, time in the Army War College Course cannot be spared in which to dwell excessively long on matters that are not primarily United States Army affairs.[23]

This did not permit General Almond to follow completely the recommendations of the Civilian Advisory Group regarding expansion of national and international affairs in the War College curriculum. However, he did expand this coverage as much as possible within the restrictions imposed by a subsequent letter from the Chief of

Staff to the Commanding General, Army Field Forces, which
defined succinctly the focus expected of the War College course of
instruction:

> . . . . The Army War College curriculum is properly concerned
> with the Army's preparation for and conduct of war. To prepare
> properly for war, students of the Army War College must search
> for and examine all the problems that may possibly confront an
> army in future wars. Primary emphasis must be placed upon the
> study of new weapons and their impact on modern warfare.
> Instruction on the conduct of war must develop through knowl-
> edge and capabilities as follows:
>   1. primarily as a commander of large units.
>   2. secondarily, as a staff officer of such commanders or as
>   a staff officer in the Department of the Army, Depart-
>   ment of Defense, or in other governmental agencies to
>   which Army officers are assigned . . . .
>
> The curriculum will include instruction in other departments of
> the government but such subjects should be examined primarily
> in the light of the effect upon the operations of the Department
> of the Army. Although the student must understand the capabil-
> ities, limitations, and employment of other services, primary
> emphasis will be placed upon army command and staff
> positions.[24]

An additional problem was raised by a memorandum circulated
by the Deputy Chief of Staff for Operations and Training indicating
that the Army war College was to be considered ". . . as a potential
source for special studies in connection with proposed Department
of the Army policies, plans, and programs." [25] The memorandum further stated that the College ". . . is prepared to designate specially
selected committees from members of the faculty and the student
body to study such problems as may be submitted by the Army
staff." [26] Although no immediate effect was felt, eventually this memorandum was to engender an additional workload on the faculty and
result in establishment of a faculty group whose primary assignment was preparation of these special studies for higher headquarters. This policy may be viewed as a partial return to the pre-World
War I situation and a reversal of the policy for which McAndrew and

McGlachlin had argued and fought in the early years following World War I.

General Almond and his Deputy Commandant, Brigadier General Arthur Trudeau, investigated the possibility of having the Army War College accredited and authorized to award a graduate degree to its students, but decided to drop the idea after discussion with educational councils. The possibility of devising a graduate program jointly with a civilian university also was investigated. George Washington University offered to establish a program which would provide credit for some portions of the Army War College course and offer graduate level courses to student officers to enable them to obtain a graduate degree while at the War College or soon thereafter. The concept was not adopted. After a thorough study of the proposal, it was decided that the concurrent study required for the two courses would be too much of a load on the student officer. Furthermore, there was question as to the coordination required and the demands which might be made by George Washington University insofar as the content and conduct of the War College curriculum were concerned.[27] Additional discussions with the American Council of Education indicated that it might be possible for the War College to award a graduate degree, if the courses encompassing area studies, national policy, and international affairs were expanded. However, after the departure of both Almond and Trudeau during the 1952-53 academic year, interest in the project lagged and remained dormant for a number of years.

The curriculum for 1952-53 was again an improvement over that of the previous year, although few major changes were made. The comments received from Army Field Forces had negated Almond's intent to make a major revision in the course of study. Consequently, the general outline for the year paralleled the course of study for the previous two years.

Almond returned to a three-phase division of the curriculum: National Security and Policy, the Army, and War Planning. A rearranged sequence of the subcourses provided a better integrated overall curriculum. The course began with a strategic intelligence study of world powers, followed by a study of National Policy. Phase I concluded with detailed analysis of US organization for national security.

Two trips were made during this phase: one to Washington, D.C., for briefings by Department of the Army and State Department officials; the second to the United Nations in New York City.

Phase II consisted of subcourses on logistics, manpower, and operations. These studies were designed to provide the background information required for the next phase of the course of instruction. Not only were Army doctrine, policies, and procedures reviewed, comparisons were made with the methods of the other services and with historical precedents tested in large-scale conflict. The student committee problems for this phase were a decided contrast to those used in Phase I. Here the emphasis was on purely military studies, such as "Army Program Management and Budget Performance" and "The Impact of the Development of New Weapons on Modern Warfare." In Phase I, the emphasis had been on studies such as "US Policy Toward China," "US Economic Support of the NATO Nations," and "Foreign Policy Formulation."

The third phase of the course of instruction pertained to war planning and was divided into subcourses on strategic planning, Army planning, and theater planning. Strategic planning concerned the Joint Chiefs of Staff Strategic Concept and required student preparation of a portion of the Joint war plans. Army planning studies included mobilization, budgeting, and logistics and required student preparation of portions of various Army supporting plans. Theater planning involved preparation of plans of operations for several theaters and wargaming of one plan.

During the year, 132 lectures were scheduled. This was 30 percent less than the number scheduled in the 1951 academic year and reflected the comments of the Civilian Advisory Group. Normally, no more than one lecture was scheduled for any one day. Afterlecture discussions with the speaker continued with the student groups held to a small number.

Despite the evolutionary modifications in the overall course of instruction, the greatest change was made in the individual study program. The minimum length was increased to 6,000 words, and the subject selection list was broadened to include a wide variety of topics. The span extended from foreign policy into domestic affairs as well as including many topics strictly military in nature. Study topics received from Department of the Army and Army Field Forces were included in the list recommended to the student officers; however, choice was largely up to the individual student. Of the 94 different subjects selected by the students, 68 had originally been recommended by the faculty and only two by Department of the Army. For the first time in the postwar period of the War College, the student was given the opportunity of requesting approval of a topic of his own concept; 24 students conducted studies of this nature.

The correspondence with both Army Field Forces and Department of the Army in this and subsequent years indicates a dual attitude on the part of the War College. On the one hand, the College indicated a desire to cooperate with higher headquarters study requirements by assigning them to faculty members, individual students, or student committees for research. On the other hand, the War College commented frequently and strongly against the use of faculty time for higher headquarters studies and resisted their efforts to dictate completely the student research subjects. Since only two students selected study topics from the list prepared by Department of the Army, the War College recommended that suggested study topics be screened stringently before they were sent to the College. The interest in studies made by the students was apparent, for copies of many studies were requested. The Faculty Board noted however, that "a number of staff officers in these headquarters have indicated in private conversations general disappointment, at least at the "Indian" level, partly because of lack of time to winnow any useful ideas out of all the wordage."[28]

The organization of the faculty reflected the organization of the course of instruction. Five officers were assigned to a General Staff Group, and eight to each of three faculty groups which corresponded to the three phases of the course of instruction. Each subcourse was supervised by a course director who selected the lectures to be given, corresponded with guest lecturers, prepared the course directive, and conducted the course with the assistance of other members of the faculty. From three to eight problems were assigned the students in the various courses. Considerable research on the part of the course director and his assistants was required to assure that the subject was appropriate to the curriculum, the scope and purpose of the problem were clearly explained, and the problem could be fully supported by documents in the War College Library or readily available from outside sources.

Once the course was prepared, the course director was responsible for faculty monitorship of student committees to assure adequate faculty guidance of committee work on a graduate level and to provide faculty members with intimate knowledge of the students' abilities directly as well as through their written work. The small size of the committees fostered the personal and intimate student-faculty relationships which were and are an important asset of the Army War College methodology.

In contrast to the academic activities of the three faculty groups, the General Staff Group had a variety of functions. It advised all faculty members on matters falling within the sphere of the various staff sections (G1, G2, G3, and G4) and was responsible that a proper balance of staff work in these fields was maintained in all student committee work. Special studies in the fields of strategy and doctrine were undertaken by the General Staff Group, as directed by the Commandant. For the most part, these studies were in response to requirements from Department of the Army or the Army Field Forces. The General Staff Group also reviewed current and proposed Army doctrine and was responsible for operation of the War Room. Members of the Staff Group assisted in the conduct of the various courses and served as committee advisers. The entire individual research program for student officers was supervised by the General Staff Group, and this function was of prime importance. In addition to these many duties, Group members were also used as special consultants on specific geographic areas of the world and advised students and faculty on ". . . political, economic, and military development" in these areas![29] This requirement may have been based on the Civilian Advisory Group's recommendation to develop faculty expertise beyond military capabilities. However, the vastness of the requirement almost precluded any special expertise for a particular country or area, and this duty was assigned to other faculty members the following year.

The Joint Advisory Group, with its representation from the Department of State, the Navy, and the Air Force, continued to advise and assist the Commandant, the faculty, and the students on matters relating to their respective departments. Its members also served as committee advisers and assisted course directors in the preparation of the various courses.

General Almond fostered within the faculty a constant self-evaluation of the War College. Such analysis was not made a formalized project by appointing a committee or group to review the curriculum. Instead, for the most part, individual members of the faculty forwarded their comments to the Commandant or the Deputy Commandant. Although General Almond was reassigned in December 1952, his successors continued to support the self-evaluation he initiated.

One such evaluation was a comprehensive study by Colonel James K. Polk, whose stated purpose was to determine ". . . those policies or projects which can be undertaken to enhance the prestige of the Army War College and are commensurate with the mission . . ."[30] Although the proposals made were intended to assure "a high degree of acceptance for the graduate," the prime intent of the study was to place the College on a firm and secure base as an essential and meaningful element of the Army educational system.

The study was divided into analyses of three major subjects: military operation of the College, local community relations, and national recognition. The study of "military operations" encompassed all activities which could be accomplished by Department of Army. Colonel Polk reviewed the following:

1. Maintenance of high academic standards at AWC.
2. Insistence on continued input of superior quality student officers.
3. Provision for maximum standards for administration and personal well being of students and their families.
4. Location of the Office, Chief of Military History, at Carlisle Barracks.

5. Publication of an officially sponsored AWC periodical review or digest.
6. Initiation of a special short course for senior officers of the reserve components.
7. Provision for selected civilian component officers to attend a selected portion of the total course at the AWC on an active duty basis.
8. Participation in the combat developments program under OCAFF [Office, Chief Army Field Forces].
9. Provision for one or more resident civilian Professors on the Faculty.[31]

Polk's detailed study of these topics and his analysis of the advantages and disadvantages of each resulted only in his recommending that high academic standards be continued, that the selection process not be eased, that a periodical be sponsored by the College, that officers of the civilian components be permitted to attend portions of the regular course, and that the faculty be expanded to include civilian professors. His reasons for not recommending adoption of the other considerations were an estimated increased workload for the faculty or, insofar as moving the Army Military History group to Carlisle was concerned, inability of post facilities to accommodate additional activities.

The review of national recognition of the War College pertained to other suggestions which included:

1. Establishment of a Board of Civilian Consultants.
2. Initiation of yearly Strategic Seminars with participation by distinguished civilians.
3. Publication of outstanding lectures delivered at the AWC in nationally known periodicals.
4. Publication of authoritative articles about the AWC by nationally known or by Faculty authors.
5. Publication of student individual studies in unofficial military publications.
6. Publication of original articles by members of the Faculty of the AWC.
7. Affiliation with the national educational system in order to award recognized academic degrees to graduates.[32]

This portion of the study began with the comment that "Nationally, the AWC is almost an unknown quantity. Carlisle Barracks is identified with the Indian school . . .!'' After analyzing each of these proposals, Colonel Polk recommended to the Commandant that a permanent board of consultants be established, that articles be written about the War College, and that student and faculty alike be encouraged to write for publication. He did not recommend publication of lectures because of the benefits to be gained by retaining the non-attribution policy so long a part of the War College lecture program. Although the strategic seminar had many advantages, Colonel Polk felt that the existent College facilities would not support such an effort. Publication of student individual research studies was not recommended because of their broad scope and primarily military slant, but "sanitized" versions were recommended as a substitute. Reference was made to the Trudeau study on graduate degrees in recommending against that concept.

Colonel Polk indicated that some of the actions he recommended could be undertaken immediately without undue strain on the faculty or the existing facilities at Carlisle Barracks but that others ". . . will require careful planning, coordination, and budgeting and, hence, should be initiated carefully on a long term basis . . . ."[33]

The recommendations were carefully studied by the Deputy Commandant before being submitted to Major General James E. Moore, the new Commandant. The recommended permanent Civilian Advisory Board was not approved, but a policy of inviting a different group periodically was adopted. The proposed AWC publication was referred to a faculty study committee, because it was believed that additional staff and faculty personnel would be needed to undertake such a publication. The proposal to add civilian professors to the faculty also was referred to a study group for further analysis. As a result, the major proposals recommended by Colonel Polk were not adopted although they were revived in substance many times in later years. Polk's study, however, did cause a second Civilian Advisory Group to be invited to the College in January 1954.

The six months of the new academic year preceding the visit of the Advisory Group were to prove a busy time for the War College. Although no extreme changes had been programmed for the curriculum, evolutionary development had again brought alterations within the framework of the course of instruction. Phase I was redesignated from "National Policy and Security" to "National and International Affairs," the first time in the postwar tenure of the College that open recognition was given to the importance of studying the world situation. The first course was devoted to a study of national policy formulation and included analysis of US Government organization, its membership in international organizations, and its own national interest. The second course gave the student a detailed analysis of the Soviet bloc for the first time, and included study of the ideological, political, geographic, social, military, and economic structure of the USSR and its satellites. Course 3 concerned US foreign policy and included discussion of policy problems faced in various areas or countries.

Exactly what brought this change in title and stress in the first phase of the course of instruction is not clear, for there is no detailed discussion in the minutes of Faculty Board meetings. Possibly, contemporary events brought about a growing awareness of the importance of international affairs in the press of the country undoubtedly had an effect on the War College as much as on the average American. An increased awareness of foreign affairs thus resulted in a reassessment of the importance of international studies for the War College student officers. The courses included in Phase I for the 1954 academic year reflected this changed attitude.

General Moore addressed the student body at the close of the course on National Policy Formulation and summarized the role of the military by saying:

> The military should furnish the advice as to what the security of this country requires. Secondly, if they are not given the means which they think necessary to provide that security, they should advise as to what the consequences will be. Thirdly, having been given the means, they must make them work to the best of their ability and provide the greatest security possible.[34]

Phase II again was devoted to study of the Army and its problems, policies, and doctrines. Although the organization of this phase remained unchanged from the 1953 academic year — three courses covering manpower, logistics, and operations — the internal content removed much of the technical Army procedure stressed the previous year. This procedural study was covered, instead, in a fourth course entitled "General Army Orientation." By removing the study of technical coverage, the time devoted to the remaining courses could be concentrated on the problems and doctrine involved in each of the major Army staff areas.

The third phase of the curriculum once again was devoted to war planning; three courses covering strategic planning, Army planning, and theater planning. Because of the elimination of the course on strategic intelligence, intelligence estimates were included in the course on strategic planning. Little change was made to the other two planning courses. Significant changes, however, were made in the problems assigned to the student committees. Strategic studies were research and development of new weapons, and to midrange estimates designed to provide justification for development of force objectives and requirements. For the first time, a student committee problem was devoted to "Strategic estimates and plans . . . . for military operations short of global war."[35] This problem reflected faculty discussions and was:

> . . . generated by the nagging possibilities of nuclear 'plent' and 'stand off,' the implications of the atomic era, the prevailing tempor of the 'cold war,' and a host of controversies internal to the War College . . . . Thereafter the earlier emphasis on general war as the most important possible policy problem for the graduate experienced a dilution in favor of the more immediate and possibly more confusing problems of military-political pressures short of general war.[36]

The individual study topics included problems in all fields of consideration contained in the curriculum, including command, manpower, intelligence, operations, training, organization, logistics, military strategy, weapons systems, research and development, international affairs, and public relations. Each student was given the option of selecting a topic area from those recommended or of pro-

posing an original topic. In either case, the study was required to be
"One of high level importance and of current or future interest to
the Army, a problem which will require original and creative thought
and research."[37] The maximum length was increased once again,
this time to 7,000 words. Each student was required to present a
summary of his research to a small seminar group. Selected subjects were presented to the entire College.

Colonel Polk's study and recommendations were studied in detail by various faculty committees in the early months of the 1954
academic year. One committee recommended to the Faculty Board
that ". . . it is not the mission of the Army War College to develop
doctrine or to be an operative agency."[38] This recommendation was
caused by increased demands from Army Field Forces for the War
College to conduct studies of various types and was supported by the
Faculty Board. Although General Moore did not agree with this concept, he fully sympathized with the faculty opinion that the number
of officers assigned would not permit any definitive research. Moore
believed that the College should make such studies for Department
of the Army, but only if the faculty were provided with additional
officers for that specific purpose. He directed that a study be made
to determine the feasibility of establishing a small group to study
military strategy and Army doctrine. The report made by this faculty committee was the basis of a letter, from Moore to the Chief of
Staff, which stated Moore's opinion that:

> . . . The Army is at a relative disadvantage with respect to the
> other services because a lack of emphasis on advanced study
> in such areas as strategy, the future use of land power, and
> the development and employment of large Army units.[39]

Furthermore, Moore proposed:

> . . . establishment of an Advanced Study Group to undertake a
> continuing program of long range thinking on strategy and land
> power. The Army War College is believed better equipped to
> pursue such studies than civilian organizations or other schools
> in the Army system.[40]

PRESENTATION OF THE PATTON PORTRAIT

Major General James E. Moore, right, received the portrait of George S. Patton as a student at the War College in 1932 from General Patton's daughter and son-in-law, Colonel and Mrs. James W. Totten.

Moore asked for five additional faculty members for this purpose. The proposal was approved in June 1954, and the Advanced Study Group was organized soon thereafter.

Shortages of officer spaces authorized for the faculty caused great concern during this period. Although vacancies were filled annually, usually during the summer months, losses occurred constantly during the academic year because of reassignment or promotion of individual officers. Eight colonels were promoted to general during the 1952 academic year; three, during the 1953 year. Although there was no complaint about these promotions, General Moore and the College Secretary made strong and frequent comment to the Office of Career Management about the failure of that agency to replace the promoted officers. Additional losses were caused by overseas requirements or by command positions being offered individual officers.

Faculty meetings at this time were devoted largely to a discussion of War College procedures and the use of graduate level techniques. The advantages and disadvantages of using the case study method for operational problems were discussed; however, a decision was deferred until faculty members could obtain more information on the preparation of these studies. The number of lectures which ought to be scheduled was a subject of frequent discussion. Finally the decision was made in December 1953 to limit the number to four each week.[41]

The student workload was discussed at length and often with some heat. One course director maintained that the afterlecture conferences were of value to the student only if the guest lecturer was present. The course director stated that, in his opinion, the practice of requiring student afterlecture discussions monitored by a faculty member was of questionable value "unless properly handled by the faculty member." General Moore added a note to his Deputy Commandant "Why not train him [the faculty monitor] up to it? This is the chairman's responsibility."![42]

Because the faculty was preparing outlines for the 1954-55 course at this time, new concepts and changes were suggested by the course directors and faculty group chairman. One officer suggested dividing the class into groups to pursue different courses of study. This suggestion was phrased as a question, "Should all students continue taking the same course or should variations be taught which are tailored to individual needs?"[43] The question was then rephrased in an effort to determine whether the Army War College mission was to "develop skills, impart knowledge, train speakers, seek solutions for Department of the Army problems, develop habits of thought, or encourage study, analysis, and creative thought." The faculty member concluded that the War College should not develop individual skills, train speakers, or seek solutions for Department of the Army problems per se but should impart knowledge to its student officers by encouraging individual study, detailed analysis, and creative thought.[44] He recommended against establishment of any number of varied courses and continuation of a single curriculum.

This was the Army War College that was visited by the second Civilian Advisory Group in January 1954. It was an academic institution much different in some ways from that reviewed by the first Group two years before; an organization unchanged in other ways. The 1954 Civilian Advisory Group consisted of seven men from various fields. Retired General Harold R. Bull was a member, as was Dean Rusk, Assistant Secretary of State for Far Eastern Affairs, and Professor John W. Masland from Dartmouth College. Many of the comments and recommendations of the Group reflected the internal dissatisfaction and controversy within the faculty; others fully supported War College efforts for improvement which had not been approved by Army Field Forces or by Department of the Army.

The report of the Advisory Group expressed its ". . . respect for the openness with which the Commandant and his colleagues have invited criticism.[45] This was interpreted as an encouraging sign of the responsible attitude of the Commandant, the faculty, and the student body. However, the Advisory Group also indicated that it was ". . . hesitant to comment on the program and the methods of instruction on the basis of a relatively short visit."[46] The advisory Group felt that it could make only "a superficial examination of the number of problems raised,"[47] even though everything possible was done to make information available.

The recommendations and comments of the Advisory Group

were divided into five major categories: Provision of Intellectual
Leadership, the Curriculum, Methods of Instruction, Officer Personnel, and Miscellaneous Matters. Each category contained a number
of suggestions, comments, or recommendations.

In the opinion of the Advisory Group, the Army War College
should be identified as the center for application of original and
vigorous study to the problems of the Army as a whole. The proposed establishment of the Advanced Study Group received strong
endorsement and the Advisory Group indicated that ". . . It should be
their function to examine problems of urgent importance, both short
and long range, for which high-level planners have little time for
systematic study and evaluation."[48] The need for a War College periodic publication was noted and commended "as indicative of the interest of the College in the continuing intellectual welfare of its
graduates and of the leadership of the Army." Both of these activities, the Advisory Group stated, could be developed within the mission of the Army War College as then defined in Army regulations.

The Advisory Group first reviewed the curriculum of the War
College to determine whether the course of instruction fulfilled the
mission assigned the College. The conclusion was made that the degree of emphasis on national and international affairs, policy formulation, and joint and strategic war plans "appears to us to be in the
right proportion to support the mission of the Army War College."[49]
The courses devoted to the Army and to war planning were considered properly adjusted to the mission, although the Advisory Group
believed that some attention should be devoted to study of the relationship of the personality and psychology of the commander to the
exercise of command.

Recognizing that they were not fully qualified as a group to judge
completely the military content of the curriculum, the Civilian Advisory Group concentrated on the part of the curriculum devoted to
the study of national and international affairs. Much of its discussion
was devoted to a fundamental dilemma which had previously been
studied in detail by the War College faculty: the problem of balancing
breadth and depth of coverage. The Advisory Group admitted recognizing fully the value of the broad coverage provided in the courses

taught in Phase I of the curriculum, National and International Affairs, particularly because this was the last opportunity most of the student officers would have to ". . . examine the full range of problems facing the United States and the global nature of our strategy."[50] The Advisory Group was split in its conceptual analysis of the Phase I subjects. Some members were satisfied with the organization of the phase and the coverage provided, feeling that a fine balance between breadth and depth had been achieved. Others saw a need for greater attention in depth with less emphasis on completeness of coverage. These members felt that broad coverage in itself was not sufficient to give the student full feeling for the wide range of factors involved and the interrelationships of these various factors. They maintained that a few lectures and a committee study could not give an officer a full ". . . appreciation of how a high-level command responsibility is adjusted to the political situation in an area"[51] and that it was far more important to stress fundamental principles and relationships than descriptive material alone and to develop ". . . habits of mind in coping with complex politico-military situations."[52] A number of ways in which depth might be stressed were suggested.

A lack of realism, insofar as the course on the Soviet bloc was concerned, was commented on. It was pointed out rather emphatically that the lack of consideration of the military factor at the same time as other factors of Soviet national power were studied was detrimental to the overall value of the course, even though the Soviet military factor was studied as part of the strategic war planning course. The Advisory Group recommended that one lecture, at a minimum, should be devoted to this topic.

In reviewing the College instructional techniques, the Advisory Group commented most favorably upon the individual research program. The Group urged that every effort be made to improve the program quality and to develop better facilities and means for evaluating the individual student research effort. The comment was also made that, if necessity should force reduction of any part of the War College program, such reduction or curtailment should not be made by eliminating the student research effort.

The Group recommended against scheduling too many lectures

and urged greater use of the committee system as the principal means of instruction. The seminar type of committee presentation was particularly recommended. Separate listings, comments, and annotations for course bibliographies were suggested as well as a necessity to encourage general reading by the students.

The turnover rate of faculty personnel was noted, and the Advisory Group recommended that not more than one-third be replaced annually and that the faculty be kept at full strength at all times. To supplement the military faculty, the Advisory Group recommended that two highly competent civilian faculty members be approved by Department of the Army.

Field trips were encouraged and the necessity for improved physical facilities was noted. The backlog of uncataloged materials in the Library again was noted and the suggestion made that the Commandant request assistance from the Library of Congress or the American Library Association to eliminate the backlog.

The departure of the Advisory Group resulted in renewed efforts by the faculty to ready the curriculum for the 1955 academic year. Changes in the curriculum followed the general recommendations made by the Advisory Group. The course on the Soviet bloc added coverage of the military factor of Soviet power. The Phase II courses relating to the Army remained almost unchanged. However, Phase III, was retitled "Strategy and War Planning" and the former course on strategic planning was changed to a course on strategy. This course was designed to develop an understanding and appreciation of strategy as it related to the military aspects of deterrence and the conduct of war. The historical concepts of strategy in the past were translated into concepts for strategy in the future. Among the lectures scheduled were "The Causes of War and Deterrents," "Fundamentals of Military Strategy," "The Philosophy and Influence of Clausewitz, Hahn, and Douhet," and "The Opposing Strategies of the Cold War."

The remainder of this phase of the curriculum paralleled previous courses, including Army and theater planning and a wargame of student plans. Another innovation adopted a suggestion made by Colonel Polk in his 1953 study. The War College sponsored a strategy seminar in March to which 58 distinguished citizens, both military and civilian in background, were invited. Four lectures on "Modern Strategy," "Concept of Future Land Warfare," "The Current Military Situation," and "Current Strategic Problems" were delivered to the visiting group and its hosts. Students and guests met in round table seminar sessions after each lecture to discuss the material covered. The committee solutions developed were presented to all conference participants in the final plenary session.

This was the first effort of the War College to sponsor an activity of this scope with both civilian and military participants. The seminar was successful, although conflicts in timing did not permit participation by some Government officials from Washington. However, the overall success warranted consideration of a repetition the following year.

Another proposal fostered by General Moore and encouraged by the Civilian Advisory Group was establishment of an Advanced Study Group within the faculty. Initially, only two additional officers were assigned when the Advanced Study Group was organized in May 1954. Following the normal assignment of new officers to the faculty during the summer months, the five officers requested by General Moore and approved by Department of the Army were allocated to the section. The assigned mission of the Group was to ". . . study broad problems whose solutions will provide long-range guidance for Army policies."[53] The first specific study given the group was to "Determine a desirable, feasible, and acceptable organization and deployment for the United States Army which will enable the United States Army to be used to deter aggression and war or to fight successfully under all conditions of limited or global hostilities."[54] The study, however, was to be developed in outline form rather than in detail. Its intent was to provide the basis for more detailed investigation at a later date in such conceptual areas as "grand strategy in an era of nuclear plenty and the role of land power in the foreseeable future."[55]

Another recommendation which Moore made to Army Field Forces and Department of the Army — publication of an Army War College periodical — did not meet with approval in either headquarters. Although the War College action officer had carefully prepared a detailed study of the resources required to publish a quarterly magazine, and despite the fact that an overwhelming majority of War College graduates had indicated their desire for and support of such a publication, the request was again denied. The precedent already established by the previous disapproval was to prevent authorization for nearly ten more years.

Many other small projects were accomplished during General Moore's term as commandant. Students merely raised their hands at afterlecture conferences to indicate they wished to ask a question. The next-recognized student often asked a new question rather than one related to the on-going discussion. A simple but effective "signal" system was devised to indicate to the faculty monitor whether the student had a new question or a "related" question. A related question was indicated by the student forming an "O" for his fingers; a new question by an open palm. Still in use, this system solved the problem and resulted in far improved continuity of questions for visiting lecturers.

Interest in Army history and the historical background of Carlisle Barracks was also fostered during General Moore's incumbency. This took many outward forms. One project marked the major building and historical sites at Carlisle Barracks. Another project was the brainchild of Colonel W. P. Yarborough and Colonel Albert O. Connor. They recommended that the student coffee shop be decorated to indicate the ties between the Army War College and the Army. Their solution was to hang small "commanders' plaques" bearing the insignia of units commanded by student officers or faculty members before or after graduation from the War College. Each plaque also carries the name of the officer concerned. The collection today numbers over 800 plaques and represents units of all branches of the Army and of all sizes from battalion to corps. It has become what Yarborough and Connor intended, a symbolic and visible representation of the tie between the College and the Army.

The annual visit to the Gettysburg Battlefield, initiated by General Almond in 1951, was expanded to include an historical skit by officers of the faculty. Although, in some ways, this Gettysburg

GETTYSBURG SKIT

Annually, officers of the Army War College faculty present a skit narrating the events leading to and the action taking place at the battle of Gettysburg. The skit is followed by a tour of the battlefield. The above photograph shows the final scene of the 1967 presentation.

trip may be considered a descendent of the pre-World War I visits
to the Civil War battlefields, it had one great and very marked dif-
ference: the original trips were strictly for the military students
and faculty; the modern version includes the families of the officers.
The concept adopted by General Almond had been developed by a
faculty member of the Army Information School in 1949-50, Major
John Elting. War College improvements included a more comprehensive pretour orientation by officers uniformed to represent Union
and Confederate generals, a running narrative by faculty tour directors during the visit, and a picnic lunch at the battlefield.

General Moore was not present to see many of his concepts and
recommendations become fact instead of theory. He was reassigned
in February 1955. In the next nine months, the War College had two
commandants before Major General Max S. Johnson was appointed
in October 1955, Brigadier General Thomas W. Dunn and Major
General Clyde D. Eddleman.

During the 1955 academic year, Colonel John A. Berry, secretary of the War College, took time to make a number of proposals
which reflect the attitude and thoughts of the faculty. "Thinking of
the future," he said, "and considering the comment of our advisory
groups and consultants, I have tried to visualize the long range and
intermediate measures we should initiate in order to establish the
intellectual leadership of the Army which this College should right-
fully exercise."[56]

After discussing doctrinal concepts and procedures of the College, Colonel Berry made a number of important recommendations.
He advocated that a study be prepared and forwarded to the Chief
of Staff "giving the optimum structure of the College for the period
1960-70,"[57] as well as establishing intermediate steps to reach that
goal. One of the steps he advocated was establishment of a nonresident or correspondence course to give future students basic Army
War College knowledge. Berry intended this course to eliminate the
need for a substantial amount of material in the curriculum and thus
make more time available for more detailed and advanced study in
depth. Berry also urged establishment of a periodical and the under-
taking of a detailed study to determine the curriculum content for

1960 when ". . . the pool of College trained officers will meet the worldwide requirements [of the Army] and needs only to be maintained."[58]

The short-range actions considered by Berry were primarily in the nature of curriculum refinement: improved committee studies and lectures integrated more fully into a specific course or sub-course. Also recommended were better faculty selection processes, improved faculty training techniques, expansion of the scope covered by the Advanced Study Group, and development of specialities by faculty members. Unfortunately, little if any action was taken on Berry's proposals at that time, although many were adopted in later years.

The 1956 academic year was well underway when General Johnson arrived in October 1955. As might well be expected, the brief tenure of two commandants between General Moore's departure in February and Johnson's arrival in October resulted in retention of the previous year's curriculum almost unchanged. Course sequence had been changed with little internal content variation. The year began, however, with a new course, "The World Scene and the Army." With the intent of providing a background for subsequent courses, the broad orientation on fundamentals underlying the East-West power struggle was designed to broaden understanding of command and managerial functions within the United States security organization as well as to provide a comparison of sea power, air power, and land operations. Two other courses on operations and intelligence and logistics and manpower were included in Part I of the overall course of instruction.

Part II was devoted to international relations. After a course devoted to the Soviet Bloc, the student officers reviewed US national security organization and foreign relations. The discussion of the policies of the United States toward other nations and areas of the world led to the first course in Part III, "Strategy." This course was devoted to developing understanding of military strategy for the conduct of war and as an instrument of national policy to deter war. Studies of historical strategic concepts were included as well as development of military strategies for the future. A course on Army,

Joint, and theater war planning, with a wargame, concluded the regular course of instruction.

The academic year ended with the National Strategy Seminar in mid-June. Student committees reviewed and refined selected problems from the earlier course on United States foreign relations and extended the committee solutions based upon the military discussion and programs developed in the war planning courses prior to the arrival of the guest participants. The outline national strategies thus developed were presented to committee guests and discussed in seminar sessions. The final plenary session considered the proposed national strategy developed jointly by one student-guest committee and was followed by a general question period. The changes in procedure and greater participation by Government personnel from Washington resulted in an improved seminar, which faculty analysis indicated to be for more beneficial for the students and guests alike.

During the year, relationships with the Continental Army Command, successor to the Army Field Forces, deteriorated. In many ways, the contacts between the War College and its immediate supervisory headquarters were similar to the situation which existed during the controversial McAndrew-Haan discussions in 1921. CONARC insisted that the War College follow general educational directives which were prepared for all schools in the Army educational system. For example, on 24 February 1956, CONARC directed the War College to institute a 10 to 15 hour block of instruction on the Army's role in civil emergencies in the United States.[59] This requirement was particularly difficult for the War College to include in its curriculum. The timeblock of instruction directed did not fit War College procedures. If normal Army school methods were used, a special two day course would be required. If the lecture and committee discussion technique was followed, an even longer period would be taken from the already full War College schedule. Neither way was desirable from the War College point of view. The College compromised by scheduling a lecture on the subject, by conducting short committee discussions soon thereafter, and by including civil emergency topics in the list of individual research subjects.

A previous requirement for an individual research paper by
faculty members had been discarded earlier in the year, primarily
because the Advanced Studies Group was fully functional and had
taken over many of the studies directed by CONARC and Department
of the Army. However, the requirements for research by the Advanced Study Group were increased greatly in January 1956 by another CONARC directive which stated:

> It is the intention of this headquarters to establish the Army
> War College as the agency responsible for developing studies
> depicting the role of the Army in modern warfare. It is envi-
> sioned that these studies will be developed on a continuing basis
> as required to keep pace with doctrinal changes resulting from
> developments in weapons, tactics, and techniques.[60]

This requirement, together with specific study topics directed
by CONARC, generated a much heavier workload on the five man
Advanced Study Group, and other faculty members were given some
of the special research projects. This additional faculty requirement
resulted in prolonged discussions with CONARC and a subsequent
request for additional personnel. CONARC concurred, but Department of the Army would not approve the request. Consequently, the
Advanced Studies Group and other faculty members continued to prepare studies assigned by CONARC, and the extracurricular faculty
requirements thus generated continued to plague the Commandant
and his assistants.

Faculty Board discussions of this period included a study of the
role of the War College in any future major conflict involving the
United States. A plan was developed on the assumption that the College would continue to function as an educational institution during
such a war, despite the opposing precedents established in 1917 and
1940. The proposal, which was not forwarded to Department of the
Army, provided for two courses annually with 200 student officers
in each course. Curriculum content was to be devoted primarily to
Army and Joint planning and procedures. The plan was based on an
anticipated requirement for additional War College graduates to
meet the needs of an expanded Army, an estimate founded on the

shortages encountered by Pershing during World War I and by the major commanders of World War II.

Continued efforts were made to obtain approval for civilian members for the faculty and for publication of a War College periodical. The latter requirement was forwarded to CONARC as a dual request: authorization for an annual catalog outlining the course of instruction and providing a description of the War College and its background; and a request for a periodical containing articles prepared by students, faculty, and graduates. Both requests were disapproved. Approval was given for establishment of one civilian faculty position, but the grade structure provided was so low that the position could not be filled with a competent educator. Although efforts were made to have the position upgraded, the authorization later was withdrawn by Department of the Army.

Means of improving War College procedures continued to be a topic of almost constant discussion. Case studies were again considered, this time in conjunction with the logistics portion of the curriculum. Their use was encouraged, at least on a trial basis. The time required to prepare such studies, however, was recognized as critical, particularly when added to the CONARC research projects already required of the faculty and the Advanced Studies Group. Additional discussions on procedures resulted in a decrease in the number of student presentations to the entire class and an increase in seminar or committee presentations. The size of the committees was reduced to approximately 15 officers to stimulate individual participation and discussion. Additional individual requirements replaced committee written reports.

Another proposal often discussed and studied in previous years was revived again: the institution of a course for officers of the reserve components. A special committee was named to investigate the feasibility of establishing either a short resident course or an extension course to meet this requirement.

The curriculum for the 1957 academic year eliminated the three phases of preceding years in an effort to provide a more integrated course of instruction. National and international studies were returned to the beginning of the school year, followed by courses on the Army, Joint, and theater war planning. The year again ended with the National Strategy Seminar. At the recommendation of General Johnson the guest list for the 1957 Seminar included many individuals who had not participated in the two previous sessions. The percentage of civilian guests was increased to equalize their participation with that of military and retired military personnel. An effort was made to include representatives of labor, management, educational institution, industry, news media, Government, and other civilian activities. Military representatives were invited from each of the armed services.

The end of the first year of General Johnson's tenure as commandant may be viewed as the end of a distinct phase in the modern history of the Army War College. Although the curriculum varied little from the course of earlier years, decided changes were forthcoming. Whitson presents an excellent summary of the early years in his doctoral dissertation, "The United States Army War College and National Security":

> From early curricula the tentative conclusion may be derived that, at first, the focus was on no particular role, executive (command) and planning (G3 primarily) roles both receiving somewhat more emphasis than intelligence but all being considered primarily for Department of the Army or theater levels. In later curricula, planning roles appeared to have gained the primary focus of all courses with a joint (either National or theater level) perspective receiving much greater emphasis than before.[61]

The first seven years of the post-World War II College represent a period of transition and change which reflects the events of the world outside the academic community. The conclusion of the Korean conflict, intensification of the cold war, development of the US deterrent capability, increased foreign assistance programs, and changed concepts of the land power — all these were reflected in changes within the curriculum. The continuous discussions within the faculty regarding depth versus breadth of instruction, the efforts to add civilian members to the faculty and to sponsor a publication, and the constant stress on improved procedures that would be more consistent with a graduate educational system are indicative of the intense desire of the commandants and their faculties to improve the overall caliber of instruction at the War College.

The change in assigned mission of the College also reflects the change in attitudes of and toward the Army and its role within the national military establishment. From a requirement in 1950 to prepare officers for duty in Army headquarters at Army group or higher level, the mission had been altered to a requirement to prepare officers ". . . for the highest command and general staff positions in the Army, and for such high level positions within the Department of Defense or other governmental agencies as the Army might be called upon to fill."[62] This change in mission was reflected by equivalent changes in the curriculum.

Faculty discussions generally centered about five very basic fundamental questions which, although not clearly defined as such in any faculty discussion, constantly appeared as problem areas from year to year. Whitson summarizes these problems in this manner:

> What is the nature of the problem the graduate may be required to handle?
> At what staff levels may he expect to operate?
> Broadly, what roles can he expect to play at those levels?
> What capabilities should he possess in order to perform those roles most effectively?
> What other missions should the War College have?[63]

Almost every change made to the curriculum, every variation attempted in College procedures, every effort made to obtain approval for projects such as a War College publication was based on an effort to arrive at a solution of these problem areas. Whitson's analysis of problem areas is well-founded and is as applicable now as it was ten years earlier. In an effort to solve these basic and fundamental enigmatic problems, General Johnson conducted a detailed self-analysis of the College which was to result in major changes to the curriculum and the entrance of the Army War College into a period concerned with the role of the Army in supporting the national strategies of the United States.

In Support of National Strategy:

1957-1963

IN discussing proposed revisions of the curriculum, Johnson and his faculty isolated the fundamental concepts into three distinct categories: differences in basic theories regarding content of the curriculum, arrangement of courses, and the distribution of time among the various courses. Essentially, the basic theories discussed related to role of the studies in the social sciences as a part of the curriculum versus the place of strictly military subjects in the course of instruction.

Strangely enough, the argument for including national and international studies in the curriculum contended that ". . . that portion of the mission which directs preparation of the student 'for the highest level of command and staff positions in the Army' is the primary element which justifies the inclusion of any non-military subjects at this senior service school level."[1] Both of the Civilian Advisory Groups — in 1952 and 1954 — had urged an increase in coverage in nonmilitary subjects. Despite some additions, particularly in coverage of international affairs, many of the faculty contended that even more time should be devoted to the social studies. One member commented that ". . . the level of instruction in International Relations did not compare favorably with that presented to cadets at West Point."[2] The proponents for the social studies, however, fully admitted the necessity for military subjects and urged that the War College ". . . strike an appropriate balance between military and non-military subjects in its curriculum."[3]

The advocates of more military subject matter based their

arguments — ironically — upon the same wording in the War College mission used by the social studies proponents to justify nonmilitary coverage: ". . . highest command and general staff positions in the Army." However, their argument was also founded on an additional statement in the mission which indicated that the War College was to ". . . develop tactical and logistical doctrine relating to the employment and operations of the Theater Army and Army and Army Group . . ."[4]

Some of the more avid advocates for more military coverage still insisted that a return to the "Leavenworth" methods, rejected by General Swing in 1950, would provide optimum training for War College Students. Most of the military subject supporters preferred courses devoted to the functions and methods of the major staff section with emphasis on planning techniques and wargaming. Although many of the group admitted the necessity for some coverage of international and national affairs, they maintained that a comprehensive study of the social sciences could not be accomplished, even if the entire year was devoted to such a course. Since coverage of such studies of necessity had to be broad, they considered a brief exposure to be sufficient.

This dilemma was analyzed thoroughly by the faculty committees. The rationale behind the recommendation to General Johnson stated:

In simplest terms, military doctrine cannot be intelligently developed, nor the planning for the employment of military forces effectively accomplished, without an appreciation of war's political object . . . . competence in ' the highest level command and staff positions' requires more than military capability. Today, and in the future, the Army's top level leaders and the staff officers who must provide their immediate support must have also acquired the appreciations necessary to the correlation of military thinking and activity with the other forms of national power and with the institutions which develop them and control their use.[5]

The report emphasized that including a national strategy requirement would increase the curriculum scope both in substance and in method. Furthermore, it was stressed that the requirement in itself would provide unity for the first part of the recommended curriculum, the nonmilitary subjects. The report maintained that:

> . . . although the mission could be interpreted in terms of a great many academic requirements, such as the need for a study of economics — as a discipline; or the need for a study of intelligence — as a staff function, the mission of the College would be better served by developing the curriculum around a broader — and yet, more tangible — theme.[6]

This rationale resulted in development of a unifying theme for the curriculum which reflected a tangible interpretation of the College mission and was unique to the War College and its course of instruction. The theme was in two parts and corresponded to two different and distinct "levels" of consideration which had been an implied part of the War College curriculum since 1950. The theme of the first half of the course in 1956 was the national strategy of the United States; the theme for the second half was a supporting national military program. Although the curriculum for 1956 had not been separated into two formal parts or phases, the courses for the entire year had been divided into the two natural groupings upon which the twofold theme was based. The essential purpose in recommending formalizing these two themes was to assure that the courses which contributed to each part actually were a progressive development of student understanding of the overall purpose and intent of the curriculum. If this were true, the faculty report maintained that "On this basis it would be possible to evaluate any particular course in terms of its essential and non-essential elements."

As a result of the comprehensive and objective review of the War College curriculum and procedures, General Johnson instituted changes which were to have a profound effect on the College. These changes were begun toward the end of the 1957 academic year and continued until his departure in February 1959. The major alterations, however, were made to the curriculum for the 1958 academic year.

The course was divided into two major phases: "The United

States and Its National Policy" and "Military Doctrine, Strategy and Readiness." Within this organizational framework, ten courses were scheduled. The year ended with the National Strategy Seminar in June. Although not clearly specified in any of the published curricular discussions, the integrated theme concept was used throughout the entire year. Each course was conducted with the end thought in mind of the contribution the course subject matter made either to the national strategy of the United States or to a military program to support such a strategy.

The first three courses were designed to develop fuller understanding of national and international affairs and the problems associated with developing and implementing a realistic national strategy for the United States in the coming decade. After studying the national strategy of the United States, the student officers compared the national interests and power of the United States with those of the Soviet Union. This provided the foundation and background for a review of US international relations and foreign policy. Existing techniques — lecturers, seminars, committee studies, and individual problems — were augmented by a new teaching method — the use of discussion topics. These were a seminar-type discussions based on a preindicated topic and recommended readings. An example of the discussion topic can be found in Course 2, "International Relations and United States Foreign Policy," where two discussion topics were assigned: "The Nation-State System and International Relations" and "International Economics."

In the second part of the course of instruction, the emphasis changed from the international-national studies to military topics associated with development of a military program for the United States adequate to meet the nation's military security requirements for the next decade. Four courses provided a review of military doctrine, military strategy, and readiness. The first course of the military bloc pertained to "The Army in Combat" and stressed the principal elements and factors likely to influence the organization and employment of Army forces in conjunction with Naval and Air forces in future combat. After a one-week wargaming session, an analysis of theater, theater Army, and Army group operations occu-

THE STATUE OF FREDERICK THE GREAT

a. Presented to the War College by Kaiser Wilhelm, the statue stood in front of the War College building at Fort McNair.

b. The statue was moved to Carlisle Barracks in the 1950's and now stands on the "Old Parade."

pied the students. This was followed, in turn, by a course devoted to military strategy which included study of the scope, nature, and prupose of the strategy guidance required of the Joint Chiefs of Staff and the Department of the Army in the furtherance of national objectives. The last course of the regular academic year was "Military Readiness," a review of the Nation's readiness to provide for its security, with emphasis on the Army's capabilities to meet these requirements.

The summation of the entire year was the preparation for and conduct of the annual National Strategy Seminar. Student officers prepared national strategies based on the second phase. The resultant strategies and supporting programs were presented to the Seminar guests for comment and discussion. Revisions were made and a final prospective national strategy and its supporting military program prepared in individual committee sessions wherein student and guest alike expressed his opinions about the draft papers. One committee was selected by lot to present its efforts to the College and its guests at the final Seminar plenary session.

This curricular pattern was followed for the next five years. True, there were changes within the core design; but, basically, the pattern established by General Johnson dominated the War College curriculum during this period. The only significant change occurred in the 1959 academic year just prior to Johnson's departure. In many ways, this was not a change at all but, rather a redesignation and reallocation of time. Part I of the curriculum was retitled "National Power and International Relations" instead of "The United States and Its National Strategy." The time devoted to this phase was shortened four weeks. Part II remained virtually unchanged but was also curtailed two weeks. The time taken from the curriculum of the previous year was used for the summation course, "National Strategy and a Supporting Military Program." The increase in time permitted the student committees to develop more fully a better, more realistic national strategy and its supporting military program.

There were, however, other changes and improvements made. The individual student research program became a "thesis" program. This change in terminology is in itself symtomatic of the major procedural and substantive changes made to the core curriculum. The student thesis reflected the vastly increased College emphasis on individual student efforts and the extension of philosophical, technological, and other lines of inquiry almost without limit. Each officer was provided thirty pages of suggested topics from which he could select his area of research. If the student so desired, he might request approval of his own subject. The maximum length was increased to 10,000 words with provision for extension beyond this limit, if the student could justify such an increase. Many suggested topics, however, remained unchanged from the previous year's list. There were more areas relating to nuclear warfare, and, for the first time, a suggested study area related to automatic data processing. In keeping with the curricular theme concept, several titles related directly to "national security" in its various aspects.

The trend followed by Johnson and his three immediate successors, Major Generals William P. Ennis, Jr., Thomas W. Dunn, and William F. Train, was toward increased international and national studies with a corollary decrease in the amount of curricular time devoted to purely military topics. Despite the apparent lessening of emphasis on military coverage, extensive effort was made throughout the curriculum to stress the roles and missions of the armed services in furthering the national policies of the United States.

Student evaluations were of continual concern to the commandants and members of the faculty. The importance of the student's final academic report was realized fully, and every effort was made to provide a comprehensive and accurate accounting of each student officer's year of study. The basic evaluation system devised by General Swing in 1950 provided for a combination narrative-adjectival rating of each student by the faculty committee advisers. At the end of the academic year, each student would have been evaluated in each of his courses, usually by a different member of the faculty in each instance. To these ratings was added the evaluation of the student's individual research paper. Although there were many minor variations, the general system devised by Swing continued in use. Some interesting rating concepts were developed and discarded from time to time. One attempt was made to quantify student participation on the basis of the number of questions asked and comments made in question periods, after-lecture conferences, and committee discussions. Needless to say, this project was discarded in very short order, for its overall value was negligible, and the chore of tabulating the questions and comments was onerous. Another suggestion considered by the Faculty Board was to establish "peer rating" system with mutual evalutions made by students. After a lengthy study, a faculty committee recommended against adopting such a system, because some officers would be rating their superiors and the problem of devising valid rating criteria would be almost insurmountable.

During 1959, George Washington University agreed to establish a program of concurrent instruction for the members of the Army War College. Although the primary intent of the program was additional study toward a degree of Master of Arts in International Affairs, arrangements also were made to permit work at the baccalaureate level. The cited purposes of this program were:

> To complement the Army War College curriculum in the international affairs field.
> To further mid-career development of officers in the United States Army and other military services and governmental agencies while at the US Army War College.
> To provide academic recognition, in the form of a degree, for successful candidates.[7]

The agreement between the two institutions provided for award of nine credit hours for the Army War College curriculum and an additional six credits for the War College thesis. The Trudeau-George Washington University discussions in 1952 had indicated that the University would award 15 credits for the "successful conclusion of your present curriculum"[8] and an additional six credits for an acceptable thesis prepared under University supervision. Despite substantial increases in the study of international and national affairs, the University had lessened the number of credits for the War College curriculum. Furthermore, the University now recognized that the War College student research effort was of thesis nature, a decided change from the opinion of the University regarding the War College research requirement in 1952.

Any member of the War College enrolling in the George Washington University Program was required to pursue the additional studies required by the University of his own "nonduty" time. It was specifically stated by the War College that such work was to have no adverse impact on either the work of the individual student or the War College curriculum. The George Washington University Program was divided into three trimesters. Two were conducted during the War College academic year, and the third, during the two months immediately following graduation from the War College.

The agreement between the two institutions was renewed annually until the conclusion of the 1966 War College academic year. During the six years the program was conducted by the University, approximately 370 officers earned degrees. The number of War College personnel enrolled in the George Washington University courses in any one year varied from less than 100 to approximately 180. Subjects studied during the 1965 academic year are typical of the curriculum:

> Theories of Economic Development (Underdeveloped Countries)
> Diplomacy since World War II
> International Law
> International Organization
> Comparative Governments and Politics [9]

Problems created by concurrent conduct of two courses of instruction brought many discussions between the War College and the University. Generally, these problems fell into six areas: the University thesis requirement; scheduling to permit coordination with the War College activities; the amount of student time required for the University courses; the length of the summer trimester; content of the War College curriculum; and the qualifications of University professors.

The Army War College Commandant, Major General Thomas W. Dunn, near the conclusion of the first year George Washington University Program, stated that the thesis had been a major problem.

"From the inception throughout the initial phases," he said, "there was never any indication that the University expected the Army War College student to write a GWU-on-campus type thesis . . ."[10] although this was the position stated during the year by University personnel. General Dunn stated that these efforts had only one result, insofar as the War College was concerned, ". . . to adversely effect the Army War College thesis, an important professional requirement . . ."[11] Dunn indicated two major effects: a reduction in the number of military subjects selected by War College students and incompatability with the Army War College curriculum.

The thesis problem was solved by compromise although neither institution was completely satisfied with the results. On the one hand the University agreed to accept the thesis prepared as a War College requirement, wherever possible, and to approve the thesis topic early in the year. On the other hand, the War College revised its thesis format and procedures to more closely approximate on-campus requirements for college academic writing. Students were allotted additional time to prepare their War College theses and were permitted, with justification, to exceed the 10,000-word War College limitation. Although this joint effort eliminated much of the difficulty surrounding the thesis, the problem did continue to come up time and time again during the six year period the University program was conducted.

Another difficult problem involved the amount of time required by the War College student to prepare for his George Washington courses. A War College survey in 1962 indicated that, for one University course, students were applying an average of 11 hours study for one class session. University requirements in another course included six term papers; two other courses required papers prepared in thesis format. In additon to written requirements, all courses required oral presentations. General Dunn indicated in his 1961 letter that, "The continued use of mid-term and end-of-course examinations, term papers, oral presentations, and an intensified thesis requirement will increase the workload to the point where it may not be possible to continue the program."[12] Although the University did make some effort to understand the War College position and did lessen, to a certain extent, course requirements for War College students without lowering University standards, the problem of preparation time· was never solved to the complete satisfaction of both institutions. For example, at one discussion, University officials took the stand that the students would have enough study time for both the War College and University Courses if they ceased engaging in extracurricular activities. The War College contended that the extracurricular activities were an important part of the education of the officer and an essential part of the College mission; that informal discussions outside the War College classroom added to the officer's overall development. The lack of common appreciation of each other's viewpoint relative to University course requirements and their absorption of the student's time continued and the problem still existed almost unchanged in 1966.

During the first year, completion dates for many University requirements conflicted with major War College activities. Arriving at a common scheduling program may appear to be an easy matter requiring only a few discussions, but a series of conferences was required to resolve the problem even though the solution was simple. The War College provided the University with its schedule as early in the year as possible, emphasizing dates on which student and committee written requirements were due. Thereafter, the University resident coordinator scheduled his requirements so there was no conflict and rescheduled his classes if unexpected War College requirements appeared.

The University also contended that a longer summer trimester was required. The War College pointed out that it was impossible to retain the individual officers more than a few weeks after completion of the War College course. Duty requirements also precluded acquiescing to the University suggestion that a similar summer session be held prior to the start of the War College instruction, as well as after. Eventually, it was recognized that the summer trimester could be scheduled only after the regular War College course, and that it would have to be kept relatively short. Periodic efforts by the University to extend total summer trimester time were unsuccessful.

As has already been mentioned, many discussions took place between University and War College representatives regarding the accreditation offered for the War College courses. This had been established by the University as nine credits, with six additional available for an acceptable thesis. The War College position was that more credit should be given for its curriculum. This was substantiated by an informal indication from the American Council for Education that the curriculum might be considered for up to 30 credits. The War College did not recommend or request such a drastic increase in credit hours for its curriculum; it asked only that its students be given twelve instead of nine credits.[13] The University did not agree to this request, on the basis that "To do so would jeopardize both the program itself and The George Washington University in the eyes of sister institutions . . . ."[14] This ended discussions on additional credit for the War College course.

The War College objected strongly to the University's examining students on the content of War College courses during its final testing. "Not only is this contrary to our agreement," said General Dunn, "but results in an impossible preparatory task for our graduates."[15] The Commandant also stated that the nine credit hours for the War College curriculum ". . . stood alone — with their substantive quality a responsibility of the Army War College,"[16] from the beginning of the program. He reasoned that, such being the case, the comprehensive examination should be reduced in length, but the University would not agree. This conflict also continued throughout the lifetime of the program.

Another problem arose over qualifications of the George Washington professors who conducted courses at Carlisle Barracks. As the representative of the Department of the Army, the War College had the responsibility for supervising the offduty educational program, and considered approval of qualifications of the instructional group a part of such supervision. Although the University initially retained two and later one resident professor at the War College, the other professors came either from the on-campus academic staff in Washington or, by contract, from other colleges near Carlisle Barracks. The War College attempted several times to have the University agree to a doctoral degree as a prerequisite for instruction at Carlisle Barracks, but the University would not agree. However, it did submit names of the proposed staff to the War College annually, primarily to facilitate security clearances required by the College.

In some ways, the George Washington University program supplemented the War College curriculum by providing study in depth in related fields. However, the time entailed infringed on student application to meet the academic requirements of the War College. Anticipated increase in student requirements, based upon planned improvements and changes to the War College curriculum, resulted in termination of the program at the end of the 1966 year. It was stated at that time that concurrent participation in the additional demanding study program of the University would make it extremely difficult for future students to concentrate sufficient effort on the War College curriculum.[17]

This situation is not unique. All other senior service schools have sponsored graduate courses similar to the George Washington University Program. All have had experiences and problems paralleling those between the Army War College and George Washington University. All have become concerned over the amount of time required of the student officer to meet both his military schooling requirement and the graduate study work concurrently.[18] The Army War College decision, made only after long and extensive study, was dictated by the realization that programmed changes in the College curriculum would place increased demands on students. The decision was made with recognition of the contributions made by George Washington University during the existence of the joint program. As the Commandant, Major General Eugene A. Salet, indicated in recommending Professor William Lonsdale Tayler, Director of the George Washington University Center at the War College, for the Distinguished Civilian Service Award, "There is no question . . . . that the contribution has been extensive in scope and in value to the United States Army."[19]

The early 1960's brought many evolutionary changes in internal organization of the staff and faculty, faculty improvement, the War

College mission, and curriculum variations to the War College. Most of them were the result of continuing self-analysis on the part of the College, although some were caused by Department of the Army action.

Supervisory responsibility for the War College was transferred from the Continental Army Command (CONARC) to the Deputy Chief of Staff for Operations, Department of the Army in 1960.[20] This action taken at the personal direction of the Chief of Staff of the Army, General L. L. Lemnitzer, after discussions with the War College Commandant and the CONARC Commanding General, actually returned the College to its pre-World War II organizational location. Since its reinstitution in 1950, the College had differed constantly with its next superior headquarters on two very basic fundamental matters: content of the War College curriculum and the assignment of doctrinal studies to the College.

Both problems were generated primarily by a lack of understanding by officers on the CONARC staff of the functions and requirements of the College. As a result, CONARC included the War College in directives to schedule instruction which actually were designed for branch schools or the Command and General Staff College. The War College resisted assignment of such subjects, with their narrow, near-technical requirements compared to the postgraduate level of the War College. Not one commandant during the entire ten year period agreed with the CONARC concept, and all strongly and vociferously resisted the CONARC effort to superimpose these technical requirements on the graduate level program.

The requirement to conduct special studies already had forced the College to change its internal organization by establishing the Advanced Study Group within the faculty. The number of officers available for this Group never was sufficient to meet the CONARC study demands. Thus, the studies placed an additional workload on other faculty members who had to assist in their preparation. CONARC also generated another heavy requirement for the War College: preparation of field manuals for the ROTC program.

Additional factors contributed to the organizational change. As a subsidiary installation of the Continental Army Command, the War

College was under Headquarters, Second Army, at Fort Meade, Maryland, for administrative and logistic support. This arrangement often made it impossible for the War College to obtain approval, funding, or even support for necessary projects directly related to the functions of the College or to the welfare of its students and faculty.

Many advantages accrued, other than elimination of the problems created by the relationships with CONARC, under the new organizational arrangement. For example, the College could now go directly to Department of the Army agencies for help in developing its curriculum and conducting its courses, particularly in obtaining assistance in the way of documentation and lecturers. The old arrangement had required working through CONARC or ignoring the "chain of command" completely. Final authority to approve the curriculum had always been retained by Department of the Army, but the necessity to meet CONARC requirements to obtain approval from that headquarters often caused unnecessary delay in transmitting a proposed curriculum to Department of the Army for final approval.

Department of the Army directed another major organizational change two years later when it established the Combat Developments Command in 1962. Although this action had a direct effect on the War College, it was part of a major Department of the Army reorganization. Several agencies were formed in June 1962 to accomplish the Combat Developments Command mission. One, the Institute of Advanced Studies was to be collocated with the Army War College at Carlisle Barracks [21] and was assigned the mission of preparing long-range studies on international, national, and departmental matters and on organization and strategic operations of theater army and higher echelons. The Doctrine and Studies Division of the War College was redesignated the Institute of Advanced Studies and placed under the Combat Developments Command in August 1962.[22]

This action removed the requirement for conducting doctrinal studies from the War College faculty, but the Commandant of the War College also became the Commanding General of the Institute of

Advanced Studies. The dual command function thus established permitted development of a close intimate relationship between the two institutions.

With the establishment of the Institute of Advanced Studies, the War College faculty for the first time was able to devote its entire interest and effort to the academic work of the College and to undertake many projects which the previous workload had not permitted. Members of the faculty now could expend effort toward accomplishing the responsibility assigned in September 1960 to monitor major fields of military interest. Each officer was given primary responsibility for one specific area, such as air defense or special warfare. Each was expected to screen current military and civilian publications and to maintain informal contacts with related agencies in Washington or elsewhere.[23]

Unexpected reassignment of faculty members still created constant and undesirable turmoil. The departure of one officer usually required shifting another faculty member to cover the departee's work or, a less desirable solution, having one officer do the normal work of two. A request to Department of the Army to make such reassignments only at the end of the academic year was not approved.

Additional faculty improvement came with an increase in number, not from the Army, but from the other military services. The Joint Advisory Group, established in 1951, now consisted of one representative each from the US Navy, the US Marine Corps, the US Air Force, and the State Department. The number of officers from the other services was increased in 1960 to three from the Air Force and two each from the Navy and the Marine Corps. These officers were assigned to the various academic departments of the faculty.

Another interservice activity was initiated in 1960. The heads of the service War Colleges scheduled the first annual Military Education Coordination Conference to coordinate matters of common interest. Some agenda items were methods of evaluating the curriculum and students, management principles, senior education and national objectives, methods of teaching counterinsurgency, strategy seminars and reserve programs, publications, and the use of con-

GRADUATION EXERCISES

Weather permitting, graduation exercises are held beneath the trees ringing the "Old Parade." By War College custom, the last man in the graduating class alphabetically is the first to receive his diploma.

sultants. Over the years, this interchange of concepts and ideas has resulted in a closer relationship among the various senior schools.

Continued efforts to obtain approval for an Army War College sponsored publication still met with no success. A partial solution was obtained in 1961 after discussions with the Commandant of the Command and General Staff College, Major General Harold K. Johnson. The Leavenworth school had published a magazine, Military Review, for a number of years. This publication had achieved an excellent reputation in military and civilian circles alike and had recently expanded its coverage to include Spanish and Portuguese editions. By agreement between the two Army Colleges, the content of Military Review was to be changed to include more material on national and international affairs. An officer on the War College faculty was to be designated as associate editor of the Leavenworth publication to screen War College student and faculty studies and articles and forward them to Military Review. Although this did not end War College efforts to sponsor its own publication, the Military Review provided an excellent interim outlet for faculty and student articles.

A number of minor changes were made to the mission of the War College. Most of these were the result of recommendations made by the College itself, rather than unilateral decisions by Department of the Army. The main purpose of these changes was to delineate the primary mission of the College more definitively and, futher, to establish its secondary functions more explicitly. The mission at the beginning of the 1962 academic year was:

> Prepare selected Army officers for the highest command and general staff positions in the Army, in joint, allied and combined commands, and for such high level positions within the Department of Defense and other governmental agencies at the national level as the Army may be called upon to fill. Additionally, prepare selected students from other services and governmental agencies for comparable or similar positions.
>
> Develop the tactical and logistical doctrine relating to the organization, employment and operations of Army group and theater Army to include joint and combined aspects thereof, and to provide curriculum coverage at these levels.

Prepare studies, as directed, on broad national and departmental level matters, and on optimum strategies, doctrine, organization, and equipment for current and future Army forces.

Develop interservice, interdepartmental, and interacademic understanding with emphasis on Army doctrine and operations. In furtherance of this objective liaison will be established and maintained with selected educational institutions, organizations, and agencies whose activities are in fields related to the mission of the College.[24]

Again a Civilian Advisory Group was invited to visit the War College. Among its members were the Very Reverend Laurence J. McGinley, S.J., President of Fordham University; General Cortland V. R. Schuyler, USA, Retired; Doctor Oscar T. Marzke, Vice President for Fundamental Research, United States Steel Corporation; and Doctor Arnold O. Wolfers, Director of the Washington Center of Foreign Policy Research, Johns Hopkins University. The Advisory Group visited Carlisle Barracks for three days in February 1962, received comprehensive briefings, and made a thorough study of the College. Major areas covered in its report and recommendations related to the curriculum, methods, composition of the student body, faculty, and physical plant. The Group began its report by indicating that ". . . we could not have made even a beginning appraisal of the curriculum, and methods, of the College had we not received such full and candid cooperation from the Commandant and his aides,"[25] and that the best way for the College to achieve its assigned mission was by ". . . placing a high priority upon encouraging the students to think broadly and objectively, upon stimulating them to intellectual independence and leadership, and upon enlarging their horizons within their service and beyond their service."[26]

In reviewing the curriculum, the Group noted the wide scope of lectures, committee discussions, and individual research. "No criticism is implied," its report stated, " if it is pointed out that gaps remain; it would be spreading the matter too thin if every aspect of the subject matter were actually covered."[27] The Group, however, did recommend consideration of more thoroughness in the choice of topics for the curriculum. It also recommended topics for inclusion with the understanding that adopting them might require dropping others, possibly of lesser significance.

The primary finding of the Advisory Group was that analysis of the interests and attitudes of major US allies was insufficient. Noting that no lectures on France, Germany, and Britain were scheduled, the Group also found relatively little room in other sections of the program for discussion of these countries and of Japan. One method of including material on these countries recommended by the Advisory Group was to incorporate some of the problems pertaining to these allies in the parts of the course of instruction assigned to economics or the role of science. The Group also recommended that the War College consider adding information ". . . more specifically directed towards an understanding of the American foreign policy and the role of economic, ideological, and military policy as integrated parts of this foreign policy"[28] to Course 1, "National Purpose and National Power of the United States and the Soviet Union."

Noting the division of time between military and nonmilitary subjects, the Group recommended that, ". . . because of the breadth of the nonmilitary subject that is of such crucial importance for military leaders and does not come to them from personal experience during their precollege career, . . . no effort be spared to compress the military subject matter to the minimum compatible with the mission of the College."[29] This recommendation was based on the extremely wide coverage given both national and international studies and the more detailed study of strictly military topics. To add additional depth, the Group urged the use of required readings from course bibliographies and preparation of a one page critical review by each student officer. Another recommendation was made to consider the entire Sino-Soviet bloc instead of the Soviet Union only.

In general, the Advisory Group was complimentary in its comments on College instructional techniques. It indicated that the procedures were ". . . well thought out, suited to the unique mission of the USAWC, generally dynamic, and in broad measure successful,"[30] and that its suggestions were for qualitative improvement, not for basic change. Careful briefing and supervision of student committee chairmen was recommended as a means of preventing an entire committee from falling behind on its critical time schedule, emphasizing less important phases in its discussions, or failing to provide adequate time for individual work requirements. More individual student presentations were recommended, ". . . similar to but less formal than the thesis presentation."[31] These more informal individual efforts would provide discussion and presentation at an intermediate level between the committee "bull session" and the formal presentation in the auditorium.

Another recommendation made by the Advisory Group may be considered one of the more important suggestions offered. "Since group learning is necessarily limited to its own resources and horizons," the report stated, "there should be special effort to feed in special expertise, especially in the non-military subjects . . . ."[32] Some ways to accomplish this, the Advisory Group noted, were to use consultants or civilian faculty members, a greater admixture of students from other services and governmental agencies, and scheduling of panels of experts from time to time.

Review of the student thesis program brought a recommendation for assignment of faculty supervisors with better knowledge of the subject and for giving the students a more detailed and helpful evaluation of his thesis both during and at the conclusion of his efforts. Alternative suggestion was to consider retaining experts to evaluate the student research papers. The Group further stated, "Most helpful, for the success of the thesis program, is the clear assignment of uninterrupted blocks of time for this purpose alone — and places to do it not presently available, e.g., more desks and carrels in the Library."[33]

Another recommendation was that all the war colleges consider scheduling a simultaneous visit to Washington, because many senior Government officials apparently were unable either to address all the senior schools or, in some cases, even to leave their work long enough to visit one college. Consequently, the Advisory Group recommended a two day simultaneous visit by all of the colleges which would permit ". . . full-scale participation of the President, the Vice President, the Secretary of State, the Secretary of Defense

. . ."[34] and other officials who were rarely able to contribute to War College discussions by a personal visit.

In discussing the composition of the Army War College student body, the Advisory Group referred to that portion of the mission which concerned developing officers for the highest command and general staff positions in Army, joint, and combined commands and for military leaders to fill posts in nonmilitary agencies of the Government at national and international levels. The Group noted that the 1952 and 1954 Advisory Groups recommended an increase in the percentage of non-Army students at the Army War College. Although the number of officers from the other services and students from various nonmilitary agencies of the Federal Government had increased, the Advisory Group recommended that, "the composition of the student body be altered to double the number of students from the other services . . ."[35] and that faculty composition reflect the proportion of service representation within the student body as much as possible. However, the Group recognized that this recommendation could not be adopted without a reciprocal change on the part of the other service war colleges but made it in the belief that it would broaden and generate more viewpoints for discussion as well as deepen the areas of knowledge and insight for all student officers. This mutual exchange of ideas and experiences would further develop ". . . needed interservice and interagency understanding so urgently required,"[36] thus serving the prime purpose of expanding the capacity of the student officers to think broadly and objectively in keeping ". . . with today's — and tomorrow's — needs of the Army and the other services."[37]

In addition to the expressed belief that the faculty should closely reflect the composition of the student body, the Advisory Group recommended fulltime assignment of civilian academicians to the faculty, a recommendation which had been made by the two previous consultant groups. The Advisory Group amplified this recommendation by indicating that such civilian faculty members should not be permanent but ". . . should be rotated every year or two so that it would be possible to get university people on leaves of absence."[38]

Although the Advisory Group had fully endorsed the committee system used by the War College, it also recommended greater pedagogical teaching participation by the faculty. While such additional teaching would decrease the time for committee meetings, the Group felt this would be justified by more effective learning by student officers without loss of the valuable experience of fairly extensive committee work and discussion. The Group also felt that there should be a closer and more continuous contact between faculty members and students individually. This could be accomplished by more faculty guidance during committee discussions, by more counsel in thesis preparation, and by other academic contacts with the student.

In discussing the physical plant of the War College, the Advisory Group again commented on the lack of adequate study facilities in the Library and in student rooms. It was convinced that ". . . the individual student is handicapped throughout his course of instruction by the inadequacy of space in a suitable environment for his almost daily and heavy requirement for individual research, required, and recommended reading . . ."[39] After inspecting existing library facilities, student committee rooms, and several student quarters, the Advisory Group fully endorsed War College proposals for a new academic complex and additional quarters.

At the end of its report, the Advisory Group indicated that it was desirable to develop ". . . an appreciation of the impact, the potentialities and the limitations of science"[40] in the student. The student need not become a competent scientist, but rather, should have an understanding of the force of science, an understanding which could be fostered by lectures.

The Civilian Advisory Group was scheduled to meet in February so that its recommendations could be incorporated in the curriculum and procedures for the following year. The comments made by the Advisory Group led to allocation of more time to the study of national power and international relations. This time was not obtained by curtailing the military coverage to any great extent; it was gained by shortening the last course, "National Strategy and a Supporting Military Program." Most of the time increase was given to international relations and US foreign policy. Discussion of important US allies was included. Instead of consolidating the study of the Communist bloc in one course, the War College retained the comparison of United States and Russian national purposes and power. The Chinese study remained a part of the course on international relations. This proved undesirable and led to a major alteration in the international studies part of the War College curriculum in the 1963 academic year.

Although the total time for military subjects was not lessened materially, their content was varied somewhat. The study of US global concepts and military capabilities was extended. For the first time, a distinct part of the curriculum was devoted to counterinsurgency as a phase within this course. The military block of the curriculum also included courses on concepts of future land warfare and US preparedness for war.

Another addition to the curriculum was made to give the students an appreciation of the impact, potentialities, and limitations of science. A new technique was used in scheduling this addition to the course of instruction. Normal procedure called for scheduling a course "vertically" by providing all instruction consecutively within an assigned time period. The new lecture series "Frontiers of Knowledge," was scheduled horizontally with one lecture a week for a three month period. The lectures provided a survey of significant advances in the physical and life sciences, the social sciences, and the behavioral sciences. In addition, the technological revolution was discussed in some detail. Another first also came with this course: the use of the expertise of the newly formed Institute of Advanced Studies. Although many visiting lecturers were an important part of the course, the Institute was assigned complete responsibility for its development and conduct. Student and faculty wives also were able to participate in this program for it was held in the evening.

Some Advisory Group recommendations were not adopted, although faculty committees studied every suggestion thoroughly. For example, the Advisory Group recommended written reviews of required readings. Such a requirement would have placed too heavy an additional workload on the individual student, in view of the great number of required readings assigned. Additional and more informal presentations to smaller groups were scheduled, however.

The 1962 curriculum did not reflect all the Advisory Group suggestions that were agreed to by the War College, because adopting all of them in one year would have required major organizational changes. The alterations adopted were evolutionary in nature and paved the way for even greater modification and improvement the following year. In many ways, the 1963 year was the end of the second period of the modern War College era and the beginning of a new one marked by greater and more complete integration of the courses within the curriculum.

In January 1963, another long term effort of the War College was successful. At the request of the Commandant, Major General William F. Train, Department of the Army approved establishment of a short course for senior officers of the Organized Reserve and the National Guard. The two week course was to be scheduled during the 1964 academic year.

An additional briefing course, also suggested by General Train, was scheduled for officers assigned to attend the French, Canadian, and British institutions equivalent to the Army War College. Officers selected to attend these schools, who were assigned to the War College as associate members of a College class, were brought to Carlisle Barracks for a one week briefing. This provided them with an opportunity of noting Army War College techniques and methods, meeting the students and faculty, and receiving a short but comprehensive review of the curriculum.

Because the process by which student officers are designated is highly selective, many officers with excellent records are nominated for but not appointed to a War College class. General Train requested permission to establish a correspondence or nonresident course for these officers, pointing out the advantages the Army would gain from this additional source of War College educated officers. Department of the Army did not approve this request because it was contrary to long-standing policy not to reveal the names of officers not selected since doing so might well cause great damage to their morale. A counterproposal to establish a nonresident course for all eligible officers was rejected by the War College because the physical and administrative facilities at Carlisle Barracks could not carry the additional load such a requirement would generate. As a result, the project was dropped.

A query from Department of the Army indicating a possible requirement for the War College to institute a foreign language program as a part of the curriculum was opposed because it would necessitate a minimum of three classes weekly and, preferably, five. Such an addition could result only in elimination of some topics and an even broader coverage of the already too-broad curriculum. The proposal was dropped when the Department of Defense consolidated the various service language schools into the Defense Language Institute.

The first 13 years of the post-World War II War College can be divided into two distinct periods. From 1950 through 1957 was a testing phase; a time of trial and rejection marked by almost annual changes to the curriculum and fluctuations in College procedures. The second period, from 1957 through 1963, was characterized by relative stability of the curriculum and procedures. A trend established within this latter period, however, resulted in allocation of more and more time to international and national studies with a resultant lessening in time for strictly military subjects. Stability was apparent, not only in the structure of the curriculum, but also in the organization of the faculty. Instructional methods became more refined and effective; procedures, relatively standardized.

War College efforts to initiate new programs and techniques, such as sponsoring a publication, adding civilian members to the faculty, and establishing a course for reserve component officers, for the most part were unsuccessful. Furthermore, the faculty was not able to devote its full efforts to its academic mission prior to 1962 because of requirements to prepare detailed doctrinal studies and other materials. This problem was alleviated with the organization of the Institute of Advanced Studies of the US Army Combat Developments Command. The 1963 academic year marked a turning point in War College affairs and the beginnings of a major revision of the curriculum.

XI

Emphasis on the Role of the Army
1963-1966

ALTHOUGH the course of instruction for the 1964 academic year still was divided into three major parts, the core curriculum bore little resemblance to that of the previous years. The first part retained its title, "National Power and International Relations," but changed its subcourses completely. Four new courses were scheduled to replace the two courses on "The National Purposes and National Power of the US and the Soviet Union" and "International Relations and US Foreign Policy." The first was divided into two phases—a review of the world environment and the elements of national power and a study of international relations. The second course concerned the United States and the North Atlantic Community; the third, the national power, purposes, and objectives of the Soviet Union, Communist China, and the Eastern European satellite nations. Course four devoted an entire block of instruction to the developing areas of the world.

The second part of the curriculum, which emphasized military subjects, also reflected much change. Two courses on "US Global Strategic Concepts and Military Capabilities" and "US Preparedness for War" were replaced by a course entitled "National Security," which was concerned with the formulation processes of US policy and the elements of US military power. The course on strategic military concepts and capabilities was retained, as was "Science, Technology, and Future Military Power." This second major part of the curriculum was retitled "Military Power in Support of National Security Policy."

The third section of the course remained unchanged, although reduced in time. This was preparation of student committee versions of US national strategy and the military program to support that strategy. The National Strategy Seminar remained as the final event of the academic year.

The curriculum included political, economic, psycho-social, scientific and technological, and military elements which were related to national power interwoven on a framework or theme of the design of a national strategy and a supporting military program. The military subjects stressed the Army in the context of joint, combined, and allied operations. For the first time, the entire curriculum was fully integrated to emphasize the interrelationships and interdependence of these elements of national power. This intent was explained to the student officers in their orientation course, was stressed throughout the academic year, and culminated in the National Strategy Seminar. The Frontiers of Knowledge lecture program was continued, but it was spread throughout the first eight months of the year.

Senior officers of the reserve components began a two-week period of study in February 1964. Sixteen general officers and colonels of the Organized Reserve and the National Guard were exposed to a condensed but highly concentrated review of the War College curriculum. The group joined the regular students at morning lectures, question periods, and afterlecture conferences. Afternoons were devoted to faculty presentations and to seminars covering the entire scope of the War College course of instruction. The course, considered a success by both the officers attending and the War College, was rescheduled on an annual basis. Although not noted at the time, this first session took place almost exactly 30 years after the old "special" reserve component courses at the pre-World War II War College were suspended for lack of funds during the depression years.

General Train instituted a series of faculty seminars during the 1964 academic year. Although not a complete innovation, the seminars were designed to improve faculty knowledge and understanding of national issues by examining concepts highlighted by prominent authorities. Herman Kahn, Dr. Edward Teller, and General Matthew

Ridgway visited the College for seminar discussions varying in length from a half day to two days. Other faculty seminars during the year included discussions on systems analysis, NATO strategy, automatic data processing systems, and the role of the professional military officer in national security affairs.

Continuing efforts to initiate a faculty preparation plan which would include graduate study at a civilian university met with disapproval by Department of the Army. The general basis for the Department of the Army position was the length of time—approximately two years of study followed by three years as a faculty member—these highly select officers would be removed from other military duties. Although the Army position appears to indicate a lack of understanding of the War College requirements, such was not true. The needs of the War College had to be considered on a par with other equally important military requirements. War College graduates were needed for 2,300 other assignments. The entire problem, generated at this time by the schooling request, merely emphasized a difficulty which had existed from the very establishment of the War College in 1901: lack of availability of qualified officers for the faculty.

Requirements for the modern day War College faculty only emphasized problems that had confronted every commandant and Department of the Army assignment agencies: how to obtain the best qualified, relatively senior officers for the War College when these same officers were needed equally, if not more, in other critical positions. The average age of the faculty member in 1963 was 45. He was either a senior lieutenant colonel or a colonel and was a graduate of one of the service war colleges. Most had served in both World War II and the Korean conflict, had commanded a battalion or larger sized unit, and had served on a high level staff in the Army or in a joint or combined command. Consequently, although it was difficult for the War College to view Department of Army decisions impartially and objectively, there were sound and justifiable reasons for the disapproval of the College request in this instance.

In July 1964, Major General Eugene A. Salet replaced General Train as Commandant. Plans already had been made for the 1965 academic year, and the proposed curriculum had been approved by Department of the Army.

The proposed curriculum represented a minimum change from that of the 1964 academic year. Three phases were projected, with no change in title and with only one variation in course structure. The course in national security was replaced by "Management of United States Military Power." The new course covered the capabilities and preparedness of the United States; the availability of defense resources; and procedures for planning, programming, and budgeting of resources and manpower. This stability was indicative of the care and thought used in implementing the recommendations of the 1962 Civilian Advisory Group by evolutionary development. Moreover, although the core curriculum remained almost unchanged, the content of the various courses had been modified and improved to provide even greater integration of the entire course of instruction.

After analyzing College activities, the new Commandant made a number of observations. At a Curriculum Board meeting, he discussed the need for professionalism within the faculty, referring not only to military professionalism, but also to the development of broad academic professionalism.[1] Salet indicated the need for exploration of faculty development and provided guidance for a study to determine the means by which the academic abilities of the faculty as a unit, not as individuals, could be improved.

A second study was initiated as a result of the Commandant's emphasis on development and stimulation of "creative thinking" by the student officers.[2] This study had the objective of determining procedures whereby the efforts of the student officers could be directed toward identifying opportunities and alternative courses of action related to national strategy, national security policy, defense posture, programs, operations, and the organization of the Government. The study was not to be restricted to an analysis of the thesis program alone but was to survey the entire curriculum for the following academic year. With the exception of the plan initiated by General Train for implementation of the recommendations of the 1962 Civilian Advisory Group over a two-year period, the one-year projection had been the normal curriculum development procedure since 1950.

The decision was to have a profound effect on the entire War College activity, an effect possibly as far-reaching as the McAndrew curriculum preparation in 1919. He directed that a comprehensive

study of the War College be made to determine: "Where are we today? Where are we going? Where should we be going? How do we get
there?"[3] In Salet's estimation, every organization—military or civilian, every institution had to take stock of itself with a view to the future, particularly an educational institution whose measure of success could only be judged by the success of its graduates at some
future time. "This is done," he said, "by conducting a thorough,
rigorous, searching self-analysis and self-evaluation. Properly done,
these periodic institutional soul-searchings renew vitality, develop a
sense of mission and direction, and maintain a forward look in an endeavor to keep up with the times and to meet a rapidly changing environment."[4]

It is true that the self-analysis concept was not new to the Army
War College, for this method of determining needed improvements
had been used as early as the Bliss-Wotherspoon era. However, at
no time in the history of the War College had as extensive and detailed a survey been made. In directing the Deputy Commandant,
Brigadier General Ward S. Ryan, to determine "Where are we?
Where are we going? Where should we be going? How do we get
there?", Salet established objectives for the 1970 time frame. In response to Ryan's question, "What shall we call this study?", he
thought for a moment and answered, "Army War College 70,"
adding, "That's what its end result will be—the US Army War College in the 1970's."[5]

Ryan became chairman of an ad hoc committee composed of a
large number of faculty members. The work devoted to the "Army
War College '70" (AWC 70) Study at one time or another involved almost every officer on the faculty. In scope, the study involved every
phase of the War College and its activities: the curriculum, methods,
and teaching techniques; the qualification, education, and organization of the faculty; the composition, education, and study habits of the
student body; the mission of the College and its organization to accomplish that mission.

Although the prime efforts devoted to the AWC 70 Study were internal, some of the ad hoc committee's efforts were directed away
from the College proper. One subcommittee analyzed civilian atti-

tudes toward the military profession in general and civilian concepts of the Army War College and its graduates in particular. Another group studied the faculties of other military schools, including the United States Military Academy and the other service war colleges. A third group investigated procedures followed by civilian graduate institutions.

More definitive instructions regarding the objectives of the study were forthcoming. In providing these instructions General Ryan indicated the Commandant's desire that the scope of the assessment cover all aspects of the Army War College's activities ". . . viewed within the framework of the overall career development of the Regular Army Officer and the whole Army education and training system."[6] This assessment was not to be restricted to the current time frame, but was to ". . . relate to the Nation's present and foreseeable requirements for senior professional Army officers and to the national security environment in which the USAWC and its graduates must be prepared to operate. . . ."[7]

Specifically, three basic tasks were included:

1. Determine the appropriate objectives and misson of the War College.
2. Assess the strengths and weaknesses of the War College vis-a-vis the objectives and missions developed.
3. Determine what should be done. . .to improve the effectiveness of the War College in realizing its objectives and accomplishing its mission.[8]

Initially, the work of the ad hoc committee and its subcommittees was outlined in a series of questions. The questions were consolidated according to their relationship to the three basic tasks assigned to subcommittees for study. For example, the task group assigned the study of the mission and objectives of the War College was given eight primary questions, each with a number of corollary areas, as an initial guide. Among them were the following:

What is expected of the military professional who graduates from a war college now and in the foreseeable future?
What contribution should the Army War College make to develop-

ment of the necessary professional knowledge, skills, and characteristics required of its graduates?

What, if any, other roles should the War College fulfill in addition to educating career professionals?

What should be the relationship of the Army War College to civilian educational institutions? What can the War College learn from civilian education? How should the War College program be related to the acquisition of graduate degrees? [9]

Other questions pertained to relationships with other service War Colleges and to the adequacy of the War College curriculum to accomplish its mission and objectives. Realizing that the proposed study would require extensive time, a schedule was established that had several objectives in itself. The initial survey by each task group was to be completed and presented as a basic concept study by the end of November 1964. The mission and objectives study was given first priority and a completion date of December. The assessment of the strengths and weaknesses of the War College and the evaluation of the current curriculum and methods was to be completed by 15 January 1965.

The short "time-fuses" on completion dates were completely necessary to develop sufficient information early enough to start the 1965-66 War College structure and curriculum in the desired direction and assure that the relatively long-range objectives developed by the AWC 70 Study could be met in an orderly and progressive manner.

The three task groups worked closely together, exchanged information and conclusions periodically, and fully coordinated their joint efforts. Once the initial phases had been completed, the final conclusions and recommendations were to be made within six months.

The AWC 70 Study was started immediately to permit use of the preliminary findings as the basis for developing the 1966 curriculum and project the final conclusions and recommendations into the future academic years, aiming at the 1970-75 time period. This was a new concept to the War College and was a decided contrast to the first period of the modern era, when almost annual changes were made to the curriculum. It was equally in contrast to the second period, which had been characterized by the relative stability of its course of study. The trial and rejection typical of the nineteen fifties had not fostered a long-range projection of the needs of the War College. The stability of the early 1960's, on the other hand, was not caused by a survey of future needs but, rather, was only another indication of the continuation of the development of each year's curriculum based on the lessons learned during the previous year or two. To use military terminology, the AWC 70 Study was a reconnaissance in force preparatory to making an assault; the changes to be made to the 1966 curriculum, a scouting force in the direction of the objective; and the ensuing long-range program, the attack in force to seize the objective.

The study was not restricted to the War College alone. The Commandant and several faculty members visited the United States Military Academy. Their purpose was not to review the West Point curriculum but to discuss methods used, faculty development procedures, and faculty organization. General Ryan headed another group which visited Princeton University to observe its graduate methods and to discuss the AWC Study with members of the Woodrow Wilson School of Public and International Affairs. Other groups made trips to the various service War Colleges and to the Mershon Center for Education in National Security at Ohio State University.

To obtain impartial and objective opinions of the War College and the preliminary findings of the various task groups, a number of prominent civilian educators and military officials were queried by letter. Their comments and suggestions were added to the mass of data accumulated by the task groups. Further information and assistance was sought by inviting a group of consultants to visit the War College. Instead of following the precedent already established of inviting the group to visit in a body, Salet invited only two individuals at a time. This permitted detailed briefings, established a more informal relationship, and permitted the consultants to concentrate in depth on the areas in which each was most interested. Government and military consultants were Lieutenant General Ben Harrell, Assistant Chief of Staff for Force Development, Department of the Army; John M. Steadman, Deputy Under Secretary of the Army for International Affairs; Major General Max S. Johnson, USA, Retired, former War College Commandant; General Bruce C. Clarke, USA, Retired; Alain C. Enthoven, Deputy Assistant Secretary of Defense for Systems Analysis; and retired Army Lieutenant Generals Garrison H. Davidson and Arthur G. Trudeau. The consultants from academic institutions were Dr. Ivan J. Birrer, Educational Adviser of the Command and General Staff College, Professors Samuel P. Huntington of Harvard University, Laurence I. Radway of Dartmouth College, Arthur E. Burns of the George Washington University, and Edgar S. Furniss, Jr., of Ohio State University. A third group came from research institutions: Dr. Meredith Crawford, Director of the Human Resources Research Office; Dr. Frank Parker, President of Research Analysis Corporation; and Dr. Nicholas Smith, a RAC staff member. The frank, candid comments made by these consultants were of much value to the faculty task groups for the consultants based their criticisms and suggestions upon personal experience in Government, military service, research, and educational institutions.

By mid-December 1964, the overall study had reached a point that permitted assessment of its status, review of what had been accomplished, and a determination of what remained to be done. Additional responsibilities to the task groups were assigned the task groups as a result of this review.[10] Additional interim reviews were made in January and March 1965.

The final results of the AWC 70 Study were not consolidated into a single document. Instead, a series of reports and recommendations were submitted by each task group to the ad hoc committee chairman, General Ryan. Each report was reviewed by the committee, revised as necessary, and forwarded to the Commandant for approval. The major studies developed and approved from October 1964 to June 1965 included the following subject areas:

Faculty Development
Curriculum Revision
Revision of the Student Research Program
Organization of the War College
Sponsorship of a Publication
Use of Consultants
Mission and Objectives of the Army War College

CLASS PLAQUES ARE RETURNED TO THE WAR COLLEGE

Major General Eugene A. Salet, Commandant of the Army War College, left, receives the plaques of the pre-World War II classes from Vice Admiral Fitzhugh Lee, Commandant of the National War College.

A number of other studies were also prepared and included in the overall project. These included an assessment of Army requirements, an analysis of civilian attitudes toward the military, and comparisons of the Army War College with civilian graduate institutiions and the other service War Colleges. Each study contributed to the final result of the AWC 70 project: establishment of a comprehensive program for continued development and improvement of the War College and its curriculum.

As each part of AWC 70 was approved, it was analyzed to determine the actions required to achieve the results recommended. Some actions could be accomplished unilaterally without assistance or approval; others required Department of the Army concurrence. Some of the recommendations were applied immediately, some were added to the plans for the 1966 academic year, and others were of relatively long-term character. The actions taken as a result of the AWC 70 Study had, and will continue to have, a profound effect upon all phases of War College activity.

Thus far, little has been said about the content of the study. This omission has been intentional to permit a description of the wide scope of investigation and the concentrated efforts exerted by the members of the Ryan ad hoc committee. By the time the AWC 70 Study was completed, almost a full year had been devoted to analysis, investigation, interview, review, and contemplation. The study touched every facet of the War College: its faculty, the student body, curricular content, procedures, physical plant, support facilities, extra curricular activities, research, and many other areas.

Several corollary studies were conducted in response to General Salet's questions, "Where are we now? Where should we be going?" The first, mission analysis, may be termed the keystone study of the entire project. The mission cited by Army Regulation 350-5, in October 1964, was "To prepare selected senior officers for command and high level staff duties with emphasis upon Army doctrine and operations and to advance interdepartmental and interservice understanding." Basically, this assigned mission was little different from that of 1950. For that matter, it was not greatly at variance with the mission of the earlier years of the War College before World War II.

The major change had been the addition of the phrase "to advance interdepartmental and interservice understanding."

A subcommittee headed by Colonel H. W. W. Lange prepared a comprehensive analysis of the mission of the War College and the objectives derived from the mission. After a review of the assigned missions from 1950 to 1965, the Lange committee studied the missions and objectives of the other service War Colleges and the United States Military Academy. His group then approached the problem which had been divided into a number of specific areas, each defined by a question:

> Should the mission be broad and brief as now stated or, should it be couched in more detailed and specific language?
> Should the world "strategy" be included in the mission or is it sufficient that strategy be covered only in the stated scope?
> Is the mission really "to prepare selected senior officers. . . ." or is it, rather, "to conduct a course of study. . . . to enhance the preparation of selected personnel. . . .?"
> Would the phrase "for command and high level staff duties" be more accurately stated as "for the highest command and staff duties?"
> Should not the joint-combined nature of command and high level staff duties be identified in the stated mission?
> Is the current mission valid? Is it relevant in light of the present DOD tendency to consolidate service school systems whereever possible?
> Is the advancing of "interdepartmental and interservice understanding" a valid part of the mission?
> Should the mission be amplified by a scope as it now is, or should the mission statement be followed by a list of objectives?
> Should the mission state or imply an additional purpose such as a non-resident program? [11]

The mission study thus varied in nature from a review of basic format for stating the War College mission—broad and brief or detailed and lengthy— to a study of the very purpose of the College—prepare for command or conduct a course of study. To assist this committee in its efforts, other groups working on different portions of the AWC 70 project fed information to Lange. Colonel D. A. Bussey provided the Lange committee with the results of his survey on civilian opinion of the military, a survey which had included personal interviews with various Federal officials and academicians. The prime benefits of Bussey's study, insofar as Lange was concerned, were the strengths and weaknesses of the military as cited by Department of Defense and other service civilian officials. Other input to the mission study group came from the consultants who visited the War College and from the correspondence with military commanders and civilian educators.

Lange and his committee determined that the wording of the statements of the mission, generally, was adequate and acceptable for War College purposes. However, the committee recommended that it be modified to eliminate the "unsupported and unfounded allegations that the stated missions of the war colleges are too broad and. . .designed primarily for educating officers for staff. . .positions."[12]

The committee reiterated statements reminiscent of those made many years before by McGlachlin in reorienting the curriculum in 1922 with his "unremitting attempt. . .to impress the College with the idea that Command is the great thing in war, the true determinant of success or failure, and that the General Staff officer. . .is but an advisor, an agent, a subordinate coadjutor of the Commander."[13] Lange stated, "It is considered that the curriculum emphasis should be placed primarily on the educational aspects of command as opposed to the secondary aspects of preparation for staff duties."[14] This was further delineated to indicate that command, applied to the War College graduate, was intended to embrace all positions held by Army general officers worldwide. Therefore, the mission statement was changed to "highest positions of command." From the command requirement, the group defined a scope requirement to provide the requisite breadth of knowledge required by the military professional in such positions: an appreciation of the bases of military policy through the understanding of the political, economic, and social factors related to military matters. Insofar as staff duty, the secondary task of the graduate, was concerned, Lange indicated that the mission statement lacked specificity as to the levels and types of staff for which the selected officer was being trained. The committee therefore added "joint, unified, combined, and other high level staff duties" as a replacement for the simple "high level staff duties" then in the mission.

The mission recommended to the Department of the Army was brief, broad, and yet definitive:

> To prepare selected senior officers for the highest positions of command and for joint, unified, combined, and other high level staff duties, with emphasis upon Army strategic concepts, doctrine, and operations and to advance interdepartmental and interservice understanding.[15]

To support this mission, Lange's committee derived five objectives which clearly defined the proposed direction of the War College efforts in accomplishing the stated mission:

> 1. To conduct a course of study concerned with the present but oriented to the future that will expand the abilities and outlook of the officer in the appreciation, use, command, and management of military power in the nation's security.
> 2. To provide an appreciation of the component parts of a national strategy, to include a comprehensive understanding of the world environment and sources of conflict.
> 3. To study, observe, analyze, and contribute to the development of US Army strategic concepts and doctrine.
> 4. To develop the officer's powers of analysis, logical reasoning, and expression in consideration of broad problems of interest to the military profession, with emphasis upon creative thinking.
> 5. To enhance the officer's physical and mental attributes essential to meeting the demanding requirements for future military service.[16]

It might be well, at this point, to pause and take an analytical look at the mission and objectives established by AWC 70, for here can be found the key to the entire study. Two words provide that key: "command" and "military." The purpose of the College can be defined as preparing the officer for military command. The curriculum emphasizes the military aspects of international and national affairs which are needed by a <u>commander</u> to accomplish his assigned tasks. The appreciation of <u>military</u> policy, however, requires an understanding of other elements of national power, all related to <u>military</u> matters. The use of "Army strategic concepts, doctrine, and operations" further reinforces the need for curriculum emphasis on <u>command</u> implications, <u>military</u> aspects, and the role of the Army.

The restatement of the mission and the definition of the scopes derived from that mission was to have an immediate effect, not only on the balance of the AWC 70 project, but also on the War College curriculum. The trend toward greater and greater emphasis on the international and national studies was slowed—not halted, but slowed. The emphasis henceforth was to be upon the military aspects of international and national affairs. This was not a complete reversal of policy, nor was there a great upheaval in conceptual attitude for it was realized that the study of international and national affairs provided an essential background without which the study of military policy was meaningless.

What had taken place was a look to see "Where should we be going?" A mental step back to permit a closer look had taken place. From this came the realization that the emphasis of the War College curriculum had strayed from its main purpose of preparing professional military officers for the highest command to preparation for quasi-military positions. The AWC 70 studies brought the War College back to its primary mission and resulted in a reorientation before beginning the march forward to the future. Thus, one AWC 70 objective had been accomplished almost at the very outset of the comprehensive study. The War College was given a better and clearer idea of "Where it should go."

The determination of direction also brought another realization. Continuous self-evaluation is essential to assure that the mission, objectives, curriculum, procedures, and other activities continue to be responsive to the dynamics of the changing world environment and to the resultant effect of this changing environment on military doctrine and concepts. Internal self-evaluation is not only important; it is essential. This, the Commandant believed, could be done only by establishing a faculty group divorced from the actual conduct and detailed preparation of any one part of the curriculum, a group with the primary function of supervising the entire academic activity of the College. Therefore, in mid-March 1965, he established the position of Director of Instruction and Research to provide a means of directing the faculty effort in overall curriculum matters and revised the entire organization of the College.

This was not a mere reorganization, but, rather, a new and completely different approach to organizational efficiency. From the very establishment of the War College over half a century earlier, one man had coordinated both the administrative and academic supervision of College activities: the Secretary of the War College. In earlier years, this arrangement provided a feasible and efficient means of coordinating all phases of the War College activities. More recently, however, the magnitude of the Secretary's functions grew until major faculty groups assumed an ever-increasing self-determination without the detailed and "across-the-board" supervision and coordination so essential to the conduct of effective and integrated instruction.

This situation had become apparent earlier, and, although efforts had been made to rectify the problem, they had not been completely successful. Now, however, by a sweeping step, Salet established a dual organization. The Secretary was responsible for supervision of all the administration, the operation of the Library, and the personnel and logistic support of the College. The Director of Instruction and Research was given responsibility for supervision of academic activities. He also was given direct supervision of the research and publication efforts of the students and faculty and the responsibility for a constant and continuing evaluation of the current course of study and the proposed curriculum for the future.

The faculty was organized into three major instructional groups: the Department of Strategy, the Department of Strategic Appraisal, and the Department of Military Planning. Each Department chairman was responsible for supervising the preparation and conduct of a number of specific courses.

To focus on the professional skills available in and necessary to the faculty, three faculty chairs were established: The Elihu Root Chair of Strategy, the General D. Eisenhower Chair of Strategic

Appraisal, and the General John J. Pershing Chair of Military Planning. Later, a fourth chair was established for the Director of Instruction and Research, the General George C. Marshall Chair of Military Studies. The military nature of the curriculum was clearly indicated in the departmental chairs thus established.

The new organization provided a more efficient means of developing and coordinating the curriculum of the College. Each academic department was responsible for preparation and conduct of a block of courses. The Department of Strategy provided the foundation for the study of national strategy and the military implications of such strategy. The Department of Strategic Appraisal was responsible for a power appraisal of various world areas. Army and joint planning and programming and long-range strategic studies were the responsibility of the Department of Military Planning.

These primary interests, however, were for the 1965-66 academic year and for the curriculum developed for that year. The faculty organization was not inflexible nor intended to concentrate only on the responsiblities and interests first delineated. Instead, the division into three departments was designed to provide flexibility, future development, and constant improvement based on self-evaluation. Within this departmental framework, courses could be shifted, varied in content, eliminated, or added without requiring a major reorganization of the faculty. Thus, when the Frontiers of Knowledge lecture series was eliminated, no organizational change was required. The addition of a seminar program concerned with comparative military strategies required no alternation to the faculty structure.

Furthermore, the organizational structure also provided for greater integration of the curriculum. As each course director developed his particular phase of instruction, the department director was able to assure that this course meshed with the other courses supervised by his department. The Director of Instruction and Research, at the next level, could take positive steps to achieve curriculum-wide integration, to avoid undesirable duplication, and to make certain of progressive development throughout the course of instruction. The final product, curriculum for any one year, could then be presented to the Academic Board—the Deputy Commandant, the Director of Instruction and Research, the Secretary, and the three department directors—for review before it was presented to the Commandant for his approval.

Conversely, the determination that additional material should be added to the curriculum could flow effectively from the Commandant or the Academic Board to the Director of Instruction and Research. He, in turn, would analyze the material recommended, determine its value to the curriculum, and assign it to one of the academic departments for inclusion in its block of courses. The department director would then place the new material within his departmental structure in the proper course with the emphasis warranted, and with the necessary lessening or elimination of other subject matter required to make space for the new material.

To achieve overall coordination of the activities of the Secretary and the Director of Instruction, the position of Chief of Staff was established. However, it became apparent that this position was not required, and it was dropped from the War College organization in 1966.

The overall result of the reorganization was soon apparent. Faculty resources were more efficiently used. Preparation and conduct of the various courses became more efficient and more effective. Continual evaluation and coordination became the normal course of affairs rather than a spasmodic or annual effort. Thus, General Salet provided himself with a means of answering his question "Where are we now?"—intensive and continuous internal self-evaluation.

AWC 70, however, did not "put on blinders" and ignore the value of external evaluation. The use of consultants was considered in a separate study which included a detailed analysis of the values and disadvantages of a permanent board of visitors. Although a permanent group would provide continuity and would gradually develop a detailed appreciation of the mission and functions of the War College, the committee report for this portion of the AWC 70 Study recommended that the College continue to convene different groups of consultants periodically. The greater flexibility inherent in this arrangement would make it possible to select members specifically qualified to evaluate the War College on the basis of current dominant needs of the College and the Army.

The AWC 70 committee also considered the problem of how to develop a professional academic faculty. First, the role of the faculty in the conduct of the War College curriculum had to be determined. This role, however, could not be determined without a decision on the exact teaching methods to be used and a curriculum content analysis and evaluation to make certain the course of instruction fulfilled the mission and objectives of the College. This chain of interrelated factors encompassed the entire AWC study. Nowhere is it more evident than in the report of the faculty development subcommittee. One may almost provide a mathematical equation to indicate the areas this group studied and reviewed:

$$\frac{\text{Faculty}}{\text{Development}} = \frac{\text{Mission} + \text{Objectives}}{\text{Curriculum}} + \frac{\text{Curriculum Planning}}{\text{Role of Faculty}} + \frac{\text{Teaching Methods}}{\text{Role of Faculty}}$$

This, essentially, was the method of analysis used by the faculty development committee. Did the curriculum meet the requirements of the mission and the objectives of the War College? What was the role of the faculty in curricular planning and development? What was the role of the faculty in the conduct of the course of instruction? Once the exact role of the faculty had been determined, then means for developing a professional academic faculty could be explored.

The prime elements in the equation to determine faculty development were the roles of the faculty in the preparation and conduct of the curriculum. Exactly what did the faculty do? "In the past," the committee indicated, "the USAWC faculty has performed almost exclusively in the role of a 'management-type' faculty."[17] The faculty conducted very little formal instruction. This may be traced to the decision made 15 years earlier by General Swing not to have platform instruction of the "Leavenworth" type. For the most part, the committee system of instruction, with a minimum of faculty supervision, had been the mainstay of College practice. Most seminars were conducted by students, not by faculty members. The committee summed up the faculty teaching role as, "Generally, activity of this nature has been confined to faculty and course advisor duties, and, to a limited degree, moderation of a few students committee seminars early in the academic year."[18]

Immediate steps were taken to change this managerial role to more of a teaching role. Faculty members were directed to moderate many student committee seminars, partially replacing the student seminar conductor; to prepare and deliver lectures; and to work more closely with student committees through supervision of committee activities. Salet's aims were to develop a teaching faculty and increase its professional standing in the academic world. His actions were based on his conviction that assumption of a greater teaching role was essential to any meaningful faculty development program. However, as he indicated, the changes did not ". . . replace or dilute the splendid guest lecture program,"[19] which had been so effective a part of the College system; nor was any consideration given to curtailing the almost complete academic freedom enjoyed with the College.

The second faculty role was to prepare course material. In the past, the faculty member assigned as director of a course received general guidance on content and coverage from the Deputy Commandant, the Curriculum Board, and his Faculty Group Chairman. Then the course director prepared a course outline, normally based on the previous year's course; selected lecture topics, wrote the lecture scopes and listed proposed guest lecturers; prepared the student requirements and course bibliographies; and either assembled a list of assigned reading or prepared selective readings. He submitted the course material to the Faculty Group Chairman for approval and forwarding to the Curriculum Board. The approved course plan was returned to the course director for implementation. He then invited the proposed lecturers, indicated the number of committee advisers needed, and prepared the final course directive.

During actual conduct of the course, the course director supervised activities of committee advisers, lecturers, and other course events. On completion of the course, he reviewed it generally, received comments from committee advisers, and prepared his after action report. This report often became the basis for changes to the course for the next year.

The study committee analysis of the faculty's role in preparation and conduct of the curriculum indicated that the faculty needed expertise, often in a particular study area not normally available to Army officers through a normal assignment experience, to accomplish its role effectively. The committee made another study of the benefits of sending potential faculty members to civilian universities for graduate instruction. After noting that approximately 85 percent of the faculty already had graduate degrees, the committee recommended that "A total of three officer spaces, not chargeable to the USAWC, be authorized at selected civilian schools for officers designated to join the USAWC faculty."[20] Assigning these three to the War College annually eventually would provide pretrained officers for about one-fourth of the faculty. Careful coordination with Department of the Army career assignment groups could provide for selection of other officers with graduate degrees in desired disciplines for assignment to the faculty.

The committee recommended that faculty members observe students at the Army War College carefully to determine those possessing the greatest potential for later assignment to the faculty. Lists of potential faculty members from graduates of the Army War College and other service war colleges were also to be screened and updated annually. In this manner, a better selection could be made for nomination to the assignment personnel in Department of the Army.

The committee studied at length the possibility of requesting authorization for permanent professors, similar to the organization of the Military Academy, and concluded that the desired stability within the faculty could be obtained by other means. "Basically," the committee said, in recommending against permanent military personnel, "it is apparent that the dynamics of the military art demand a periodic and fresh input from the 'field' . . ."[21] Instead of asking for permanent assignments, the committee recommended Department of the Army establish and adhere to the three year basic tour for all members of the faculty, including the Commandant and the Deputy Commandant; and that seven extended tours of four years, with an option of an added year, be authorized. In making this recommendation, the committee had reviewed the entire faculty assignment tenure from 1951 to date. It noted that the average length of tour for both the Commandant and Deputy Commandant had been two years or less and that the average faculty member had remained at the College less than two and a half years. The committee recommendation would provide for an extended tour for about one-fourth of the faculty.

Although faculty members had been assigned military areas of responsibility, the committee recommended that each member of the faculty be given a special area of interest within the curriculum structure. If this were done, the committee indicated, the individual faculty member would be able to monitor new publications, prepare detailed bibliographies for student usage, provide better guidance and advice for student research, and better supervise preparation and conduct of his particular part of the overall curriculum. This recommendation was approved by the Commandant and became effective during the 1967 academic year.[22]

The committee also considered the desirability of adding civilian members to the faculty. This, of course, was not a new concept; it had been recommended by all of the Civilian Advisory Groups since 1952. The committee also considered the comments of the many consultants who visited the War College during the spring of 1965. Most of these distinguished men, particularly the civilian educators, had stressed the value of not establishing permanent civilian faculty spaces, because more qualified academicians would be available on short leaves of absence from their home institutions. The committee therefore recommended that consideration be given to establishing civilian faculty spaces on a rotational or temporary basis.

Another recommendation closely allied to faculty development represented a new concept insofar as the War College was concerned. This was the proposal to establish a fellowship program in an effort to reestablish the preeminence of the Army and the Army War College in the field of military strategy. Many senior Army officers were greatly concerned about the scarcity of military authors in this field so closely related to the daily work and missions of all of the military services. Colonel Russell O. Fudge, a former War College faculty member, had sounded a clarion call in his article, "Paging Colonel Mahan."[23] After discussing the need for military authors, Fudge had suggested that military fellowships be established under which these men would be sent to the War College for a two year period, not as students, but to be ". . . given a desk and turned loose."[24] Fudge envisioned these fellows using the library, selecting their own areas of study, and producing worthwhile treatises. Another proposal submitted as a War College student research paper modified the Fudge concept by recommending establishment of a more formal program.[25] Recommendations of the AWC 70 Study, however, proposed a more conservative program. Six students from the graduating class of the War College were to be recommended for an additional year of research at the War College. Preliminary discussions with Department of the Army indicated budgetary and space problems might make this concept impossible. The final recommendation of the AWC 70 Study, therefore, asked for four fellowship spaces.[26]

This proposed fellowship program was directly related to internal efforts to improve the War College student research program. These efforts included establishing a Research and Publications Section in the Office of the Director of Instruction and Research to monitor the entire research effort of the College, both student and faculty. Realizing that research in itself is not the end product desired because the results of research are almost worthless until put to practical use, the Commandant assigned the Research and Publication Section the additional mission of fostering publication by both students and faculty in professional journals.

The student research program was changed to offer the individual a choice of format: a thesis, two essays, or a research paper. In the thesis element, the student was to prepare a graduate level thesis on a topic of importance to the military profession. The objective of the research element was study on a military problem of interest to the Army. The essay element was to cover the more important, timely, and current-interest problem areas in the field of military strategy, hopefully for publication in professional journals. This new research program provided the student officer with the opportunity to do research in his area of interest and in the format best suited to his own particular capabilities and talents.

Another step brought into being the publication so long sought by Salet's predecessors. In September 1965, the War College prepared a small, mimeograph document called "Occasional Papers." This was a "test-case" effort to determine the reaction to a publication designed to reach the limited audience of graduates of the War College still on active duty and other selected Government officials. Two papers prepared by members of the Class of 1965 were used. The response was overwhelmingly in favor of the publication. Consequently, with Department of the Army approval, the publication effort was expanded to a printed magazine, "The US Army War College Commentary". The first issue, distributed in April 1966, contained four articles by members of the Class of 1966. The magazine has since been published on an infrequent, nonperiodic basis with the express purpose of providing a forum for expression of mature and professional thought on military strategy and other topics of significant and current military interest. Distribution is limited to current and former members of the War College faculty and student body and selected personnel of various agencies of the Federal Government. Typical of the comments received after the first issue had been distributed was that of General Earle G. Wheeler, Chairman of the Joint Chiefs of Staff. He indicated that even more important than the worthiness of the articles contained in the magazine was ". . . the provision of opportunity and encouragement to military men who have something to say to publish their observations in appropriate journals such as this. . ."[27]

To further extend the benefits of student and faculty research, the Research and Publications Division assisted in preparation of articles for general publication. The advice given—particularly on format and suitability for specific publications—resulted in a tremendous increase in the publication effort by members of the College. Three times as many articles were published during the 1966 academic year as during the previous year.

Another outgrowth of the research effort was preparation of a manuscript on "Communist China's National Strategy". Seventeen student officers of the Class of 1966 contributed to this effort, each researching specific area parts of the overall project. Colonel John B. McKinney, Chief of Research and Publications, edited the book.

The manuscript has been cleared for general publication by both the Department of Defense and the State Department. It is expected to be published soon.

Another action came as the result of a chance remark made by one of the guest participants at the 1966 National Strategy Seminar. Noting that all members of the College, both students and faculty, wore uniform, he asked the Commandant, "How do you identify the faculty from the students?" General Salet replied that the faculty was so small that he knew these men intimately. However, he realized that the visitor had no such intimate association and that some means should be provided for identifying the faculty from the students. Consequently, the Commandant asked that a means of identification be devised. The solution was a "faculty badge" to be worn on the left pocket. It was the old insigne the War College faculty wore before World War II—the mailed fist of the military holding aloft the torch of academic learning—superimposed upon a blue circular belt. The belt symbolized the College effort to develop future commanders by providing a broad general curriculum designed to foster overall development of the professional officer. Three gold stars on the belt symbolized the three periods of the College: pre-World War I, post-World War I and post-World War II.

All these parts of the AWC 70 Study were basic to the curriculum survey and its immediate outgrowth, the curriculum for the 1966 academic year. The review and recommendations regarding the missions and objectives of War College, the study of its teaching methods, the reorganization of the faculty, the plans for faculty development, and the changes to the research and publications programs all contributed to the curriculum study.

The group studying the curriculum began by analyzing the 1965 curriculum. They were assisted by the consultants invited to visit the War College during the spring of 1965. Many of their recommendations were included in the curriculum for the following year.

Some of the study areas investigated by the curriculum committee were almost basic in nature. For example, the problem of depth versus breadth—the same problem that had been reviewed so many times since 1950—again was discussed. This time the problem was studied from the viewpoint of what the Army War College graduate would face after his graduation. Should he be a generalist or a specialist? Because the mission of the College indicated specifically that the officer was to be prepared for the highest positions of command and staff, the curriculum committee concluded that the College should retain the generalist approach and focus the curriculum on study of the appropriate use of military force in support of national security policy. By taking this approach, the committee rejected the narrower view that the curriculum of the War College should concentrate only on those disciplines necessary to prepare officers for service with Department of the Army, Joint Chiefs of Staff, or Office of the Secretary of Defense organization.

The changes made to the curriculum in preparation for the 1966 academic year were not revolutionary in nature. Instead of making major renovations, the Commandant directed that a gradual evolutionary development be started with the express intent of making further developmentary changes in 1967 and 1968. Furthermore, he realized that the core curriculum was sound and essentially met the requirements placed on the War College by its assigned mission. What was needed was an evolutionary reorientation of the curriculum with more stress on the role of the military in developing national strategy rather then the requirements inherent in any military program designed to support such strategy. Salet also insisted that proper emphasis be placed on the role of the Army throughout the course of study stressing that the Army War College is the only educational institution in the United States capable of fully and objectively analyzing the Army contribution to determination and support of the national security policy of the United States.

The AWC 70 Study was far from complete when the proposed 1966 curriculum was submitted to Department of Army for approval. Some parts of the project were not completed until the spring of 1966. Nevertheless, recommendations of the committees were used. Two major trends evident in the recommended curriculum were the greater emphasis on the military throughout the curriculum and increased individual student requirements. The increased military emphasis was not accomplished by curtailing the time or coverage devoted to the study of international national affairs. It was, instead, an analysis of the international and national environments and policies from a military viewpoint; the effect of these environments on military doctrine and strategies; and, conversely, the contribution of military forces to these policies. This was not a parochial view nor a narrow analysis. The technique was the same as that used in other academic disciplines: the law student studies international relations in the form of international law; the economics major, world economies; the student of government, governmental organizations of other nations. This emphasis of the military was not a step backward. Instead, it placed a proper professional perspective on the view of international and national situations, the perspective required for the military arts and sciences.

The AWC 70 Study brought other results. The lecture program contained a greater number of faculty presentations designed to bring proper focus on the purely military aspects of the subject matter as well as to provide a better integration of the overall curriculum. Faculty members were to monitor periodic seminars and to take a more active part as committee advisers. This outgrowth of the faculty development program was not a lessening or abandonment of the committee system of instruction. It was, instead, a finite improvement already tested and proved by graduate educators throughout the academic community.

Changes in the research program gave the student more flexibility in selection of his research field and the format of his study. Following the trend started during the 1965 academic year, the research program continued to stress meaningful creative thinking, in terms of alternative proposals or courses of action, by the students in their academic endeavors. This was, to some extent, a reflection of current decisionmaking practices in the Department of Defense which required consideration of problems in terms of a solution and the alternatives to that solution. It was even more an outgrowth of the AWC 70 Study and its emphasis on deep analysis and creative contemplation.

The 1966 curriculum, approved by Department of the Army, consisted of eight courses. Although not formally divided into parts or phases, the course of study fell into three major groupings: an analysis of the world and national environment, planning and programming for future military requirements, and development of a national strategy and its supporting military program. The analysis of the world and national environment included a survey of major areas of the world and the sources of conflict, a strategic appraisal of the United States and the North Atlantic Community, a study of the strategic threat of the Communist powers, and a study of the strategic implications of the developing areas. Army and joint capabilities planning, Army and joint objectives planning and programming, and a long range strategic study were a part of the informal grouping related to future military requirements. The capstone of the curriculum was the final course which required student development of a national strategy and a supporting military program.

The entire curriculum again centered about a central theme, "A United States National Strategy and A Supporting Military Program." The curricular theme fostered integration of the entire course of instruction and emphasized the need for a cohesive and unified effort by all agencies of the Federal Government in development of a national strategy. Use of the theme permitted the College to emphasize the role of the military, particularly the Army, in development of national security policy, as well as the effects of such policy and strategy on military doctrine, concepts, and force structure.

The survey of the world environment—the North Atlantic Community, the developing areas, the Communist bloc, and other areas—clearly defined the threat to the United States and the free world and indicated ways and means by which that threat could be countered. The national power of the United States—its economic, social, industrial, technological, and scientific resources—was compared to the national power of other nations. The organization of the Federal Government for national security purposes illustrated the interrelationships of these agencies, the contribution of each to national security, and their respective functions. These international and national studies provided the background and foundation required for student development of a national strategy.

Concurrently, these same national and international segments of

WAR COLLEGE VISIT TO THE UNITED NATIONS

Since 1950, each War College class has visited the United Nations for briefings by representatives of member nations. In the above photograph, the War College class occupies delegates seats for a briefing.

the curriculum focused on the military aspects of international policy and national affairs. For example, foreign aid programs were viewed from the standpoint of economic aid and military assistance. The study of US budgetary affairs and economics was not restricted to analysis of military financial requirements, but also analyzed the entire fiscal needs of the Government and the economic situation of the nation as a whole. Consequently, the student gained an appreciation of the effect of military expenditures on the national economy, an understanding of the counter-effect of fluctuations of the national economy on military resources, and a better comprehension of the exact role of the military forces as elements of the overall national power of the nation.

These primarily nonmilitary studies provided not only a foundation but also the framework on which the military part of the curriculum was rationally developed. The results of the strategic analysis of various areas of the world and the defensive requirements of the United States provided the basis for force development and budgetary programming from both Department of Defense and Army viewpoints. The long range strategic study analyzed current and future scientific and technological advances and their application to future military power with emphasis on their effect on the conduct and support of land forces.

Both the nonmilitary and military studies facilitated development of a national strategy by the students. The overall national strategy thus prepared included both foreign and domestic policies and considered both military and nonmilitary implications of the strategy. For this part of the final course of the year, the student committees functioned as a special committee appointed by the President. The deliberations of each student committee included a reexamination and restatement of the national purpose of the United States as the basic source of guidance for national strategy. The strategic appraisal of world conditions was projected 15 years into the future. Based on the national purpose thus determined and the strategic analysis projected, each committee determined national objectives and the policies required to achieve those objectives.

Student committees assumed the role of the Joint Chiefs of Staff in developing the military program to support this national strategy. After analyzing midrange military requirements and means, the committees prepared military strategic concepts designed to provide midrange program guidance, including a statement of the military objectives and the military strategic concept, specific undertakings, and force structure required to attain the stated objectives. Significant risks generated by the proposed program were considered together with possible means of minimizing or eliminating such risks. The committees also considered the budgetary implications of their strategies and the costs of their supporting military programs. The final committee report thus provided an analysis of the world and national environment, projected this environment into the 1975-80 time period, developed a national strategy, and proposed a military program to support the strategy.

The final event of the academic year was the annual National Strategy Seminar. More than 100 distinguished citizens participated in the 1966 seminar. After an orientation, an average of six guests joined each student committee as working members. Officer students briefed the guests on the methods and rationale used to develop the committee report. The guests participated fully in examining and evaluating the final strategies and military programs in detail. Their contributions were particularly valuable in appraising the adequacy of the proposed strategies. In many cases, committee reports were amended by a corrigendum to incorporate suggestions and improvements recommended by the guests. One solution was presented by a student-guest committee at the final plenary session with both students and guests participating.

The primary changes inherent in the 1966 curriculum were the careful and detailed integration of the entire course of study, the increased emphasis on individual student effort, the continuing and added stress of the role of the military in general and the Army in particular, and increased participation by the faculty. Although the AWC 70 Study had not been completed when the initial curriculum plan for 1966 was prepared, the input from the AWC 70 committee groups prepared the way for further curricular development in later years. Consequently, curriculum development was designed

. . . to ensure the requisite coverage of that subject matter which
is considered to be essential for the development of War College students and which will enable them to achieve the degree of
professional military competence required for their assumption
of the highest command and staff responsibilities.[28]

During the 1966 academic year, a Department of the Army board,
under the direction of Lieutenant General Ralph E. Haines, Jr., was
appointed to review the Army system of officer education. This
Board's survey of the War College was of particular value, because
it provided an external investigation of the same areas covered by
the internal analysis of the AWC 70 Study. Furthermore, the Haines
Board findings more fully evaluated the position of the War College
in the overall Army educational system.

In the seven months the Haines Board spent reviewing Army officer education, it visited all Army schools and colleges, the Joint
and Defense schools, selected schools and colleges of the other services, and the three Service academies. To obtain information regarding civilian academic and industrial training techniques, the
Board visited several civilian universities and industrial executive
training agencies. It also studied the officer school systems of the
British, French, German, and Japanese armies.[29] Consequently, the
final report of the Haines Board represented a comprehensive survey
of the current Army officer education system, compared this system
to that of the other armed services and of four foreign armies, and
compared Army educational methods with those used by civilian universities and industrial corporations.

Not all the details of the Haines Board report are germane. Some
recommendations related only in part to the War College; others pertained solely to College activities. These latter recommendations
were important to the College not only because of their substantive
comment, but also because the suggested improvements in many
cases paralleled or complemented findings and conclusions of the
AWC 70 Study. As a result, official Department of Army recognition
of these problem areas provided the War College with the support
needed to undertake improvements.

The Haines Board recommendations relating to the War College can be divided into five major categories: mission and functions, faculty development, curriculum content, procedures, and miscellaneous. In addition, the report contained many comments sustaining current programs and activities of the War College. Although the majority of the recommendations made by the Board were approved by the Chief of Staff of the Army, approval of some suggestions was withheld pending further study, and some recommendations were disapproved.

In briefing the Chief of Staff, General Harold K. Johnson, on the final report of his board, General Haines indicated that

> The Army War College, along with the other senior service colleges, has been criticized in some circles as lacking focus in its curriculum, of being an 'intellectual smorgasbord,' and even of having 'all of the intellectual content of a high school civics course.'[30]

Haines stated that this criticism was ". . . more colorful than exact."[31] Such criticism, however, was indicative of concern felt by many that the Army War College was directed more toward a broad national security education rather than toward the Army's role, doctrine, and operations. In the opinion of the Board, this concern existed partially because the War College's mission was not focused on a specific goal nor tied to any Army organizational level. The Board recommended changing the mission statement to emphasize the role of the College in preparing officers for the highest positions of command and staff—but by specifically making the College responsible for developing doctrine for the theater army, which the Board considered the highest level of Army forces that would operate in the joint or combined environment. The importance of research was stressed by including student and faculty research as a part of the mission. The Board also recommended that the mission include a concept of an Army role in space in the future.

Although the Chief of Staff recognized the need to revise the War College mission, as had General Salet early in the AWC 70 Study, General Johnson did not concur with the entire mission statement submitted by the Haines Board. The revised mission assigned the Army War College was

> . . . to provide resident and nonresident instruction for senior officers of the Army and the other services in the exercise of command and in the execution of key staff responsibilities at major military and departmental headquarters and to advance the art and science of land warfare in the joint and combined environment.[32]

The mission statement itself did not contain all of the Haines Board recommendations, but the delineation of the functions of the War College did include many others and also incorporated some of the conceptual content of the mission recommended by General Salet in March 1965. To accomplish its assigned mission, the War College was to:

> Conduct an Army War College resident course, the objective of which is to enhance the competence of selected officers, with high general officer potential, to assume command responsibilities and to function in key assignments in major Army, joint, and combined headquarters and in planning and policymaking positions at the seat of Government; to stress Army doctrine, higher tactics, and operations against an appropriate background of national strategy and the joint and international environment; and to provide intellectual challenge and an opportunity for individual contribution to the advancement of the art and science of land warfare through student research.
> Conduct an orientation course for selected senior officers of the Reserve Components.
> Conduct nonresident courses as directed.[33]

Three major concepts can be discerned in the first function defined as a part of the mission of the War College: preparing selected officers for future high level duties; stressing the roles of the Army against the "background of national strategy and the joint and combined environment;" and emphasizing student research. The fact that these three conceptual statements were considered sufficiently important by both the Haines Board and the Chief of Staff to be included in the functions assigned the War College indicates the validity and thoroughness of the AWC 70 Study. The AWC Study had stressed the importance of considering the future requirements of the Army in preparing the curriculum of the War College, the necessity for stressing the Army's roles in making and supporting national security policies, and the need for student individual creative effort. These almost basic concepts were carefully considered throughout the AWC 70 Study and were given prime consideration in preparing the curriculum for the 1966 academic year.

The conduct of an orientation course for selected senior officers of the Reserve Components was not a new function, but the directive to "conduct nonresident courses" projected the War College into a new area of education. Noting that the Naval and Air War Colleges and the Industrial College of the Armed Forces all conducted extension courses, the Haines Board defined the need for such a course to be conducted by the Army War College. "Many dedicated Army officers," the Board said, "who are not selected for the resident course could enhance their military professionalism and their value to the Army by participating in an AWC extension course."[34] The Board cited the large numbers of active Army officers who participated in extension courses conducted by the other senior service schools as proof of their desire to advance their military education and of the need for the Army War College to conduct such a course.

In making this recommendation to the Chief of Staff, the Haines Board carefully considered the impact on the War College and the increase in personnel that would be required to prepare an extension course to parallel its resident course. However, the Board believed that the extension course initially "should consist of selected courses from the AWC curriculum with an eventual goal of a complete extension course paralleling the resident course."[35] The Board recommended that the course be open to active and reserve colonels and lieutenant colonels with 15-25 years of service who were graduates of the Command and General Staff College or its equivalent. Completion of the extension course was not to be equated with completion of the resident course, but the Board recommended that an entry be made in the officer's individual service record and that an appropriate diploma be awarded.

As soon as the Chief of Staff approved establishment of a nonresident course at the College, the Commandant formed a faculty committee to study the extension courses offered by the other senior service schools and to develop a plan for the Army War College nonresident course.

In considering faculty development, the Haines Board considered the composition, qualifications, and role of the faculty, and recommended that:

1. The War College be authorized a position for a civilian Educational Adviser.

2. The faculty should be augmented with several professors on sabbatical leave from their colleges or by contract arrangements with local civilian institutions.

3. The military faculty should include specialists in fields such as research and development, logistics, research and systems analysis, and project management.

4. Continuation of the arrangement with Department of the Army for assignment to the War College faculty of the Army officer studying as a Fellow at the Harvard Center for International Affairs.

5. Stabilized tours for key members of the faculty.

6. Selection of officers with advanced degrees for the military faculty.

7. Increase the military faculty by four officers whose specific mission would be research.

8. As a general rule, officers should not be assigned to the Army War College faculty unless they had an intervening tour of duty after graduation from a senior service school.[36]

The Chief of Staff did not approve all these recommendations. He acknowledged the desirability of stabilized tours for the faculty but said it could be approved only as an objective, not as a policy. The reasoning behind this partial approval was the same as that used by the Department of Army justification in handling similar War College requests in the past.[37]

The Haines Board recommended augmentation of the faculty in lieu of the fellowship program advocated by the AWC 70 Study, because it believed more meaningful research could be accomplished by officers who were assigned to the College for longer than a year.[38] The Board also recommended use of these research personnel for preparation of case studies to be used by the War College. This recommendation was approved by the Chief of Staff.

The Chief of Staff did not approve the Board's recommendation that student officers serve at least one intervening tour of duty elsewhere before being assigned to the faculty. The Haines Board noted that about one-third of the faculty were recent War College graduates and recommended that "selected specialists should be on the faculty and that, as a general rule, faculty members should have at least one intervening tour after completing a senior service college."[39] Similar comments had come from other sources. All of the Service war college faculties had been criticized by Edward L. Katzenbach, Jr., in an article in the United States Naval Institute Proceedings in which he said:

> . . . they are picked largely from classes just graduating from a war college, without experience in applying what they have learned under field or staff conditions[40]

Both Mr. Katzenbach and the Haines Board overlooked to some extent a practice common to the graduate academic community. Universities often use graduate students as "graduate assistants" to their faculties and then make them permanent faculty members when they have completed graduate schooling "without experience in applying what they have learned under field or staff conditions." It had been the custom to assign students to the Army War College faculty immediately after graduation since 1905; other service schools followed the same custom. Furthermore, although Army War College students have an average of 20 years military service, they are not considered for assignment to the faculty unless they possess specific academic and military qualifications needed on the faculty.

The Board noted that the 1966 curriculum placed greater emphasis on individual work than on the committee requirements of the previous year and recommended that the AWC should continue to employ the case study method but on an expanded basis in the course curriculum, with particular emphasis to committee problems in which group decisions derive from its use.[41] Although he approved this recommendation, General Johnson urged caution in using the committee method, since too great an emphasis on group decisions would tend to develop indecision on the part of the individual officer.

"In certain areas of the AWC course," the Board noted, "it appears that a suitable standard textbook should be provided."[42] Although the War College provided special reading assignments in a series of separate publications, the Board stated that prescribed texts would provide a solid base for study of entire subjects and thus ". . . would serve as a connecting link between presentations by guest speakers and faculty members."[43] The separate publications referred to in the Haines Board report were the "selected readings" provided by the faculty; a compendium of articles from current magazines, books, and other sources which presented various aspects and background data for the lectures and other presentations. The Chief of Staff did not approve use of standard textbooks, but he authorized the Commandant to use them as he determined would best serve the College's purposes.

The Haines Board made a number of recommendations intended to better corollate the curriculum with the mission of the College. Their prime purpose was to improve the professional preparation of the officer by more closely integrating his War College education into his career-long academic improvement. The specific recommendations were:

1. The curriculum of the Army War College should continue to be military-oriented, with increased emphasis on the Army's role, strategic concepts, and doctrine. The individual research papers should be limited to military subjects of direct interest to the Army.

2. The Army War College should establish an appropriate elective program as part of the curriculum in academic year 1967-68.

3. The Army War College should initiate an extension course program.

4. Operations research, systems analysis, and automatic data processing should be included in the core curriculum and as progressive electives in the upper three levels of officer career schooling.

5. Unless appropriate modification can be made which will eliminate the conflict between the Army War College course and the George Washington University program without any compromise of the curriculum, the graduate study program at the Army War College should be discontinued.[44]

The Haines Board noted that the curriculum was militarily oriented, but recommended that the role of the Army be emphasized even more—specifically through the individual student research efforts. "In the interest of encouraging original thought on problems of direct interest to the Army," the Board said, "and to improve the body of professional military writings, the Board considers that individual research papers should be limited to military subjects."[45] This reorientation of the curriculum to stress its military aspects and to provide even greater emphasis on the role of the Army already had been initiated as a result of the AWC 70 analysis. The Haines Board recommendation added further impetus to the trend already started.

Although the War College from time to time had considered the possibility of a "split" curriculum—the specialist approach in contrast to the generalist concept—little if any consideration had ever been given to adding electives to the course of instruction. Consequently, the Haines Board recommendation that electives be instituted posed new problems to the College. The Haines Board, however, did not make the recommendation without considering the faculty resources needed to implement an elective program. The addition of civilian faculty members and the development of expertise or specialization by the military faculty were intended to provide instructional support to the elective program. When the Chief of Staff approved this recommendation, General Salet began a study to determine which elective programs should be established.[46] The Board recommendation that the War College initiate a nonresident course of instruction also required additional study before it could be implemented by the College.[47]

The Haines Board was concerned that Army schools, as a whole, were not devoting sufficient time to the study of operations research, systems analysis, and automatic data processing. Because of the emphasis upon these techniques throughout the Department of Defense and the military services, the Board expressed its belief that the progressive professional development of the officer required frequent and academic exposure to the techniques and concepts involved. It therefore recommended that career schooling include the subjects as a part of the core curricula in the various schools, to provide every officer with the sound foundation required for his professional development, and that progressive electives be provided for officers desiring to specialize in these general fields of study.

The concern of the Board had been shared by the War College and had been discussed in detail as a part of the AWC 70 Study. Consequently, steps already had been taken to include additional coverage of operations research principles, systems analysis techniques, and automatic data processing concepts in the War College curriculum. This had been initiated in the 1966 curriculum with emphasis on application at the highest levels of command and on the value of these techniques to both the commander and the senior staff officer. Additionally, increased coverage would be provided in future years as a part of the evolutionary improvements of the War College curriculum and the programming of its planned development for future years.[48]

The Chief of Staff had withheld approval of the 1965 recommendation that the George Washington University Program be cancelled,[49] pending receipt of the Haines Board report. The Haines Board concluded that "participation in the GWU program dilutes the effort that the student puts forth in the AWC course, and the student effort in meeting both sets of requirements is often resolved in favor of the GWU requirement. . . ."[50] and that the War College curriculum was sufficiently challenging to warrant the students' fulltime attention. The Board stated, "The curriculum and the professional opportunities it offers should not be eroded by extracurricular efforts to obtain a purely academic degree."[51] Since an increasing number of student officers already had graduate degrees, the Board recommended the program be discontinued if the conflicts with War College requirements could not be resolved. Therefore, the graduate program was cancelled, with General Johnson's approval, at the end of the 1966 academic year.

The Board made other recommendations about student rating techniques, library improvement, and the position of the War College in the Army educational system. However, the Commandant already had instituted many of the major changes (particularly those concerning faculty development, curriculum content, and procedures) later recommended by the Haines Board, as a result of the self-analysis the War College made during its AWC 70 Study. The validity of this study was even more thoroughly established by the findings and recommendations of the Haines Board.

A group headed by Deputy Assistant Secretary of Defense (Education) Thomas D. Morris surveyed the education systems of all the armed services soon after the Haines Board finished its work at Carlisle Barracks. Although many activities studied by the Haines Board also were analyzed by the Department of Defense study group, its final report has not yet been distributed, and its recommendations are unknown.

The deliberate step back to gain a better perspective, through the AWC 70 review of all phases of activity, brought the mission of the College into clearer focus. Instruction methods and the role of the faculty were changed as a result of analysis of the need for faculty development. Military aspects of national strategy and national security were reemphasized, with special emphasis placed on the Army's role in making and implementing national security policies, as a result of the critical and detailed analysis of the curriculum. The first long-range program for curricular improvement was developed to better accomplish the assigned mission of the College.

Analyses made during this period were not only internally generated. Ad hoc consultants invited to the War College made candid recommendations for overall improvements which supplemented the faculty studies. The survey of the Haines Board emphasized and accelerated trends already established and programmed and suggested new fields of study and methods of improvement.

Thus, the War College was able to determine "Where are we today?" and "Where are we going?" The answers to General Salet's questions, "Where should we be going?" and "How do we get there?" were obtained by thorough and detailed self-analysis and vigorous self-evaluation. The result, in General Salet's words, was ". . . renewed vitality, a new sense of mission and direction, and a forward look to keep up with the times and to meet a rapidly changing environment."[52]

THE ARMY WAR COLLEGE CLASS OF 1966

This was the fiftieth class to be graduated by the US Army War College.

"Where Are We Today?"

G RADUATION of the Class of 1966 on 13 June 1966 marked another milestone for the Army War College for this was its fiftieth class. The 205 graduates, joining their more than 5,000 predecessors, left Carlisle Barracks for their new assignments after a year of intensive preparation—preparation, not for the immediate duties to be faced, but, rather, for their assignments five and even ten years later. The assignments to which they reported were widely varied: duty with almost every major, joint, specified, and unified command; staff positions in the Pentagon; combat commands or advisory positions in Vietnam. They carried with them the charge made by their Commencement speaker, Doctor Howard L. Rubendall, President of Dickinson College:

> Today the soldier, because of the faithful interdependence, the compulsory sharing of all elements of our life, has a civic responsibility that is more than extra-curricular. In this land of a free yet inescapable interdependence, he must exercise professional competence, not alone as a competent professional, but as a competent citizen dedicated to national goals that reflect universal values and timeless ends. . . .

> My plea to you—men who know the meaning of leadership— is to bring this quality, too, out beyond professional confines and urges you to serve our common humanity, our shared values and ends, by continuing through the years to nurture the spirit of liberal learning through assiduous attention to awareness, to cultural openmindness, to your role as informed, creative critics, and to your responsibilities as leaders of our common life. [1]

This Golden Anniversary Class was followed in August by another group of students representing all of the Armed Services and a number of civilian agencies. The curriculum facing this group was the second course of instruction developed as a result of the AWC 70 Study. Although the core curriculum resembled the 1966 course of study—because of evolutionary development rather than revolutionary change—the internal improvements and changes within the various courses truly reflected the emphasis recommended by the AWC 70 Study.

The basic framework of the core curriculum was retained almost unchanged and again centered about the curricular theme of developing a military program to support a national strategy. However, within this framework many changes were made. The course began with a review of the world environment and the sources of conflict. The second course was changed from a strategic appraisal of the United States and the North Atlantic community to an appraisal of the United States and its alliances. This change fostered a better understanding of the national power of the United States and the effects of alliances, defense agreements, and international organizations upon United States foreign policy. Throughout the course special reference was made to the military aspects and relationships resulting from these alliances and defense agreements. This course was followed by an analysis of the strategic threat of Communist power and then by a review of the strategic implications of the developing areas. The first four courses were therefore a strategic appraisal of the entire world and were designed to provide the foundation for the study and development of a United States national strategy.

The fifth course provided an understanding of the current strategic capabilities of the United States, its allies, and probable enemies in possible conflict situations in selected world areas. Study included the preparation of theater estimates and campaign plans involving both friendly and enemy viewpoints. Although this study also required an assessment of Army, joint, and combined strategic military capabilities compared to the enemy threat in specific theaters, emphasis was upon theater Army capabilities. The theater plans thus developed by the student committees were tested in an analysis seminar.

Having studied and tested theater military operations, the student then analyzed strategic objectives planning and programming of the

Department of Defense with emphasis upon the role of the Army in implementing these plans and programs. This was accomplished by reviewing several program categories of the Department of Defense program system with time-stress placed on the midrange objectives. Long-range strategic concepts and future Army capabilities formed the basis for student study in Course Seven. In this course the student was acquainted with scientific and technological developments applicable to military power and currently under study or projected for future examination. A prime purpose of this course was to stimulate the development of creative concepts leading to enunciation of bold and imaginative applications in combined land combat operations in the 1977-81 time period.

The second major portion of the course of instruction, therefore, was devoted to the study of military principles, techniques, and concepts which would provide a foundation for the development of the military program necessary to support national strategy. Three time periods were used: the immediate or short-range period for the study of theater and Army capabilities; the midrange period through 1976 for Army and joint objectives planning and programming; and the long-range period from 1977 to 1981 for the study of long-range strategic concepts. In this way students were prepared to develop their own national strategies and the necessary supporting military programs for a period of a decade and a half into the future as a part of the final course requirement.

Two new courses were added in the 1967 academic year. The Comparative Military Strategy Seminar was conducted simultaneously with the first four courses, and the Command and Management Seminar concurrently with courses five through seven. Each seminar met once a week.

The Comparative Military Strategy Seminar reviewed the history and nature of military strategy, theories of the early strategists, causes and types of warfare, objectives of war and war termination, and the nonmilitary factors affecting military strategy. World War I, World War II, and the Korean conflict were studied to determine the effect of these conflicts and the respective postwar strategic concepts on the world environment. This historical analysis led to the

BLISS HALL, CARLISLE BARRACKS

Erected before the Civil War and used as a stable, Bliss Hall provided student study facilities from 1951 to 1967. The building was demolished to provide space for new academic facilities.

study of alternative strategies for the present and the future. The alternatives studied included an investigation of Soviet and Communist Chinese military strategies and a basic view of contributing factors, such as arms control, disarmament, and civilian-military relationships. This study of comparative military strategies was designed to provide the military background to complement the courses providing the foundation for the development of the military program needed to support a national strategy.

By contrast, the Command and Management Seminar had the purpose of developing an understanding of the problem-solving and decisionmaking techniques of the Department of Defense. During this Seminar, students reviewed the essentials of the Department of Defense decisionmaking process with emphasis on the planning, programming, and budgeting system. The capabilities, limitations, and military applications of various automated data processing systems were surveyed. The Seminar also examined the theories and principles of systems analysis and operations research, including military-political wargaming concepts. This study of command and management techniques also was designed to assist the students in the development of the military programs necessary to support national strategy by providing a detailed knowledge of the present Department of Defense techniques and concepts for problem-solving and decisionmaking.

The final course of the 1967 academic year was "The United States National Strategy and a Supporting Military Program." During this course, the student committees reviewed and synthesized knowledge derived from all previous courses to meet the course requirement of developing an integrated statement of US national policy and devising a military program to support that strategy.

In delineating this national strategy and projecting it forward through the next fourteen years, each student committee was required to:

Reexamine and restate the national purpose of the United States as the basic source of guidance for national strategy.
Make a strategic appraisal of the world environment.

Develop a national strategic concept.

State the national objectives and define the national policies required to attain these objectives.

The proposed military program developed by each student committee to support its national strategy included

A worldwide military strategic appraisal projected through 1981.

An analysis of midrange military requirements and means.

The development of a midrange program guidance to include a statement of military objectives, consideration of alternative military strategic concepts and the alternative force structures required to attain these stated objectives, consideration of advantages and disadvantages of costed alternatives, and the selection and justification of a specific program including the cost of that program.

A statement of significant risks entailed in the adoption of the proposed program together with the methods of minimizing or eliminating these risks.

The course culminated in the four-day National Strategy Seminar. Over one hundred distinguished Americans, representing many fields of endeavor, participated. Each guest was assigned to a student committee as a working member. The national strategies and supporting military programs developed by the student groups were reviewed by the joint guest-student committees. One committee was selected to present its final strategy and supporting military program at the final plenary session.

The curriculum which has been described did not vary greatly from that of the 1966 academic year in basic structure. However, within the framework of that structure, there was a material realignment of subject matter to provide a more integrated course of instruction. The addition of the Comparative Military Strategy and Command and Management Seminars provided essential background knowledge which could not be included in the regular curriculum structure. Most important, however, the gradual and evolutionary changes thus made paved the way for more definitive improvements already programmed by the AWC 70 Study.

The 1967 academic year saw many changes at the Army War College. In January following the Christmas holiday period, classes were resumed in the new academic building which had been under construction for over two years. Although the Library and the auditorium remained in the old building pending the razing of Bliss Hall and the completion of auditorium and library facilities, the new building provided the War College with completely adquate accommodations for the first time since its move to Carlisle Barracks.

Student study capabilities were greatly improved. In contrast to old Bliss Hall and its crowded student committee rooms, the new academic building includes small student study rooms with three or four students assigned to each room. Each student committee is assigned a committee seminar room. These seminar rooms are fully equipped with the most modern audiovisual facilities. Although designed primarily for the use of a single committee, each room can accommodate a dual-committee session.

A large conference room has a capacity of 75 individuals. This small auditorium is used primarily for afterlecture conferences with visiting lecturers, for instruction of large groups, and for faculty seminars. This room has been dedicated to the memory of Lieutenant Colonel Wilfred C. Washcoe, the original project officer for the War College expansion program.

Although the complete decor of the Bliss Hall coffee shop could not be duplicated, many of the prints and decorations hang in the new coffee shop. In addition, the unit commanders' plaques initiated in 1955 by Colonels Connor and Yarborough have been retained. [2]

When completed, the academic complex will provide facilities for almost all Army War College activities. The new auditorium will seat 500 people; the library area will include expansion capabilities to meet future requirements. In addition, the building houses the reproduction plant and other activities formerly scattered throughout the post. The plans also provide for a physical conditioning building and gymnasium although actual construction has not yet been programmed.

The academic building was dedicated formally on 29 April 1967 and named after Secretary of War Elihu Root. Major General Ulysses

S. Grant, III, son-in-law of Secretary Root, gave the dedicatory address. Other speakers included Lieutenant General William F. Train, Commander of the 1st United States Army and former Army War College Commandant, and State Senator George N. Wade, representing both the 31st Congressional District and the Commonwealth of Pennsylvania.

As a natural outgrowth of the Army War College research program and the resultant writing efforts of both students and faculty, the Commandant recommended to Department of the Army that a military history research collection be established at the War College. He indicated that it was appropriate for the Army War College, as the senior postgraduate school of Army educational system, to sponsor research facilities in its specialized field—the military arts and sciences—in the same manner that a civilian graduate institution sponsors research in its particular specialized academic area. In May 1967, the Chief of Staff of the Army authorized the establishment of the United States Army Military History Research Collection.

This Research Collection will occupy the facilities formerly used by the Army War College Academic Library, after the Library has been moved into its new facilities in Root Hall. Initially, the Collection will consist of approximately 50,000 bound volumes and a large number of periodicals, documents, and manuscripts. The Army War College Academic Library will transfer approximately 20,000 older volumes to the Research Collection. An additional 30,000 have been made available from the National War College Library, books which were a part of the original Army War College Library prior to 1946. Although the Research Collection will not be ready for full use for approximately a year, efforts are already underway to expand the materials to be made available to scholars, both military and civilian. Plans are being made to consolidate books, documents, and other historical papers which presently are located on Army posts and in service school libraries throughout the United States and overseas. In addition, an extensive campaign is being conducted to obtain the personal papers and records of retired and active duty Army officers.

To further improve research facilities, particularly for civilian scholars who may study at the War College, General Salet established

ROOT HALL, CARLISLE BARRACKS

This architect's drawing shows the academic complex as it will be when completed. Root Hall is in the center; new Bliss auditorium at the lower right. The physical conditioning building in the upper portion of the drawing is not yet programmed.

the US Army War College Research Center in June 1967. The Research Center includes both the US Army Military History Research Collection and the War College Academic Library. The interrelation of the two activities will permit more efficient administration of common functions and will foster the use of unclassified materials in the Academic Library by civilian scholars.

To obtain a critique of the 1967 curriculum and to enable better development of the course of instruction for the 1968 academic year, the Commandant again invited a Board of Consultants to visit the War College. This Board included Stephen Ailes, former Secretary of the Army; retired General Bruce C. Clarke, Vice President of the Freedom Foundation; Dr. Howard L. Rubendall, President of Dickinson College; Laurence I. Radway, Professor of Government at Dartmouth College; Ralph L. Powell, Professor of Far Eastern Studies, American University; Lieutenant General Ralph E. Haines, Jr.; Brigadier General Melvin Zais, Director of Individual Training, Office of the Deputy Chief of Staff for Personnel, Department of the Army; and Brigadier General John R. Jannarone, Dean of the Academic Board, US Military Academy.

The Board met at Carlisle Barracks for three days in February 1967. General Salet asked for the views of the Board concerning the contribution of the War College curriculum to the current and projected fulfillment of the War College mission and the continuing improvements to be achieved by the planned evolutionary changes to the curriculum. After detailed briefings by the staff and faculty and after personal discussions with students and faculty members, the Board submitted a report covering four major areas of interest: curriculum content, faculty development, the physical facilities of the War College, and the proposed 1968 curriculum.

Noting the emphasis on the roles and missions of the Army throughout the curriculum, the Board consensus indicated that this emphasis should be continued. "However," the Board stated, "the curriculum should also place the Army in its proper milieu, as an important element of a complex national and international environment."[3] The study of land warfare, according to the Board, should take into consideration that most major military operations are joint or combined. In line with the College emphasis upon the role of the Army in national security, the Board cited seven fundamental problem areas in which future Army. leaders should have a measure of special competence: raising, training, organizing, equipping, transporting, employing, and maintaining Army Forces. Although the Board recognized that these areas might be covered in the current program, it suggested that they be identified more formally within the structure of the curriculum.

The subject of student individual research was thoroughly discussed. The Board agreed that a happy medium must be maintained between narrow parochial studies and broad-guage, individually oriented studies which have no meaningful application to the Army. The Board was assured by the Commandant that the list of subjects for student individual research would be reviewed annually to insure that they are meaningful and generally Army-oriented. The Board considered the War College individual research program of theses, essays, and case studies to have great merit. However, it cautioned ". . .the War College to insure that committee work is not derogated in the interest of individual research." [4]

After detailed examination of the sequence of courses in the curriculum, the Board concluded that the War College approach was orderly and progressive. Particular note was made of the Comparative Military Strategy and the Command and Mangement Seminars as a means of providing greater continuity and relevance to the courses which they parallel.

The Board was concerned about the workload placed upon the students as a result of implementation of the Haines Board recommendations and ". . . the enthusiasm of the Commandant and the Faculty." [5] It was recommended that there be continuous evaluation of the workload to assure that it did not become overburdening and that an environment be created which would be conducive to reflective thinking and physical well being.

Considering a highly competent and well-educated faculty to be one of the primary requisites for an outstanding curriculum, the Board noted with approval the ". . .very high quality of the faculty, and the program for maintaining and even improving this quality." [6]

In stating its support of the Haines Board recommendation for greater tenure in the faculty, the Board recommended that the War College make a study to determine the validity of the concept of placing certain selected faculty members on a permanent status comparable to that afforded to professors at the US Military Academy. The Board also suggested that consideration be given to extending the retirement date of officers who might elect to remain at the War College as professional educators.

Another of the Haines Board recommendations also received favorable comment from the Board of Consultants, the addition of four faculty spaces to expand faculty research and to improve the curriculum. The Board suggested that these new faculty members be clearly identified to assure continuity in the application of their talents as envisioned by the Haines Board.

The emphasis by the War College on the teaching role of the faculty was also noted with approval by the Board. The Board stated that it was imperative that the Army War College faculty, both military and civilian, ". . .possess the education and experience which will allow them to do more than monitor discussions and arrange administrative details."[7] This the Board believed necessary to reemphasize the need for a highquality faculty with some degree of tenure.

Because the State Department assigned officers of ambassadorial rank to the National War College, the Air War College, and the Naval War College, and because the Army War College curriculum considers national policy at the highest level, the Board recommended that an officer of ambassadorial rank be assigned to the Army War College by the State Department. The Board also urged that an additional Foreign Service Officer be assigned to serve on the faculty.

The need for a physical conditioning plant received strong support from the Board of Consultants. Noting that the War College had requested authorization for a new gymnasium building since 1965, the Board stated that:

It appears incongruous to spend large sums of money on educating officers while neglecting their physical condition. Considering that these officers are at a critical point in their careers and that many will be assigned directly from the War College to duty with troops which will require a strong and healthy body, it would appear prudent to assure that facilities are made available for regular conditioning. [8]

After inspecting the new facilities for the Academic Library, the Board indicated that these were believed adequate. The War College was encouraged to introduce new library management techniques after the Library moved to Root Hall. Increased use of microfilm, tape recordings, and audiovisual aids were recommended. The Board also urged consideration of a data processing or electronic data retrieval system.

The efforts of the War College to obtain approval for establishment of a military history research collection received special attention from the Board. [9] Stating its full support of the proposal, the Board recommended that the research facility be made available not only to the College, but to the entire military and academic community of the Nation.

The Director of Instruction and Research discussed the planned curriculum for 1968 with the Board of Consultants. The Board agreed with the War College policy of restricting electives to the normal program of instruction without imposing a requirement for extracurricular attendance and study. It recommended that students be permitted to audit electives but that the number of electives should not be increased beyond the capacity of the student and beyond the capability of the faculty to present. [10] Support was given the proposal made by the Judge Advocate General of the Army that an elective in International Law be included in the curriculum and that the course be taught by a member of the Judge Advocate General's Department.

The final comment of the Board of Consultants related to the performance of the mission of the Army War College:

It was obvious to the Board from the moment of arrival that within the Army War College there exists an atmosphere of creative and progressive thinking. The caliber of the faculty is very high and, as noted in the body of the report, it will reach even

AFTER LECTURE CONFERENCE
Visiting lecturers meet with students and faculty members following many formal briefings. The give-and-take repartee has become an important part of the Army War College program.

higher levels of academic and professional competence next year. The creativeness of the school was further reflected by the variety of instructional material presented and the imagination demonstrated in the evolvement of the curriculum from a broad base to a sharply defined end-product. While recognizing the role of the Army as only one element in the conduct of national strategy, the Army War College has highlighted the role of the Army in order to insure that graduates are well aware of the capabilities of the United States Army and the role it plays in the national scene. Furthermore, with the introduction of more individual research and a dramatic increase in the publications effort, it is obvious that the Army War College is producing a better educated and more well-rounded officer than ever before in its history...[11]

These recommendations and suggestions were carefully considered by the Commandant and the faculty in the development of the curriculum for the 1968 academic year. The plan prepared as a result of the AWC 70 Study was thus refined to add the recommendations made by the Haines Board and the suggestions of the 1967 Board of Consultants.

In consonance with the AWC 70 emphasis, the role of the Army in the development of national strategy and the maintenance of national security, the curricular theme for 1968 was changed to "A Military Program to Support a US National Strategy." The various courses, seminars, and other curricular activities are focused on this unifying theme which defines the overall objectives of the curriculum and establishes a relationship between each element of the curriculum and this ultimate purpose.

Within the core curriculum centered about this theme, nine courses, two seminars, two programs, and a series of electives have been established. An Orientation Program gives the students a basic introduction to the College and its curriculum. The Military Strategy Seminar, successor to the Comparative Military Strategy Seminar of the 1967 academic year, establishes the indispensable foundation for understanding military strategy and its relationship to national strategy and higher tactics, and permits thorough evaluation of current and future strategies. An appreciation of current Department of Defense problem-solving and decisionmaking procedures is derived from the Command and Management Seminar. Each course is designed to contribute to the considerations which are required for the student to develop a military program to support a sound national strategy in the last course of the academic year. The Individual Research Program supports and complements the overall curriculum and emphasizes research and analysis in depth, professional writing, and the advancement of the art and science of land warfare. The electives supplement the core curriculum by providing each student who wants to expand his knowledge in selected areas an opportunity for detailed individual study of subjects relating to or complementing studies in the academic courses and seminars.

The overall curriculum for the 1968 academic year may be viewed as divided into three phases although a formal phasing does not exist. During the first phase, a strategic appraisal is made of the world environment to determine the forces, trends, problems and opportunities of the contemporary world which bear on US national security considerations. Included in this phase are the first four courses: "The United States in the World Environment," "Strategic Appraisal of US Alliances and International Organizations," "The Strategic Threat of the Communist Powers," and "Strategic Implications of the Developing Areas." By reviewing the world situation and by analyzing the elements of US national power, the student is enabled to prepare his version of US national strategy during the final course of the academic year. The Military Strategy Seminar is scheduled for a weekly meeting during this first phase.

The second major phase of the course of instruction again is devoted to the study of military principles, techniques, and concepts which provide a foundation for the development of the military program necessary to support national strategy. A new course has been added, "Army Internal Defense and Development Operations." The purpose of this course is to assess Army and joint capabilities to support the full range of stability operations, including military assistance programs, civic action, internal defense and development operations, and the deployment of Army forces to bolster the efforts of weaker nations in controlling insurgency and preventing subversion. The course is also designed to foster student efforts to seek innovations and creative concepts for changes in the roles, missions and activities of the US Army in cold war. The addition of this course is another indication of the efforts of the US Army War College to continually modify its course of instruction to meet the current needs of the Army and the Nation. In the same manner that the War College responded to the changing threat in the late 1930's by modifying its studies to provide greater stress on the European situation, the War College today has added a course to provide added emphasis on what the Chief of Staff of the Army has termed the Army's "third mission."

Other courses in this second major curricular phase review Army and theater capabilities in selected world areas; study Army and joint planning and programming; and analyze long range military concepts for land power. The Command and Management Seminar schedules weekly meetings during fourteen weeks of this phase. In this way, the second phase continues the study of military principles, techniques, and concepts which provide a foundation for the development of the military program necessary to support national strategy.

For the first time the War College offers its students a choice of elective subjects. This program, initiated as a result of the Haines Board recommendations, supplements the core curriculum by providing an opportunity to study subjects related to or complementing the academic courses and seminars. Each student will participate in two elective courses, one during each half of the academic year. During the fall term, the following electives are being offered by the instructors indicated:

Communicative Arts	Professor Harold O'Brien and Professor R. T. Oliver Pennsylvania State University
Political Systems and National Security	Dr. Eugene H. Miller and Dr. Howard R. Ludden Operations Research Incorporated
Economics of National Security	Professor Robert Kuenne Princeton University

Social Factors and National Security	Dr. Jessie A. Miller Operations Research Incorporated
International Law and National Security	Colonel D. L. Shaneyfelt Office of the Judge Advocate General, Department of the Army

These will be followed in the spring term by:

Communicative Arts	Professor Harold O'Brien Professor R. T. Oliver Pennsylvania State University
Analytical Techniques of Management	Professor Robert Kuenne Princeton University
Management Information Systems	Colonel O. W. Brackman Operations Group, US Army War College
Resource Management and Control	Lieutenant Colonel J. A. Hoefling Faculty, US Army War College

The final course of the year enables each student committee to develop its own version of a military program required to support US national strategy. This course is based upon prior learning experience, study, and additional research and analysis; and requires an appreciation of both military and nonmilitary considerations. While the role of the Army is given prime emphasis, the part played by all military services in formulating a national strategy is considered, with the major endeavor being the formulation of a supporting military strategy and program.

The recommendation of the Haines Board that a nonresident program of instruction be instituted by the Army War College is being implemented. The Department of Nonresident Instruction has been established to prepare and conduct the nonresident program. A target date of early 1969 has been established for completion of the course of nonresident instruction, the preparation of text materials and grading procedures, and the determination of selection criteria for officer students.

Many other progressive and evolutionary changes have been made within the War College curriculum. Following the earlier recommendations of the AWC 70 Study and the additional stress urged by the Haines Board, increased use is being made of the case study. During the 1968 academic year, students are offered an opportunity to develop case studies as a part of the Individual Research Program. Additional cases are being used throughout the regular course of study as well.

Four additional faculty spaces have been made available to the War College as a result of the Haines Board recommendation that these officers be added to the faculty with the specific mission of research. The Research and Publications Division of the Office of the Director of Instruction and Research has been changed to a separate Department with the mission of conducting the War College research and publications efforts. This new department has three major functions: curriculum research, supervision of the student Individual Research Program, and conduct of College publication efforts.

The reorganization which added the Research and Publication and Nonresident Instruction Departments retained the organizational structure instituted in 1965. Three academic departments—Strategy, Strategic Appraisal, and Military Planning—plan and conduct the various courses of the curriculum. Although the Joint Advisory Group has been retitled the Senior Service Representatives, the membership and functions remain unchanged. The dual relationship between the Secretary and the Director of Instruction and Research has been retained. Supervision of the activities of the US Army War College Research Center and the US Army Military History Research Collection has been assigned to the Secretary.

Continuing his interest in the historical ties between the War College and the Army, the Commandant directed that the student seminar rooms be named for military men of the past. Portraits, other art work, and documents pertaining to the appropriate periods of US history will decorate the halls near the various seminar rooms. The Revolutionary War is represented by Knox and Von Steuben; the War of 1812, by Scott and Jackson; the Mexican War, by Taylor; the Civil War, by Grant, Lee, Jackson, and Sherman; the Indian Wars, by Crook and Miles; the Spanish American War, by Theodore Roosevelt; World War I, by March and McAndrew; World War II, by Patton and Krueger; Korea by Ridgway. Three rooms have been retained unnamed for future commemorative purposes.

The bronze class plaques have been placed on the outside of Root Hall. Six plaques for the pre-World War II classes are mounted on the columns of the portico; other plaques on the east wall. The decision to place them outside the building will permit a far greater number of people to view them than if they were inside Root Hall.

At the urging of many graduates, the Alumni Association of

the US Army War College was established in June 1967. The primary purpose of the organization is to foster, maintain, and strengthen a sense of fraternity among the alumni of the Army War College. Among the anticipated activities of the Association are:

Preparing suitable publications to maintain contact with and between US Army War College graduates.
Recognizing distinguished service or contributions to the advancement of the US Army War College.
Conducting appropriate correspondence, publicity, and activities to promote awareness of the US Army War College.
Sponsoring social events for members of the Association. [12]

The first project undertaken by the Association was the publication of this history of the War College, Prudens Futuri. The initial goal of 1,200 members had been exceeded in August 1967 with nearly 2,000 graduates enrolled as charter members of the Association.

The Army War College has changed greatly since 1964. The AWC 70 Study and the Haines Board recommendations affected almost every phase of War College activity. Many of the concepts and ideas generated during the detailed analysis phase of the AWC 70 Study were not new. Previous studies and reports, some from the period before World War II, were unknown to the current faculty, and consequently had not been used nor consulted. The fact that many of the concepts discussed in and the recommendations made as a result of the AWC 70 Study were not new or original is not particularly significant. The fact that actions were taken to implement the recommendations of both the AWC 70 Study and the Haines Board, however, is most significant. The foresight, professional capability, devotion, and enthusiasm of the Commandant and faculty brought profound changes to the Army War College and its curriculum. The resultant effect of the evolutionary and progressive improvements made as a result of the Army War College 70 Study and the Haines Board recommendations, however, can only be judged fully in the future by the performance of the end product, the graduate of the US Army War College.

Providing for the Future

T HERE can be little doubt that Elihu Root's initial concept of a War College envisioned the preparation of studies for the War Department as its primary function. Root used the War College Board as a substitute for a staff until Congress authorized formal organization of the War Department General Staff in 1903. Even then, however, the War College continued to function as a section of the General Staff, until a sufficient reservoir of officers had been trained in staff procedures and techniques. The War College gradually increased its academic endeavors, but General Staff study requirements were not eliminated completely until just before World War I.

This close association with and functioning as a part of the War Department General Staff created the widespread impression that the War College was little more than a staff section and that little, if any, academic instruction was conducted. This was true of Young's War College Board; it also was true of the training given the first class in 1904-05. However, after 1906, the emphasis of the curriculum turned more and more toward the academic disciplines.

During its first decade, the War College was dominated by Bliss and Wotherspoon. Unfortunately, neither has received full recognition for his contributions to the academic development of the War College. Many of the educational techniques established by Bliss and Wotherspoon have been retained through the years; many of their policies are now traditional to the College. The committee-seminar technique, the combination of group and individual effort, and the extensive use of visiting lecturers were first used during this period. Insistence that the War College look to future developments in scientific and international areas as well as in military matters developed a realization that the study of the military arts and sciences, in the broadest concept, could not be restricted to a discussion of tactics, analysis of weapons capabilities, or review of military organization. The parochial views of Army officers, nurtured and fostered by a lack of contact with the civilian community, were replaced by a broadening awareness that military affairs could not be separated from the economic, social, political, and scientific aspects of national activities. Although the primary emphasis of the War College curriculum remained military until World War I, a gradual transition began with additional stress being placed on nonmilitary matters.

This trend became even more pronounced when the War College was reopened in 1919. McAndrew's curriculum, his "uncharted course," retained a military emphasis, but this stress was tempered by increasing the coverage of nonmilitary topics. Economics, international law, labor, management, scientific developments, and sociological problems were all included in the course of instruction. Detailed analyses of international problems became commonplace, although this study of international relations was considered to be primarily an intelligence estimate of the international environment. Study of the capabilities of the United States was added to the curriculum. This analysis of the economic, industrial, and scientific potential, however, was directed toward an understanding of the use of national resources during the preparation, mobilization, and fighting phases of a conflict. Great stress was placed on joint activities of the Army and the Navy.

McAndrew and his successors viewed the War College curriculum as a modification of the planning techniques of the War Department General Staff with the additional changes generated by emphasis upon the duties and responsibilities of the commander. The curriculum included: an intelligence estimate of potential enemies of the United States; a survey of manpower, industrial, and economic resources of the United States; and the development of war plans to counter possible conflict situations using these resources. If one considers the War College curriculum for the period between the two wars using the terminology of 1967, the course of instruction can be considered to have included a survey of the international environment, an analysis of the national power of the United States, the development of a military strategy for the United States, and preparation of a military program to support that strategy.

When the Army War College was reinstituted in 1950, following a ten year hiatus, curricular emphasis returned to primarily military subjects. This is understandable for the Army had an urgent need for capable, well-trained officers on high level staffs and in command positions. By 1954, however, the stress again began to be placed upon the factors of national power and international relations with a lessening of time devoted to the purely military studies. This trend continued until 1964. With each increase in time devoted to international studies or to analyses of national power came a corresponding decrease in the coverage of military topics. Curricular emphasis was upon a review of the international environment, an analysis of the national power of the United States, the development of a national strategy for the United States and a military program to support that strategy.

Curricular stress was modified as a result of the Army War College 70 Study and the recommendations of the Haines Board. There was a gradual decrease in the time devoted to international and national affairs and an increase in military coverage. Emphasis was not only upon military participation in the development of national strategy, but also upon the role of the Army.

The 1967 military emphasis differs greatly from the military character of the 1951 curriculum. The present emphasis is upon the effect of military activities upon national policy and the resultant effect of national policy upon military activities, not on the professional techniques and military methods involved in making or executing plans. Full consideration is given to all of the various factors of national power and to the interrelational use of these factors in attaining national objectives.

To provide depth to the curricular study, electives and special seminars have been added. These studies provide a definitive background for the student which enables him to develop a personal intellectual foundation of knowledge upon which to build his own personal study of the international environment and the factors of US national power from which are derived a military program to support the national strategy.

In some ways there is little resemblance between the Army War College of 1967 and the College of the past. In other ways, however, there are many similarities. Instructional methods are similar, similar but changed by evolutionary development and by the constant improvement brought by addition and absorption of modern techniques. McAndrew's intelligence estimate was a survey of the international situation but it was not as comprehensive nor as detailed as the present study involving the factors of national power of friendly and inimical nations and the analysis of international organizations. Connor's study of national resources had the objective of determining how the manpower and the industrial capabilities of the United States could be used in preparing for or fighting a war. The 1967 analysis considers the contribution of the military forces to the national power of the United States and, conversely, the importance of the various factors of national power upon the development of military forces. Throughout the curriculum, stress is placed upon the military aspects of each area of study with particular emphasis upon the role of the Army.

Throughout the years, the Army War College has had essentially the same primary mission: preparing its student officers for positions of high command and staff duty. The needs of the Army and the military requirements of the Nation have changed over the years; the curriculum of the War College also has changed to keep pace with these needs and requirements. In the final analysis, the true worth of this institution must be measured in the accomplishments of its graduates. One-third of all the officers who studied at the War College have become general officers. Many have served as Chief of Staff of the Army; others have commanded large forces in peace and in war. Army War College graduates from the other military services—the Marine Corps, the Navy, and the Air Force—have had equally distinguished careers.

Military rank, however, does not in itself fully indicate the contribution of an individual to the national security of his country. Many War College graduates did not attain general officer rank. Each graduate, regardless of rank, has had a part in the formulation and moulding of national policy because of the responsible positions he has been given after graduation from the Army War College.

The conclusion cannot be drawn that only the Army War College had an influence upon the development of these officers or that the War College alone should receive credit for their accomplishments after graduation. The many other factors affecting an officer during his career development preclude any such narrow interpretation. Nevertheless, there can be little question that the Army War College exercises a significant influence on the professional development of its graduates. The true measure of the role played by the War College in preparing its graduates to contribute to the advancement of the national security of our country can be made only with the aid of the perspective provided by time. Meanwhile, the US Army War College will continue to serve the Nation and the Army as it has in the past by providing for the future—Prudens Futuri.

APPENDICES

Appendix A

PRESIDENTS AND COMMANDANTS

Major General S. B. M. Young, 1 July 1902 - 15 August 1903, (Army War College Board)

Brigadier General Tasker H. Bliss, 16 August 1903 - 24 June 1905

Lt Colonel W. W. Wotherspoon, 25 June 1905 - 3 December 1905, (acting)

Brigadier General Thomas H. Barry, 4 December 1905 - 21 February 1907

Colonel W. W. Wotherspoon, 21 February 1907 - 8 October 1907, (acting)

Brigadier General W. W. Wotherspoon, 9 October 1907 - 19 June 1909

Brigadier General Tasker H. Bliss, 21 June 1909 1 December 1909

Brigadier General W. W. Wotherspoon, 1 December 1909 - 1 February 1912

Brigadier General Albert L. Mills, 2 February 1912 - 31 August 1912

Brigadier General William Crozier, 1 September 1912 - 1 July 1913

Brigadier General Hunter Liggett, 1 July 1913 - 22 April 1914

Brigadier General M. M. Macomb, 22 April 1914 - 12 October 1916

Brigadier General Joseph E. Kuhn, 1 February 1917 - 25 August 1917

> Classes were suspended following graduation of the
> Class of 1917 and were not resumed until 1919..

Major General James W. McAndrew, 15 June 1919 - 6 July 1921

Major General E. F. McGlachlin, Jr., 14 July 1921 - 30 June 1923

Major General Hanson E. Ely, 1 July 1923 - 30 November 1927

Major General William D. Connor, 20 December 1927 - 30 April 1932

Major General George S. Simonds, 1 May 1932 - 31 January 1935

Major General Malin Craig, 4 February 1935 - 1 October 1935

Brigadier General Walter S. Grant, 3 October 1935 - 29 June 1937

Major General John L. DeWitt, 30 June 1937 - 30 November 1939

Brigadier General Philip B. Peyton, 1 December 1939 - 30 June 1940

> Classes were suspended by the Secretary of War on 11 June 1940.
> The Army War College was reactiviated in 1950.

Lieutenant General Joseph M. Swing, 1 April 1950 - 31 July 1951

Lieutenant General Edward M. Almond, 16 August 1951 - 5 December 1952

Brigadier General Verdi B. Barnes, 6 December 1952 - 19 April 1953, (acting)

Major General James E. Moore, 20 April 1953 - 5 February 1955

Brigadier General Thomas W. Dunn, 6 February 1955 - 26 May 1955, (acting)

Major General Clyde D. Eddleman, 27 May 1955 - 9 October 1955

Major General Max S. Johnson, 10 October 1955 - 15 February 1959

Major General William P. Ennis, Jr., 16 February 1959 - 31 July 1960

Major General Thomas W. Dunn, 8 August 1960 - 16 March 1962

Major General William F. Train, 1 May 1962 - 30 June 1964

Major General Eugene A. Salet, 1 July 1964 - 22 August 1967

Major General William J. McCaffrey, 15 September 1967 - 1 July 1969

Major General George S. Eckhardt, 7 July 1969 - 14 March 1971

Brigadier General Wallace C. Magathan, 15 March 1971 - 3 May 1971

Major General Franklin M. Davis, Jr., 4 May 1971 - 26 June 1974

Major General DeWitt C. Smith, Jr., 1 July 1974 - 31 July 1977

Major General Robert G. Yerks, 1 August 1977 - 31 July 1978

Major General DeWitt C. Smith, Jr., 1 August 1978 -

Appendix B

SENIOR DIRECTORS' DIRECTORS' ASSISTANT COMMANDANTS' AND DEPUTY COMMANDANTS

SENIOR DIRECTORS

Brigadier General W. H. Carter, 1 July 1902 - 14 August 1903

Colonel Alexander Mackenzie, Corps of Engineers, 15 August 1903 - 22 January 1904

Major William D. Beach, Cavalry, 23 January 1904 - 27 June 1904

Colonel Arthur L. Wagner, Infantry, 17 September 1904 - 17 June 1905

Lieutenant Colonel William W. Wotherspoon, Infantry, 18 June 1905 - 18 October 1905

Lieutenant Colonel Smith S. Leach, Corps of Engineers, 19 October 1905 - 3 December 1905

Lieutenant Colonel William W. Wotherspoon, Infantry, 4 December 1905 - 29 September 1906

Lieutenant Colonel Smith S. Leach, Corps of Engineers, 30 September 1906 - 20 February 1907

Colonel William W. Wotherspoon, Infantry, 21 February 1907 - 26 December 1907

Lieutenant Colonel Robert K. Evans, Infantry, 27 December 1907 - 29 November 1909

Major Eben Swift, Cavalry, 30 November 1909 - 15 August 1910

Lieutenant Colonel Hunter Liggett, Infantry, 16 August 1910 - 30 June 1913

Major Benjamin A. Poore, Infantry, 1 July 1913 - 18 January 1916

Lieutenant Colonel George H. Cameron, Cavalry, 19 January 1916 - 26 July 1916

DIRECTORS

Lieutenant Colonel George H. Cameron, Cavalry, 27 July 1916 - 8 December 1916

Lieutenant Colonel Henry Jervey, Corps of Engineers, 9 December 1916 - 26 May 1917

Classes were suspended following graduation of the Class of 1917 and were not resumed until 1919.

ASSISTANT COMMANDANTS

Colonel Harry A. Smith, Infantry, 22 July 1919 - 9 May 1922

Lieutenant Colonel George S. Simonds, Infantry, 10 May 1922 - 1 July 1924

Colonel Herbert B. Crosby, 2 July 1924 - 20 March 1926

Colonel Lytle Brown, Corps of Engineers, 6 August 1926 - 30 June 1928

Colonel John L. DeWitt, Infantry, 1 July 1928 - 3 February 1930

Colonel Herbert J. Brees, Cavalry, 3 March 1930 - 29 October 1930

Colonel Joseph P. Tracy, Coast Artillery Corps, 30 October 1930 - 1 September 1931

Colonel Leon B. Kromer, Cavalry, 2 September 1931 - 29 June 1933

Colonel Evan H. Humphrey, Cavalry, 30 June 1933 - 27 April 1935

Colonel Walter S. Grant, Cavalry, 28 April 1935 - 31 May 1936

Colonel Ned B. Rehkopf, Field Artillery, 1 June 1936 - 15 June 1941

Classes were suspended beginning 11 June 1940 by order of the Secretary of War. The US Army War College was not reinstituted until 1950.

DEPUTY COMMANDANTS

Brigadier General Arthur G. Trudeau, 10 April 1950 - 1 March 1952

Brigadier General Verdi B. Barnes, 20 August 1952 - 11 July 1954

Brigadier General Thomas W Dunn, 25 August 1954 - 18 June 1956

Brigadier General Edgar C. Doleman, 19 June 1956 - 10 July 1959

Brigadier General Bruce Palmer, Jr., 12 August 1959 - 30 June 1961

Brigadier General Harry L. Hillyard, 30 August 1961 - 20 July 1962

Brigadier General Ward S. Ryan, 20 July 1962 - 19 March 1965

Major General Jaroslav T. Folda, Jr., 3 June 1965 - 13 June 1966

Brigadier General Robert B. Smith, 15 August 1966 - 8 January 1968

Brigadier General Michael J. L. Greene, 9 January 1968 - 20 December 1969

Brigadier General Wallace C. Magathan, 21 December 1969 - 3 March 1972

Colonel Henry A. Barber, III, Infantry, 4 March 1972 - 2 August 1972

Brigadier General Edward C. Meyer, 3 August 1972 - 20 August 1973

Brigadier General Calvert P. Benedict, 21 August 1973 - 21 August 1974

Brigadier General Robert G. Yerks, 26 August 1974 - 10 July 1975

Brigadier General Edward B. Atkeson, 10 July 1975 - 1 July 1976

Brigadier General Joseph H. Kastner, 5 August 1976 - 5 August 1977

Brigadier General Robert C. Gaskill, 6 August 1977 - 25 Sep 1978

Brigadier General Alfred L. Sanderson, 7 November 1978 -

Appendix C
SECRETARIES

Major William D. Beach, Cavalry, 1 July 1902 - 14 August 1903

Major Samuel Reber, Signal Corps, 15 August 1903 - 26 November 1906

Major Millard F. Waltz, Infantry, 27 November 1906 - 10 March 1907

Major Charles J. Bailey, Artillery, 11 March 1907 - 4 May 1908

Major John K. Cree, Coast Artillery Corps, 5 May 1908 - 13 December 1908

Major Henry D. Todd, Jr., Coast Artillery Corps, 14 December 1908 - 17 July 1910

Captain Joseph D. Leitch, Infantry, 18 July 1910 - 28 July 1913

Major Charles Crawford, Infantry, 29 July 1913 - 12 December 1915

Major Andrew Moses, Coast Artillery Corps, 13 December 1915 - 30 June 1916

Lieutenant Colonel Godfrey H. MacDonald, Cavalry, (Retired), 1 July 1916 - 16 January 1918

Major George P. Ahern, Infantry, (Retired), 24 January 1918 - 15 August 1919

EXECUTIVE OFFICERS
(From 1919 to 1941, the Secretary was called the Executive Officer)
Major James B. Gowen, Infantry, 16 August 1919 - 24 July 1922

Major Gilbert H. Stewart, Ordnance Corps, 25 July 1922 - 26 November 1922

Lieutenant Colonel Henry Gibbins, Quartermaster Corps, 27 November 1922 - 24 July 1924

Lieutenant Colonel John Fulmer, Infantry, 25 July 1924 - 21 January 1919

Major Simon B. Buckner, Infantry, 22 January 1929 - 4 July 1922

Colonel Kerr T. Riggs, Cavalry, 5 July 1932 - 4 July 1933

Major William F. Freehoff, Infantry, 5 July 1933 - 20 July 1936

Major Robert A. McClure, Infantry, 21 July 1936 - 28 June 1940

Lieutenant Colonel Peter J. Lloyd, Infantry, 29 June 1940 - 23 December 1941

SECRETARIES

Colonel Harry H. Critz, Artillery, April 1950 - September 1951

Colonel James M. Worthington, Artillery, September 1951 - August 1953

Colonel John A. Berry, Artillery, August 1953 - June 1955

Colonel George V. Underwood, Jr., Artillery, June 1955 - July 1957

Colonel Hal Hardenbergh, Infantry, July 1957 - June 1960

Colonel Donald H. McGovern, Infantry, June 1960 - June 1962

Colonel John H. Montgomery, Jr., Infantry, June 1962 - June 1963

Colonel Richard A. Broberg, Artillery, June 1963 - March 1965

Colonel William J. Gallagher, Artillery, March 1965 - 31 July 1967

Colonel Paul L. Bogen, Armor, 1 August 1967 - 30 June 1968

Colonel Robert A. Martin, Armor, 1 July 1968 - 3 June 1970

Colonel Richard A. Bresnahan, Infantry, 4 June 1970 - 14 September 1971

Colonel John O. Batiste, Infantry, 15 September 1971 - 1 May 1974

Colonel Adolph L. Belser, Quartermaster Corps, 1 May 1974 - 31 May 1976

Colonel William F. Schless, Infantry, 1 June 1976 -

Appendix D

DIRECTORS OF INSTRUCTION AND RESEARCH

Colonel Wilmot R. McCutchen, Corps of Engineers, 1 July 1965 - 28 February 1966

Colonel James G. Holland, Jr., Infantry, 1 March 1966 - 24 August 1967

Colonel Donald P. Boyer, Jr., Armor, 25 August 1967 - 1 April 1968

Colonel Urey W. Alexander, Artillery, 2 April 1968 - 21 July 1968

DIRECTORS OF INSTRUCTION

Colonel Urey W. Alexander, Artillery, 22 July 1968 - 14 June 1970

Colonel James A. Munson, Artillery, 15 June 1970 - 31 July 1970

Colonel Henry A. Barber III, Infantry, 1 August 1970 - 31 January 1973

DIRECTORS OF ACADEMIC AFFAIRS

Colonel Henry A. Barber III, Infantry, 1 February 1973 - 17 June 1973

Colonel Harold B. Birch (Acting), Infantry, 18 June 1973 - 5 May 1974

Dr. Charles M. Hersh, 6 May 1974 -

NOTES

NOTES

I. PRUDENS FUTURI

1. Ralph Waldo Emerson, "Civilization," Complete Works of Emerson, Vol. 7, p. 4.

II. HALLECK AND UPTON: THE PRELUDE

1. Russell F. Weigley, Towards an American Army, p. 166.
2. Henry W. Halleck, Elements of Military Art and Science, p. 406.
3. Ibid, p. 408.
4. Weigley, op. cit., p. 58.
5. Emory Upton, The Armies of Europe and Asia, p. iv.
6. Peter S. Michie, Life and Letters of General Emory Upton, p. 418.
7. Upton, op. cit., p. 367.
8. Stephen Ambrose, Upton and the Army, p. 122.
9. William H. Carter, Creation of the American General Staff, p. 1.
10. US War Department, Annual Report of the Secretary of War, 1899, p. 45.
11. Ibid., p. 49.
12. Carter, op. cit., p. 2.
13. US War Department, Special Order No. 42, 19 February 1900.

III. ROOT, LUDLOW, AND CARTER: 1899-1904

1. US Army, The Adjutant General, "Letter of Instruction to Brigadier General Ludlow," 20 February 1900.
2. William Ludlow, Report on Principles and Practical Methods Pursued in the Organization, Training, and Administration of the German, and Other Armies of Europe, 26 February 1901, p. 1.
3. Otto L. Nelson, Jr., National Security and the General Staff, p. 45.
4. Phillip C. Jessup, Elihu Root, p. 220.
5. US War Department, General Order No. 76, 1 June 1900.
6. William Ludlow, Letter Report to the Adjutant General, US Army, 31 October 1900.
7. Ibid.
8. Ibid.
9. Ibid.
10. William H. Carter, Memorandum for the Secretary of War, 14 October 1901.
11. Ibid.
12. US War Department, General Order No. 155, 27 November 1901.
13. US War Department, Annual Report of the Secretary of War, 1901, p. 25.
14. US War Department, Annual Report of the Secretary of War, 1902, p. 31.

15. Elihu Root, Statement before the Military Affairs Committee, US Senate, 17 December 1902, as cited in Establishment of a General Staff in the Army, Government Printing Office, 1902, p. 53.

16. Ibid., pp. 53-54.

17. US War Department, Annual Report of the Secretary of War, 1903, p. 8.

18. US Army War College, Ceremonies at the Laying of the Cornerstone of the Army War College Building, p. 10.

19. Ibid., p. 15.

20. Carter, Creation of the American General Staff, p. 54.

21. Ibid.

22. US War Department, General Order No. 2, 15 August 1903.

23. US Army, Letter from the Chief of Staff to the President, US Army War College, 27 October 1903.

24. US War Department, Annual Report of the Secretary of War, 1903, Vol. IV, p. 94.

25. Ibid., p. 95.

26. Ibid., p. 95.

27. Ibid., p. 97.

28. Ibid., p. 98.

29. M. Bartow Mercer, Memoranda Pertaining to the Establishment and Operation of the Army War College, pp. 17-20.

30. US War Department, General Order No. 115, 27 June 1904.

31. Ibid.

32. Ibid.

33. US War Department, General Order No. 155, 17 September 1904.

IV. BLISS AND WOTHERSPOON: 1905-1917

1. Mercer, op. cit., p. 26.

2. US Army War College, Memorandum of the President of the Army War College, 26 September 1904.

3. Ibid.

4. George B. Ahern, Army War College Chronicle, Vol. II, p. 39.

5. Ibid.

6. Tasker H. Bliss as quoted in Ahern, Ibid., p. 39.

7. Ibid.

8. US Army War College, File 619.1, Statue of Frederick the Great.

9. US Army War College, Scrapbook, pp. 10, 21, 59.

10. US War Department, General Order No. 115, 27 June 1904.

11. US Army, Letter from the Military Secretary of the General Staff to the President of the US Army War College, 9 June 1905.

12. Elihu Root as quoted by Ahern, op. cit., p. 45.

13. US Army War College, Memorandum No. 1, 20 October 1905.

14. US Army War College, Memorandum from the President of the US Army War College to the Chief of Staff, US Army, 12 October 1906.

15. Ibid.

16. Mercer, op. cit., p. 37a.

17. Ibid.

18. US Army War College, Memorandum of the President, US Army War College, 1 November 1906.

19. Ibid.

20. US Army War College, Letter from Lieutenant Colonel Smith S. Leach to Major Landis, 15 January 1907.

21. US Army War College, Exercises and Problems, 1906-07.

22. US War Department, Special Order No. 123, 1907.

23. US War Department, General Order No. 116, 28 May 1907.

24. US Army War College, Memorandum from the President of the US Army War College to the Chief of Staff, US Army, 28 May 1907.

25. US War Department, General Order No. 116, 28 May 1907.

26. US War Department, General Order No. 208, 9 October 1907.

27. US Army War College, Memorandum of the Secretary, 28 October 1907.

28. Mercer, op. cit., pp. 56-57.

29. Ahern, op. cit., p. 83.

30. US War Department, General Order No. 104, 24 June 1908.

31. US War Department, Second Section, Memorandum, 27 June 1908.

32. Ahern, op. cit., p. 73.

33. US Army War College, Memorandum from the President of the US Army War College to the Chief of Staff, US Army, 10 February 1908.

34. US Army War College, Memorandum from the President of the US Army War College to Army War College Personnel, 30 October 1908.

35. Ibid.

36. US Army War College, Lectures, 1908-09.

37. Elihu Root as quoted in The Army Navy Journal, 14 November 1908.

38. Elihu Root, The Military and Colonial Policy of the United States, p. 127.

39. Ahern, op. cit., p. 116.

40. US War Department, General Order No. 141, 19 June 1909.

41. Ahern, op. cit., p. 120.

42. Ibid., p. 123.

43. John A. Lejeune, Reminiscenses of a Marine, p. 187.

44. Ibid.

45. William W. Wotherspoon, Lecture to the Naval War College, August 1910.

46. US War Department General Staff, Memorandum from the Chief of the Second Section to the Chief of Staff, US Army, 31 August 1910.

47. Ibid.

48. Ibid.

49. US Army War College, File 352.01, Coat of Arms.

50. US War Department, General Order No. 115, 27 June 1904. See also Supra., p. 39.

51. US War Department, General Order No. 116, 28 May 1907.

52. US Army, Memorandum of the Chief of Staff, 26 September 1910.

53. Ibid.

54. US Army War College, Memorandum from the President of the US Army War College to the Chief of Staff, US Army, 23 July 1912.

55. US War Department, Annual Report of the Secretary of War, 1912, p. 235.

56. Ahern, op. cit., pp. 198-199.

57. Ibid.

58. Ibid.

59. US War Department, Special Order No. 130, 15 June 1913.

60. US Army, Memorandum from the Chief of Staff to the President of the US Army War College, 26 September 1913.

61. US War Department, General Order No. 13, 27 February 1914.

62. Ahern, op. cit., p. 204.

63. George A. Nugent, "The US Naval War College," The Journal of the US Artillery, XXXVII (March-April 1912).

64. US Army War College, Memorandum from the President of the US Army War College to the Chief of Staff, US Army, 4 February 1914.

65. US Army War College, Lectures, 1914-15.

66. US War Department, Letter from the Secretary of War to the President of the US Army War College, 17 April 1915.

67. Ahern, op. cit., p. 246.

68. Tasker, H. Bliss, Memorandum for the Record, as cited by Frederick Palmer in Bliss, Peacemaker, p. 106.

69. Ibid.

70. US War Department, Bulletin No. 16, 22 June 1916.

71. Ahern, op, cit., p. 262.

V. THE TESTING OF THE BLADE: WORLD WAR I

1. US Army, Annual Report of the Chief of Staff, 22 September 1917, p. 127.

2. US War Department, Annual Report of the Secretary of War, 1903, Vol. IV, p. 95. See also Supra., p. 32.

3. Leonard P. Ayers, The War with Germany, A Statistical Summary, pp. 16, 25-35, 37-48, and 101-118.

4. Computed from raw data in Memorandum from Chief, Historical Section, US Army War College, to Commandant, 22 October 1923.

5. US Army, Annual Report of the Chief of Staff, 1917, p. 127.

6. US War Department, Annual Report of the Secretary of War, 1918, p. 84.

VI. McANDREW CHARTS A NEW COURSE: 1919-1940

1. US War Department, Annual Report of the Secretary of War, 1919, p. 27.

2. Ibid.

3. Ibid.

4. Ibid.

5. US Army General Staff College (Later redesignated US Army War College), Annual Report of the Commandant of the US Army General Staff College, 22 July 1920, p. 1.

6. Ibid.

7. James W. McAndrew, Lecture at the US Naval War College, 22 October 1919, p. 2.

8. Ibid.

9. Nelson, op. cit, pp. 282-290.

10. McAndrew, op. cit., p. 5.

11. Ibid.

12. Ibid., p. 8.

13. US Army General Staff College (US Army War College), Memorandum from the Commandant to the Chief of Staff, US Army, 26 July 1919.

14. McAndrew, op. cit., p. 7.

15. Ibid., p. 9.

16. US Army General Staff College (US Army War College) Memorandum from the Commandant to the Chief of Staff, US Army, op. cit.

17. McAndrew, op. cit., p. 9.

18. US War Department, Circular No. 286, 3 June 1919.

19. Ibid.

20. US War Department, General Order No. 99, 7 August 1919.

21. US War Department, General Order No. 112, 23 September 1919.

22. US War Department, General Order No. 7, 3 January 1920.

23. US War Department, General Order No. 40, 15 August 1921.

24. Peyton C. March, Address at the Opening Ceremony, US Army General Staff College (US Army War College), 2 September 1919.

25. R. M. Johnson, Memorandum to the Commandant, US Army General Staff College Staff College (US Army War College), 30 July 1919.

26. US Army, Letter from the Adjutant General to the Commandant, US Army General Staff College (US Army War College), 24 September 1919.

27. US War Department, Letter from Chief of the War Plans Division, General Staff, to the Commandant, US Army General Staff College (US Army War College), 23 April 1919.

28. Ibid.

29. US Army General Staff College (US Army War College), Series of Memoranda from Faculty to the Commandant, reference Haan letter, April 1919.

30. US Army General Staff College (US Army War College), Letter from the Commandant to the Chief, War Plans Division, US War Department General Staff, April 1920.

31. US War Department, Letter from the Chief of the War Plans Division, General Staff, to the Commandant, US Army General Staff College (US Army War College), 18 March 1921.

32. US War Department, Letter from the Chief of the War Plans Division, General Staff, to the Commandant, US Army General Staff College (US Army War College), 12 July 1920.

33. George C. Marshall, Letter to the Commandant, US Army General Staff College (US Army War College), 9 July 1920.

34. US Army, Memorandum from the Chief of Staff to the Joint Board, 30 March 1920.

54. Ibid.

55. US Army War College, Letters from the Commandant to the Chief of Staff, US Army, 6 December 1921 and 18 April 1922.

56. US Army, Letter from the Chief of Staff, US Army, to the Commandant, US Army War College, 2 June 1922.

57. US Army War College, Correspondence between the Commandant and the Chief of Staff, US Army, May-July 1922.

58. US Army, Letter from the Chief of Staff, US Army, to the Commandant, US Army War College, 2 June 1922.

59. Edward F. McGlachlin, Address at Graduation Exercises for the Class of 1923, 28 June 1923.

60. Ibid.

61. Ibid.

62. Ibid.

63. Ibid.

64. Ridley McLean, Letter to the Secretary of the Navy, 3 January 1922.

65. Ibid.

66. Ibid.

67. G. J. Meyers, Memorandum to the Secretary of the Navy, 1 June 1924.

68. John J. Pershing, Address to the Class of 1925, 2 September 1924.

69. Ibid.

70. Ibid.

71. US War Department, Correspondence between the Chief of the War Plans Division, General Staff, and the Commandant, US Army War College, November 1924.

72. US War Department, Correspondence between the Secretary of War and the Commandant, US Army War College, March 1925.

73. Ibid.

74. US Army, Letter from the Adjutant General to the Commandant, US Army War College, 22 December 1927.

75. US Army, Correspondence between the Chief of Staff, US Army, and the Commandant, US Army War College, April 1927.

76. US Army, Correspondence between the Adjutant General and the Commandant, US Army War College, 1933-1939.

77. William D. Connor, Letter to the Chief of Staff, US Army, 25 August 1916.

78. William D. Connor, Address to the Class of 1929, 1 September 1928.

79. US Army, Correspondence between the Adjutant General and the Commandant, US Army War College, October 1938.

80. Troup Miller, Correspondence with the Commandant, US Army War College, June 1936.

81. Ibid.

82. US Army War College, Student Comments, 1936-37.

83. A. J. Young, Correspondence with the Commandant, US Army War College, December 1938.

84. US Army War College, The German Campaign in Poland, 1 February 1940.

85. US Army, Letter from the Adjutant General to the Commandant, US Army War College, 11 June 1940.

VII. THE SECOND TESTING: WORLD WAR II

1. D. E. Cummings, Memorandum for Naval Instructors at the US Army War College, 23 May 1935.

2. Army Almanac, p. 111.

3. US Army War College, Statistical Analysis, 1920-1940.

4. Dwight D. Eisenhower, Address to the US Army War College, 21 August 1966.

5. Winston Churchill, Address to the General Staff, US Army, 19 April 1946.

VIII. THE JOINT ERA: 1945-1950

1. US War Department, Report of the War Department Military Education Board, 1946, p. 10.

2. Ibid., p. 27.

3. Ibid., p. 10.

4. US War Department, Circular No. 117, 23 April 1946.

5. US War Department, Final Report of the War Department Policies and Programs Review Board, 11 August 1947.

6. US Army, Memorandum from the Acting Director of Organization and Training to the Chief of Staff, US Army, 28 July 1948.

7. US Army, Report of the Department of the Army Board on an Education System for Officers, 15 June 1949, pp. 12-13.

8. US Army, Modifications to the Report of the Department of the Army Board an Education System for Officers, 11 October 1949.

9. Ibid.

10. Harry L. Hillyard, Does the Army Need a War College?

11. Ibid.

12. E. M. Starr, Memorandum for the Director of Organization and Training, Depart of the Army, 10 October 1949.

13. US Army, Letter from the Adjutant General to the Board for Establishment of an Army War College, 4 October 1949.

14. US Army, Interim Report of the Board for Establishment of an Army War College, 24 October 1949.

15. John R. Beishline, Memorandum for Record, Office of the Secretary of the General Staff, US Army, 30 November 1949.

16. W. H. Hastings, Letter from Office of Chief of Engineers, US Army, to the Commandant, US Army Command and General Staff College, 4 March 1949.

17. US Army Command and General Staff College, Telegram from the Commandant to the Chief of Engineers, US Army, 22 May 1949.

IX. A NEW ERA BEGINS: 1950-1957

1. US Army Command and General Staff College, Memorandum of the Deputy Commandant, 10 February 1949.

2. US Army Field Forces, Report of Board on Army Education System for Commissioned Officers, 20 January 1949.

3. Ibid.

4. US Army Command and General Staff College, Report of Committee for Curriculum for Army War College, 8 March 1949.

5. Ibid.

6. US Army Command and General Staff College, Letter from the Assistant Commandant, 16 September 1949.

7. US Army, Report of Department of the Army Board on an Educational System for Officers, 15 June 1949.

8. US Army Command and General Staff College, Report of Board of Officers on Army War College, November 1949.

9. Ibid.

10. Melvin Zais, Interview, 14 February 1967.

11. US Army War College, Curriculum, 1950-51.

12. Ibid.

13. US Army War College, Report of the President, US Army War College, as cited in the Annual Report of the Secretary of War, 1903, p. 95.

14. US Army War College, Curriculum, 1951-52.

15. US Army War College, Report of the Civilian Advisory Group, January 1952.

16. Ibid. (All quotations used in the discussion of the 1952 Civilian Advisory Group have been takent from their report.)

17. Department of the Army, Special Regulation 350-5-4, 30 July 1953.

18. Department of the Army, Special Regulation 350-20-1, 17 March 1952.

19. Department of the Army, Circular No. 16, 3 March 1952.

20. Ibid.

21. US Army War College, Final Report, Course 4, "Operations and Training," 31 January 1952, p. i.

22. Ibid., p. 24.

23. US Army Field Forces, Letter from the Commanding General to the Commandant, US Army War College, 8 February 1952.

24. US Army, Letter from the Chief of Staff, US Army, to the Commanding General, Army Field Forces, 11 April 1952, as cited by Whitson in US Army War College and National Security, p. 170.

25. US Army, Memorandum of the Deputy Chief ot Staff for Operations and Administration, 15 August 1951.

26. Ibid.

27. US Army War College, Correspondence with the George Washington University and the American Council of Education, January-March 1952.

28. US Army War College, Minutes of Faculty Board Meeting, 23 July 1953.

29. US Army War College, Memorandum, Duties of General Staff Group of the Faculty, 22 July 1952.

30. James H. Polk, Memorandum, Projects to Enhance the Prestige of the Army War College, 25 June 1953.

31. Ibid.

32. Ibid.

33. Ibid.

34. US Army War College, Final Report, Course 1, 19 October 1954.

35. US Army War College, Curriculum 1953-54, p. 9.

36. Whitson, op. cit., p. 173.

37. US Army War College, Curriculum, 1953-54, p. 11.

38. US Army War College, Minutes of Faculty Board Meeting, 6 July 1953.

39. US Army War College, Letter from the Commandant to the Chief of Staff, US Army, 5 January 1954.

40. Ibid.

41. US Army War College, Minutes of Faculty Board Meeting, 10 December 1953.

42. US Army War College, Final Report, Course 1, 23 October 1953.

43. US Army War College, Memorandum from Chairman, Faculty Group I, to the Deputy Commandant, 9 November 1953.

44. Ibid.

45. US Army War College, Report of the Civilian Advisory Group, January 1954.

46. Ibid.

47. Ibid.

48. Ibid., p. 1.

49. Ibid.

50. Ibid., p. 7.

51. Ibid., P. 8.

52. Ibid.

53. US Army War College, Memorandum, 24 September 1954.

54. Ibid.

55. Ibid.
56. US Army War College, Report of the Secretary, 22 October 1954.
57. Ibid.
58. Ibid.
59. US Army Continental Army Command, Instruction of the Army's Role in Civil Emergencies in the United States, 24 February 1956.
60. US Army Continental Army Command, Letter to US Army War College, Preparation of Doctrinal Material, 7 January 1956.
61. Whitson, op. cit., p. 175.
62. US Army War College, Curriculum 1955-56.
63. Whitson, op. cit., p. 170.

X. IN SUPPORT OF NATIONAL STRATEGY: 1957-1963

1. Chester L. Johnson, Memorandum, The Role of Studies in the Social Sciences as a Part of the AWC Curriculum, 5 February 1957.
2. Whitson, op. cit., p. 179.
3. Johnson, op. cit.
4. US Army War College, Curriculum, 1956-57.
5. US Army War College, Memorandum for the Commandant, Comprehensive Review of Army War College Curriculum, 13 September 1957.
6. Ibid.
7. US Army War College, Review of the George Washington University Program, 14 March 1963.
8. Cloyd L. Marvin, Letter from the President, The George Washington University, to the Commandant, US Army War College, 23 January 1952.
9. US Army War College, Letter to Members of the Class of 1965, 15 March 1964.
10. US Army War College, Letter from the Commandant to the President, The George Washington University, 14 May 1961.
11. Ibid.
12. Ibid.
13. US Army War College, Letter from the Commandant to the President, The George Washington University, 20 July 1961.
14. The George Washington University, Letter from the President, The George Washington University, to the Commandant, US Army War College, 29 August 1961.
15. US Army War College, Letter from the Commandant to the President, The George Washington University, 22 May 1961.
16. Ibid.
17. The decision was made subsequent to and at the recommendation of the 1966 Department of the Army Board to Review Army Officer Schools (Haines Board). Other Board actions, recommendations, and decisions will be reviewed elsewhere.
18. US Army War College File, Office of the Director of Instruction and Research, 1965.
19. US Army War College, Letter from the Commandant to the Deputy Chief of Staff for Personnel, Department of the Army, 19 April 1966.
20. US Army, General Order No. 19, 16 June 1960.
21. US Army Combat Developments Command, General Order No. 5, 21 June 1962.
22. US Army War College, General Order No. 1, 20 June 1962.

23. US Army War College, Memorandum from the Deputy Commandant to the Faculty, 30 September 1960.

24. US Army War College, Curriculum, 1961-62.

25. US Army War College, Report of the Civilian Advisory Group, February 1962, p. 1.

26. Ibid.

27. Ibid., p. 2.

28. Ibid.

29. Ibid., p. 4.

30. Ibid., p. 7.

31. Ibid., p. 8.

32. Ibid.

33. Ibid., p. 10.

34. Ibid., p. 11.

35. Ibid., p. 13.

36. Ibid.

37. Ibid.

38. Ibid.

39. Ibid., p. 16.

40. Ibid., p. 19.

XI. EMPHASIS ON THE ROLE OF THE ARMY: 1963-1966

1. US Army War College, Minutes of the Curriculum Board Meeting, 27 June 1964.

2. US Army War College, Minutes of the Curriculum Board Meeting, 8 September 1964.

3. Eugene A. Salet, Interview, 9 March 1967.

4. Ibid.

5. Ibid.

6. Ward S. Ryan, Memorandum, November 1964.

7. Ibid.

8. Ibid.

9. Ibid.

10. US Army War College, Minutes of the Curriculum Board Meeting, 21 December 1964.

11. US Army War College, Report of the Lange Committee, 7 December 1964.

12. US Army War College, Letter from the Commandant to the Assistant Chief of Staff for Force Development, Department of the Army, 15 March 1965.

13. US Army War College, Closing Address of the Commandant to the Class of 1923. See also Supra., p. 115.

14. US Army War College, Letter from the Commandant to the Assistant Chief of Staff for Force Development, Department of the Army, 15 March 1965.

15. Ibid.

16. Ibid.

17. US Army War College, Report of the Committee on Faculty Development, 15 March 1965.

18. Ibid.

19. Ibid.

20. Ibid.
21. Ibid.
22. US Army War College, Memorandum No. 600-2, 15 September 1966.
23. Russell O. Fudge, "Paging Colonel Mahan," Army, January 1961.
24. Ibid.
25. George S. Pappas, The Voice of the Turtle Is Heard, April 1966.
26. US Army War College, Letter from the Commandant to the Assistant Chief of Staff for Force Development, Department of the Army, 15 March 1965.
27. Earle G. Wheeler, Letter to the Commandant, US Army War College, 16 May 1965.
28. US Army War College, Letter from the Commandant to the Assistant Chief of Staff for Force Development, Department of the Army, 15 March 1965.
29. US Army, Report of the Department of the Army Board to Review Army Officer Schools, Vol. I, "Summary and Recommendations," February 1966, p. 4.
30. Ralph E. Haines, Jr., Briefing for the Chief of Staff, US Army, February 1966.
31. Ibid.
32. US Army, Army Regulation No. 350-5, 26 October 1966.
33. Ibid.
34. US Army, Haines Board Report, Vol. II, p. 223.
35. Ibid.
36. Ibid.
37. See discussion, Supra. p. 224.
38. See discussion, Supra. pp. 243-244.
39. US Army, Haines Board Report, Appendix 5, p. 492.
40. Edward L. Katzenbach, Jr., "The Demotion of Professionalism at the War Colleges," United States Naval Institute Proceedings, Vol. XCI, No. 3, March 1965, p. 36.
41. US Army, Haines Board Report, Ibid.
42. Ibid.
43. Ibid.
44. Ibid., pp. 78-496.
45. Ibid., P. 491.
46. See discussion, Infra. p. 281.
47. See discussion, Supra. p. 220.
48. See discussion, Infra. p. 269.
49. See discussion, Supra. pp. 203-208.
50. US Army, Haines Board Report, p. 494.
51. Ibid.
52. Salet, op. cit.

XII. "WHERE ARE WE TODAY?"

1. Howard L. Rubendall, Graduation Address to the Class of 1966, US Army War College, 13 June 1966.
2. See discussion, Supra. p. 187.
3. US Army War College, Report of the Board of Consultants, 23 February 1967, p. 3.
4. Ibid.
5. Ibid.

6. Ibid., p. 2.
7. Ibid., p. 3.
8. Ibid., p. 4.
9. See discussion, Supra. p. 272.
10. See discussion, Infra. p. 258.
11. US Army War College, Report of the Board of Consultants, op. cit., p. 4.
12. Eugene A. Salet, Letter to the Alumni, US Army War College, 2 June 1967.

BIBLIOGRAPHY

BIBLIOGRAPHY

Ahern, George B. Army War College Chronicle. First Draft. Bound typescript in the US Army Military History Research Collection, Carlisle Barracks, Pa.

———————— Army War College Chronicle. Second Draft. Bound typescript in the US Army Military History Research Collection, Carlisle Barracks, Pa.

———————— Army War College Chronicle. Vol I., 1899-1917. Unpublished manuscript in the US Army Military History Research Collection, Carlisle Barracks, Pa.

Almond, Edward M. Army War College Curriculum, 1952-53. Briefing for the Commanding General, Army Field Forces, 12 June 1952. US Army Military History Research Collection, Carlisle Barracks, Pa.

Ambrose, Stephen E. Upton and the Army. Baton Rouge: Louisiana State University Press, 1964.

Armstrong, DeVer. Study on the Army War College, 13 August 1953. Bound typescript in the US Army Military History Research Collection, Carlisle Barracks, Pa.

Army Almanac. Harrisburg, Pa.: The Stackpole Company, 1959.

Army Navy Journal, 14 November 1908.

Ayers, Leonard P. The War with Germany, A Statistical Summary. Washington, D. C.: US Government Printing Office, 1919.

Bailey, Edward A. Analysis of the Thesis Program, US Army War College, 1950-58. Unpublished thesis study, US Army War College, 1958.

Baldwin, Hanson. "President Presses Merger of Services' War College." The New York Times, 20 January 1960, p. 1.

Beishline, John R. Memorandum for the Record, Office of the Secretary of the General Staff, US Army, 30 November 1949. US Army Military History Research Collection, Carlisle Barracks, Pa.

Bernard, Henry. Military Schools and Courses of Instruction in the Science of Art and War.

Berry, John A., Jr. Report of the Secretary, US Army War College, 22 October 1954. US Army Military History Research Collection, Carlisle Barracks, Pa.

Bingham, T. A. "The Prussian Great General Staff and What It Contains That Is Practical from an American Standpoint." Journal of the Military Service Institution, Vol. XIII, July 1892, pp. 666-76.

Brown, Lytle. "The United States Army War College." The Military Engineer, Vol. XIX, No. 106, July-August 1927, pp. 294-97.

Carter, William H. The American Army. Indianapolis, Ind.: Bobbs-Merrill Company, 1915.

———————— "Can the General Staff Corps Fulfill Its Mission?" Journal of the Military Service Institution, Vol. LVIII, No. 201, May-June 1916, pp. 337-351.

———————— Creation of the American General Staff. Senate Document No. 119, 68th Congress, 1st Session. Washington: US Government Printing Office, 1924.

———————— "Elihu Root—His Services as Secretary of War." The North American Review, Vol. CLXXVIII, No. 566, January 1904, pp. 110-121.

———————— "The Evolution of Army Reforms." The United Service, Vol. III, May 1903, pp. 1190-1197.

Chappel, Paul. Memorandum, "Peer Rating System," 29 July 1957. US Army Military History Research Collection, Carlisle Barracks, Pa.

Churchill, Winston S. "Address to the General Staff of the US Army." Congressional Record, 19 April 1946, pp. A2308-09.

Conn, Stetson. The Army War College, 1899-1940. Bound typescript in the US Army Military History Research Collection, Carlisle Barracks, Pa.

Connor, William D. Address to the Class of 1929, US Army War College. 1 September 1928. US Army Military History Research Collection, Carlisle Barracks, Pa.

————— Letter to the Chief of Staff, US Army, 25 August 1916. National Archives, Record Group 165.

Cummings, Damon E. Memorandum for Naval Instructors at the US Army War College, 23 May 1935. US Army Military History Research Collection, Carlisle Barracks, Pa.

————— "William Wotherspoon." Shipmate, Vol. XXVII, No. 2, February 1964, pp. 6-11.

Dodson, M. B. US Regular Army Officers and Graduate Degrees. 8 March 1963. Unpublished thesis study, US Army War College, Carlisle Barracks, Pa.

Eisenhower, Dwight D. Address to the US Army War College. 21 August 1966. US Army Military History Research Collection, Carlisle Barracks, Pa.

Emerson, Ralph Waldo. "Civilization." Complete Works of Emerson, Vol. VII. Riverside Edition. Boston: Houghton, Mifflin Co., 1899.

Establishment of a General Staff in the Army. Washington, D. C.: US Government Printing Office, 1902.

Fudge, Russel O. "Paging Colonel Mahan." Army, Vol. II, No. 6, January 1961, pp. 58-64.

Ganoe, William A. The History of the United States Army. Revised Edition. New York: D. Appleton-Century Co., 1943.

George Washington University. Letter from the President, The George Washington University, to the Commandant, US Army War College, 29 August 1961. US Army Military History Research Collection, Carlisle Barracks, Pa.

Haines, Ralph E., Jr. Briefing for the Chief of Staff, US Army, February 1966. US Army Military History Research Collection, Carlisle Barracks, Pa.

Halleck, Henry W. Elements of Military Art and Science. 3d ed. New York: D. Appleton & Co., 1863.

Harbord, John G. "The American General Staff." The Saturday Evening Post, 13 March 1926, pp. 31, 189-190, 193-194, 197-198, 201.

Hardin, J. T. Memorandum to Deputy Commandant, US Army War College, "Curricular Theme," 27 March 1959. US Army Military History Research Collection, Carlisle Barracks, Pa.

Hastings, W. H. Letter to the Commandant, US Army Command and General Staff College, 4 March 1949. US Army Military History Research Collection, Carlisle Barracks, Pa.

Hillyard, Harry L. Does the Army Need a War College? Unpublished thesis study, Air War College, Maxwell Air Force Base, Ala., 1949.

Hittle, J. D. The Military Staff. 2d ed. Harrisburg, Pa.: Military Service Publishing Co., 1949.

Hooper, E. C. Words without End. 22 April 1966. Unpublished thesis study, US Army War College, Carlisle Barracks, Pa.

Jessup, Phillip C. Elihu Root. New York: Dodd, Mead, & Company, 1938.

Johnson, Chester L. Memorandum, The Role of Studies in the Social Sciences as a Part of the AWC Curriculum, 5 February 1957. US Army Military History Research Collection, Carlisle Barracks, Pa.

Johnson, R. M. Memorandum to the Commandant, US Army General Staff College, 30 July 1919. US Army Military History Research Collection, Carlisle Barracks, Pa.

Johnson, Virginia W. The Unregimented General, A Biography of Nelson A. Miles. Boston: Houghton Mifflin Company, 1962.

Katzenbach, Edward L., Jr. "The Demotion of Professionalism at the War Colleges." United States Naval Institute Proceedings, Vol. XCI, No. 3, March 1965, pp. 36-41.

Leach, Smith S. Letter to Major Landis, 15 January 1907. US Army Military History Research Collection, Carlisle Barracks, Pa.

Lejeune, John A. Reminiscences of a Marine. Philadelphia: Dorrance and Company, 1930.

Leopold, Richard W. Elihu Root and the Conservative Tradition. Boston: Little Brown and Company, 1954.

Logan, E. O. Is a Thesis a Necessity at the Army War College? 25 January 1960. Unpublished thesis study, US Army War College, Carlisle Barracks, Pa.

Ludlow, William. Letter report to the Adjutant General, US Army, 31 October 1900. US Army Military History Research Collection, Carlisle Barracks, Pa.

——————— Report on Principles and Practical Methods Pursued in the Organization Training, and Administration of the German and Other Armies of Europe, 26 February 1901. Unpublished report in the National War College Library, Ft. McNair, Washington, D. C.

McAndrew, James W. Lecture at the US Naval War College. 22 October 1919. US Army Military History Research Collection, Carlisle Barracks, Pa.

——————— Orientation of the Class of 1921. 2 September 1921. US Army Military History Research Collection, Carlisle Barracks, Pa.

McGlachlin, Edward F., Jr. Closing Address at Graduation Exercises for the Class of 1923, US Army War College. 28 June 1923. US Army Military History Research Collection, Carlisle Barracks, Pa.

McLean, Ridley. Letter to the Secretary of the Navy. 3 January 1922. US Army Military History Research Collection, Carlisle Barracks, Pa.

March, Peyton C. Address at the Opening Ceremony, US Army General Staff College. 2 September 1919. US Army Military History Research Collection, Carlisle Barracks, Pa.

Marshall, George C. Letter to the Commandant, US Army General Staff College, 9 July 1920. US Army Military History Research Collection, Carlisle Barracks, Pa.

Marvin, Cloyd L. Letter to the Commandant, US Army War College, 23 January 1952. US Army Military History Research Collection, Carlisle Barracks, Pa.

Mercer, M. Bartow. Memoranda Pertaining to the Establishment and Operation of the Army War College. 1907. Unpublished manuscript in the National War College Library, Ft. McNair, Washington, D. C.

Meyers, George J. Memorandum to the Secretary of the Navy. 1 June 1924. US Army Military History Research Collection, Carlisle Barracks, Pa.

Michie, Peter S. Life and Letters of Emory Upton. New York: D. Appleton and Co., 1885.

Military Education Coordination Conferences, 1960-67. These reports discuss agenda items reviewed at the annual conferences of the commandants of the senior service schools of the various Armed Forces. US Army Military History Research Collection, Carlisle Barracks, Pa.

Miller, Troup. Correspondence with the Commandant, US Army War College. June 1936. US Army Military History Research Collection, Carlisle Barracks, Pa.

Mohlere, E. D. USAWC Graduate Requirement Study—Some Preliminary Considerations. 18 January 1963. US Army Military History Research Collection, Carlisle Barracks, Pa.

Nelson, H. E. Proposed Changes in the Curricular Theme and the Final Course of the Curriculum, 1963-64. US Army Military History Research Collection, Carlisle Barracks, Pa.

Nelson, Otto L., Jr. National Security and the General Staff. Washington, D. C.: The Infantry Journal Press, 1946.

Nugent, George A. "The U.S. Naval War College," The Journal of the U.S. Artillery, Vol. XXXVII, March-April 1912, pp. 148-152.

Palmer, Frederick. Bliss, Peacemaker. New York: Dodd, Mead, & Company, 1934.

Pappas, George S. The Voice of the Turtle Is Heard. Unpublished thesis study, US Army War College, April 1966.

Pershing, John J. Address to the Class of 1925, US Army War College. US Army Military History Research Collection, Carlisle Barracks, Pa.

———————— Address at the Graduation Exercises, US Army General Staff College. 29 June 1920. US Army Military History Research Collection, Carlisle Barracks, Pa.

———————— Report of the Commander-in-Chief, American Expeditionary Forces. Included in the Annual Report of the Secretary of War, 1918.

Pochyla, Benjamin H. To Develop an Outline for Civil Defense Coverage in USAWC Curriculum 1958-59. 3 June 1958. US Army Military History Research Collection, Carlisle Barracks, Pa.

Polk, James H. Projects to Enhance the Prestige of the Army War College. 25 June 1953. US Army Military History Research Collection, Carlisle Barracks, Pa.

Reeves, Ira L. Military Education in the United States. Burlington, Vt.: Free Press Printing Co., 1914.

Root, Elihu. The Military and Colonial Policy of the United States. Cambridge, Mass.: Harvard University Press, 1926.

———————— Establishment of a General Staff in the Army. Washington, D. C.: US Goverment Printing Office, 1902.

Rubendall, Howard L. Graduation Address to the Class of 1966, US Army War College. 13 June 1966. US Army Military History Research Collection, Carlisle Barracks, Pa.

Ryan, Ward S. Memorandum. November 1964. US Army Military History Research Collection, Carlisle Barracks, Pa.

Salet, Eugene A. Commandant, US Army War College, Interview, 9 March 1967.

———————— Letter to the Alumni, US Army War College, 2 June 1967. US Army Military History Research Collection, Carlisle Barracks, Pa.

Saunders, Oswald H. "The Army War College." The Military Engineer, Vol. XXVI., No. 146, March-April 1934, pp. 101-104.

Schwan, Theodore. Report on the Organization of the German Army. Washington, D. C.: US Government Printing Office, 1894.

———————— Duties of the General Staff Based upon Study of the German Army. Address before the General Staff. Washington, D. C.: US Government Printing Office, 1903.

Sims, William S. Lecture at the US Army General Staff College. 23 September 1920. US Army Military History Research Collection, Carlisle Barracks, Pa.

Bibliography

Spalding, Oliver L. The United States Army in War and Peace. New York: G. P. Putnam's Sons, 1937.

Spencer, P. N. Reflections of a Student Officer and the Reply of the Commandant of the US Army .War College. 2 July 1963. US Army Military History Research Collection, Carlisle Barracks, Pa.

Stansfield, George J. History of the Army War College at Washington, D. C., 1899-1917. Unpublished manuscript, August 1964.

————————— Army War College, 1901-1941. Unpublished manuscript, March 1964.

Starr, E. M. Memorandum for the Director of Organization and Training, US Army. 10 October 1949. US Army Military History Research Collection, Carlisle Barracks, Pa.

Stuart, C. E. Educational Philosophy and the US Army War College. 1958. Unpublished thesis study, US Army War College, Carlisle Barracks, Pa.

Summerall, Charles P. Brief History of the General Staff. Unpublished manuscript in the US Army Military History Research Collection, Carlisle Barracks, Pa.

Swift, Eben. "An American Pioneer in the Cause of Military Education, Arthur L. Wagner." Journal of the Military Service Institution, Vol. XLIV, No. 67, January-February 1909, p. 67.

————————— "Military Education of Officers in Time of Peace." Journal of the US Artillery, Vol. XXXIII, No. 3, May-June 1910.

US Army Combat Developments Command. General Order Number 5. 21 June 1962.

US Army Command and General Staff College. Instructions from the Commandant, US Army Command and General Staff College, to Board Planning the Advanced Course, 6 September 1949.

————————— Letter from the Deputy Commandant. 16 September 1949.

————————— Memorandum of the Deputy Commandant. 10 February 1949.

————————— Report of Committee for Curriculum for Army War College. 8 March 1949.

————————— Report of Board of Officers on Army War College. November 1949.

————————— Telegram from the Commandant, US Army Command and General Staff College, to the Chief of Engineers, US Army, 22 May 1949.

US Army Continental Army Command. Letter, Headquarters, CONARC, to the Commandant. US Army War College: Preparation of Doctrinal Material. 7 January 1956.

————————— Letter, Headquarters, CONARC: Instruction of the Army's Role in Civil Emergencies in the United States. 24 February 1956.

US Army Field Forces. Letter from the Commanding General to the Commandant, US Army War College. 8 February 1952.

————————— Report of Board on Army Educational System for Commissioned Officers. 20 January 1949. US Army War College Files, Carlisle Barracks, Pa.

US Army War College. Entries under each major category (Letters, Memoranda, Reports, etc.) are arranged chronologically by date. The source materials listed can be found in the US Army Military History Research Collection, Carlisle Barracks, Pa., unless otherwise indicated. All references to the US Army General Staff College are listed under the US Army War College.

Advantages and Disadvantages of Placing the Army War College Directly under Department of the Army, 8 February 1956.

Annual Report of the Commandant, US Army General Staff College. 22 July 1920.

Appointment of Civilian Directors of Studies to Faculty of Army War College. 29 March 1955.

Bibliography

Army War College Chronicle. Vol. II. (Vol. I is listed under Ahern, George B.) Unpublished manuscript in the US Army War College Library, Carlisle Barracks, Pa.

Army War College Graduates in World War I. Bound typescript prepared by the Historical Section, US Army War College.

Buildings and Grounds, 1950-1967.

Ceremonies at the Laying of the Cornerstone of the Army War College Building. Washington, D. C.: US Government Printing Office, 1903.

Certificates, Degrees, and Diplomas.

Coat of Arms.

Comments of Committees on the Historical Ride, 1911-1912. Bound typescript in the US Army War College Library, Carlisle Barracks, Pa.

Correspondence between the Commandant, US Army War College, and the Chief of Staff, US Army. May-July 1922.

Correspondence with the George Washington University and the American Council of Education. January-March 1952.

Course of Instruction, 1905-1940. Bound typescript volumes containing course outlines, lectures, problems, exercises, individual and committee reports, and other course materials.

Curriculum Guidance, 1964-65.

Curriculum Substance and Methodology, 1964.

Curriculum Pamphlets, Course Directives, and miscellaneous publications issued annually for each course of instruction, 1950-1967.

Doctrinal Studies Depicting the Role of the Army in Modern Warfare.

Establishment of the Plans and Policy Group. 11 February 1959.

Establishment of the US Army War College Faculty Committee for Strategic Analysis. 9 April 1964.

Factors Affecting Curricular Concept for 1957-58.

Faculty Report. 25 June 1953.

Faculty/USACDCIAS Seminar Program Directive. 1 August 1964.

Files of the Director of Instruction and Research, 1965.

Final Reports. Submitted at conclusion of each course of instruction, 1951-1967. These reports include a summary of the course, student and faculty comments, and the recommendations of the course director.

General Order 1, 20 June 1962.

The German Campaign in Poland. 1 February 1940.

Graduation and Opening Exercises.

Guide for Preparation of Student Papers, 1952.

The Heaton Picture of Von Steuben at Valley Forge.

History of the General Staff and Organization Charts. 1912. Bound typescript in the US Army War College Library, Carlisle Barracks, Pa.

Individual Studies To Be Prepared by Faculty Members. 24 August 1954.

Letter from the President, US Army War College, to P. P. Buck. 13 September 1906. National Archives, Record Group 165.

Letter from the Secretary, US Army War College to the President, US Army War College. 17 April 1915.

Letter from the Commandant, US Army General Staff College, to the Chief, War Plans Division, War Department General Staff. April 1920.

Letter from the Commandant, US Army War College, to the Assistant Chief of Staff, US Army. 1 November 1921.

Letter from the Commandant, US Army War College, to the Chief of Staff, US Army. 6 December 1921.

Letter from the Commandant, US Army War College, to the Chief of Staff, US Army. 18 April 1922.

Letter from the Commandant, US Army War College, to the Chief of Staff, US Army. 8 February 1952.

Letter from the Commandant, US Army War College, to the Chief, Career Management, Department of the Army. 5 August 1953.

Letter from the Commandant, US Army War College, to the Chief of Staff, US Army. 5 January 1954.

Letter from the Commandant, US Army War College, to the President, the George Washington University. 14 May 1961.

Letter from the Commandant, US Army War College, to the President, the George Washington University. 22 May 1961.

Letter from the Commandant, US Army War College, to the President, the George Washington University. 20 July 1961.

Letter to Members of the Class of 1965, US Army War College. 15 March 1964.

Letter from the Commandant, US Army War College, to the Assistant Chief of Staff for Force Development. 6 November 1964.

Letter from the Commandant, US Army War College, to the Assistant Chief of Staff for Force Development, Department of the Army. 15 March 1965.

Letter from the Commandant, US Army War College, to the Deputy Chief of Staff for Personnel, Department of the Army. 19 April 1966.

Memorandum of the President of the US Army War College. 26 September 1904.

Memorandum, 20 October 1905.

Memorandum from the President of the US Army War College to the Chief of Staff, US Army. 12 October 1906. National Archives, Record Group 165.

Memorandum of the President of the US Army War College. 1 November 1906.

Memorandum from the President of the US Army War College to the Chief of Staff, US Army. 28 May 1907. National Archives, Record Group 165.

Memorandum of the Secretary, US Army War College. 28 October 1907.

Memorandum from the President, US Army War College, to the Chief of Staff, US Army. 10 February 1908.

Memorandum from the President, US Army War College, to War College Personnel. 30 October 1908.

Memorandum of the President, US Army War College. 29 November 1908. National Archives, Record Group 165.

Memorandum from the President of the US Army War College to the Chief of Staff, US Army. 23 July 1912.

Memorandum from the President of the US Army War College to the Chief of Staff, US Army. 4 February 1914.

Memorandum from the President, US Army War College, to the Chief of Staff, US Army. 10 April 1915. National Archives, Record Group 165.

Memoranda from Faculty Members to the Commandant, US Army General Staff College re: Haan Letter. April 1919.

Memorandum from the Commandant, US Army War College to the Chief of Staff, US Army. 26 June 1919.

Memorandum from the Commandant, US Army General Staff College, to the Adjutant General, US Army. 29 September 1919.

Memorandum from the Commandant, US Army General Staff College, to the Adjutant General, US Army. 29 June 1920.

Memorandum from the Commandant, US Army War College, to the Chief of Staff, US Army. 26 July 1921.

Memorandum of the Commandant. 26 July 1921.

Memorandum from the Chief, Historical Division, US Army War College, to the President, US Army War College. 22 October 1923.

Memorandum: Duties of the General Staff Group of the Faculty. 22 July 1952.

Memorandum. 24 September 1954.

Memorandum from the Deputy Commandant, US Army War College, to the Faculty. 2 June 1953.

Memorandum from the Deputy Commandant, US Army War College, to the Chairman, Faculty Group I. 9 November 1953.

Memorandum from the Chairman, Faculty Group I, to the Deputy Commandant, US Army War College. 9 November 1953.

Memorandum for the Commandant: Comprehensive Review of the Army War College Curriculum. 13 September 1957.

Memorandum from the Deputy Commandant, US Army War College, to the Faculty. 30 September 1960.

Memorandum from the Deputy Commandant, US Army War College, to the Faculty. 12 December 1960.

Memorandum 600-2, 15 September 1966.

Minutes of the Academic Board Meetings, 1920-1940.

Minutes of the Curriculum Board Meeting, 1963-67.

Minutes of the Faculty Board Meetings, 1953-1963.

Missions, Functions, and Responsibilities of the Army War College.

Movement of the Army War College to Carlisle Barracks, Pa. 10 April 1951.

Organization Charts. 1950-1967.

Organization of the US Army War College, 1950-67.

Orientation Lecture of the Commandant to the Class of 1922. 6 September 1921.

Policy File, 1957-67.

Professional Development of the USAWC Faculty Member, 1964.

Record Files 1901-17, 1919-40, and 1950-67. These files contain information regarding the internal activities of the Army War College as well as correspondence with individuals and agencies outside the College.

Redesignation of the US Army War College as a Class II Activity, 1960.

Report of the Board of Consultants. 23 February 1967.

Report of the Civilian Advisory Group. January 1952.

Report of the Civilian Advisory Group. January 1954.

Report of the Civilian Advisory Group. February 1962.

Report of the Committee on Faculty Development. 15 March 1965.

Report of the Lange Committee. 7 December 1964.

Reports of Staff and Faculty Meetings, 1959-63.

Report of the Secretary, US Army War College. 22 October 1954.

Responsibilities and Support Requirements of the Army War College, 1957.

Review of the George Washington University Program. 14 March 1963.

Senior Reserve Component Officers Course of Instruction, 1964-67.

Statistical Analysis.

Statistical Comparisons Prepared by the Special Studies Group. 20 September 1963.

Statue of Frederick the Great.

Student Comments 1936-40.

Subjects of Major Importance to the Professional Army Officer. 26 February 1964.

Summary of the History of the General Staff with Supporting Exhibits. 1915. Bound typescript in the US Army War College Library, Carlisle Barracks, Pa.

Support Requirements and Establishment of the Advanced Study Group, 1957-58.

Tactical Guide for Instruction in Tactics, 1908-1909. Bound typescript dated 13 November 1908 in the US Army War College Library, Carlisle Barracks, Pa.

USAWC Background Files, Studies, and Projects, 1964.

USAWC Periodical, 1952-58.

USAWC Positions for the Department of the Army Board to Review Army Officer Schools and Other Background Papers for the Haines Board. 1965.

US Army War College Scrapbook. Collection of clippings and photographs, National War College Library, Ft. McNair, Washington, D. C.

War Department General Staff and Its Relation to Other War Department Agencies. Typescript lecture, author unknown, 30 September 1929.

The White Paper of the Army War College, Class of 1914-15. Bound typescript in the National War College Library, Ft. McNair, Washington, D. C.

US Department of Defense. Assistant Secretary, Manpower. Officer Education Study. July 1966.

US Department of the Army. Entries under each major category (General Orders, Letters, Memoranda, etc.) are arranged chronologically by date. The source materials listed can be found in the US Army Military History Research Collection, Carlisle Barracks, Pa., unless otherwise indicated.

Army Regulation 350-104, 15 December 1958.

Army Regulation 350-104, 29 July 1960.

Army Regulation 350-2, 25 January 1966.

Army Regulation 350-5, 26 October 1966.

Pamphlet 20-21: The Army School Catalog. June 1953, June 1954, May 1957, May 1961, August 1962.

Pamphlet 350-10: US Army Formal Schools Catalog. February 1965.

Circular 16, 3 March 1952.

Circular 621-1, 12 January 1966.

General Order 19, 16 June 1960.

General Order 19, 22 April 1963.

Interim Report of the Board for Establishment of an Army War College. (Eddy Board). 24 October 1949.

Letter from the Adjutant General: Letter of Instruction to Brigadier General Ludlow. 20 February 1900.

Letter from the Adjutant General to the Board for Establishment of an Army War College. 4 October 1949.

Letter from the Chief of Staff, US Army, to the Commanding General, Continental Army Command, 3 June 1960.

Letter from the Deputy Chief of Staff for Personnel, Department of the Army, to Officers Selected for the Army War College. 14 March 1963.

Memorandum from the Acting Director of Organization and Training, US Army, to the Chief of Staff. 28 July 1948.

Memorandum of the Deputy Chief of Staff for Operations and Administration. 15 August 1951.

Modifications to Report of the Army Board on an Education System for Officers. (Eddy Board). 11 October 1949

Report of the Army Board on an Education System for Officers. (Eddy Board). 15 June 1949.

Report of the Conference of Commandants of the Army Service Schools. 1 February 1951.

Report of the Officer Education and Training Review Board. (Williams Board.) 1 July 1958.

Report of the Department of the Army Board to Review Army Officer Schools. (Haines Board). February 1966.

Special Regulation 350-20-1, 17 March 1949.

Special Regulation 350-20-1, 17 March 1952.

Special Regulation 350-5-4, 30 July 1953.

US Joint Board. (Army-Navy). Number 346, Serial Number 98. 15 July 1920.

US War Department. Same as Department of the Army.

Annual Report of the Chief of Staff, US Army, 1917.

Annual Report of the Secretary of War, 1899-1940.

Army Register, 1905-67.

Bulletin 16, 22 June 1916.

Circular 286, 3 June 1919.

Circular 117, 23 April 1946.

Correspondence between the Chief of the War Plans Division, War Department General Staff, and the Commandant, US Army War College. November 1924.

Correspondence between the Secretary of War and the Commandant, US Army War College. March 1925.

Correspondence between the Chief of Staff, US Army, and the Commandant, US Army War College. April 1927.

Correspondence from the Adjutant General to the Commandant, US Army War College. 1933-39.

Establishment of a General Staff Corps in the Army. Statements by the Secretary of War to the House and Senate Committees, 1902. Washington, D. C.: US Government Printing Office, 1902.

Final Report of the War Department Policies and Programs Review Board. (Haislip Board). 11 August 1947.

General Order 76, 1 June 1900.

General Order 155, 27 November 1901.

General Order 2, 15 August 1903.

General Order 115, 27 June 1904.

General Order 155, 17 September 1904.

General Order 116, 28 May 1907.

General Order 208, 9 October 1907.

General Order 104, 24 June 1908.

General Order 141, 19 June 1909.

General Order 13, 27 February 1914.

General Order 99, 7 August 1919.

General Order 112, 23 September 1919.

General Order 7, 3 January 1920.

General Order 56, 14 September 1920.

General Order 40, 15 August 1921.

General Staff Corps. Washington, D. C.: US Government Printing Office, 1912.

General Staff Corps Regulations. 1909.

Legislative History of the General Staff of the Army of the United States. Washington, D. C.: US Government Printing Office, 1901.

Letter from the Chief of Staff to the President, US Army War College. 27 October 1903. National Archives Record Group 165.

Letter from the Military Secretary of the General Staff to the President, US Army War College. 9 June 1905.

Letter from the Secretary of War to the President, US Army War College. 17 April 1915.

Letter from the Chief, War Plans Division, War Department General Staff, to the Commandant, US Army General Staff College. 23 April 1919.

Letter from the Adjutant General to the Commandant, US Army General Staff College. 24 September 1919.

Letter from the Adjutant General to the Chiefs of the Arms and Services. 4 September 1920.

Letter from the Chief, War Plans Division, War Department General Staff, to the Commandant, US Army General Staff College. 12 July 1920.

Letter from the Chief, War Plans Division, War Department General Staff, to the Commandant, US Army War College. 18 March 1921.

Letter from the Chief of Staff to the Commandant, US Army War College. 2 June 1922.

Letter from the Adjutant General to the Commandant, US Army War College. 22 December 1927.

Letter from the Adjutant General to the Commandant, US Army War College. 11 June 1940.

Manual of the War College Division, General Staff, 1915.

Memorandum of the Chief of the Second Section, War Department General Staff, 27 June 1908.

Memorandum from the Chief, Second Section, War Department General Staff to the Chief of Staff, US Army. 31 August 1910.

Memorandum of the Chief of Staff, US Army. 26 September 1910. National Archives, Record Group 165.

Memorandum from the Chief of Staff, US Army, to the President, US Army War College. 26 September 1913.

Memorandum from the Chief of Staff, US Army, to the Joint Army-Navy Board. 30 March 1920.

The National Defense. Documents Relating to the Reorganization Plans of the War Department and the Present National Defense Act. Washington, D. C.: US Government Printing Office, 1927.

Organization of the Land Forces of the United States. Washington, D. C.: US Government Printing Office, 1912.

Report of Board of Officers Appointed to Prepare Programs of Instruction for General and Special Service Schools. (Fisk Board). 1922.

Report of Proceedings of Board of Officers Appointed to Study the Army School System. (McGlachlin Board). 1922.

Report of the War Department Military Education Board. (Gerow Board). 1946.

Special Order 42, 19 February 1900.

Special Order 123, 1907.

Special Order 130, 15 June 1913.

The Staff Departments of the United States Army. Washington, D. C.: US Government Printing Office, 1900.

Staffs of Various Armies. Washington, D. C.: US Government Printing Office, 1899.

Upton, Emory. The Armies of Europe and Asia. New York: D. Appleton and Co., 1878.

————————— The Military Policy of the United States from 1775. Washington, D. C.: US Government Printing Office, 1904.

Vincent, Thomas M. A Plea for the Staff of the Army of the United States. March 1870. Pamphlet in the National War College Library, Ft. McNair, Washington, D. C.

Wagner, Arthur L. "An American War College." Journal of the Military Service Institution, Vol. X, No. XXXIX, July 1889, pp. 287-304.

Wainwright, Jay M. Address to the Class of 1921, US Army General Staff College. 1 June 1921.

Wallace, David C. Training for Higher Staff and Command As Practiced at the Army War College in the Fall of 1953. Unpublished thesis study in the Army War College Library, Carlisle Barracks, Pa.

Weigley, Russel F. Towards an American Army. New York: Columbia University Press, 1962.

————————— History of the United States Army. New York: MacMillan and Company, 1967.

Wermouth, Anthony L. P. Memorandum: AWC Publications, 9 July 1959.

Wheeler, Earle G. Letter to the Commandant, US Army War College. 16 May 1965.

Whitson, W. W. Role of the United States Army War College in the Preparation of Officers for National Security Policy Formulation. Thesis presented to the faculty of the Fletcher School of Law and Diplomacy. 1 May 1958.

Wilkinson, Spencer. Brain of an Army. London: Constable & Company, 1913.

Wood, Leonard. America's Duty, As Shown by Our Military History, Its Facts and Fallacies. Chicago: Reilly & Lee Co., 1921.

————————— The Military Obligation of Citizenship. Princeton: Princeton University Press, 1915.

Wotherspoon, William W. Lecture to the Naval War College. August 1910.

Young, A. J. Correspondence with the Commandant, US Army War College. December 1938.

Zais, Melvin. Office of the Deputy Chief of Staff for Personnel, Department of the Army. Interview, 14 February 1967.

Zalinski, E. L. "The Army Organization, Best Adapted to a Republican Form of Government, Which Will insure an Effective Force." Journal of the Military Service Institution, Vol. XIV, No. 65, September 1893, pp. 926-977.

INDEX

INDEX

A

Aberdeen Proving Ground, Maryland, 107.
Academic Board, 107,239.
Academic Degrees, 131-132,170,175,203, 207
Academic Freedom, 159.
Adjutant General, 5, 123.
Adjutant General School, Carlisle Barracks, Pennsylvania, 159.
Adler, Julius Ochs, 163.
Advanced Course (Army War College Course), 146,154.
Advanced Study Group, 181,183,186,190, 192,193,209.
Aeronautics, 51.
Ahern, George Patrick, 43,82.
Ailes, Stephen, 274.
Air University, Maxwell Air Force Base, Alabama, 148.
Air War College, 144,147,256,276.
Airpower, 122.
Alexander the Great (Statue), 45.
Almond, Edward Mallory, 161,162,165-170,174,187.
Alumni Association, 283-284.
American Council on Education, 170,207.
American Expeditionary Forces, 92,95, 100.
American Historical Association, 75.
American Library Association, 185.
American Red Cross, 119.
American Relief Expedition, 79.
American Telephone and Telegraph Company, 80-81.
Antietam Battlefield, 53,107.
Archibald, James F. J., 42.
Armed Forces College, Fort Leavenworth, Kansas, 142.
Armed Forces Staff College, Norfolk, Virginia, 143,144,165.
Army
  Administrative Services, 102-103,105-106.
  Chief of Staff, 31,33,36,58,64,74,76,84, 124,166.
  Doctrine, 179,210,232,259.

Educational System, 89-90, 140-141, 143-145,152,227,253,263.
  History, (See Military History).
  Mobilization Requirements, 161.
  Mobilization Training Doctrine, 157.
  Second Army, 210.
  Technical Services, 102-103,106.
Army Air Force School of Tactics, Orlando, Florida, 140.
Army Field Forces, 151,169,170,172.
Army Ground Forces, 139,140.
Army Industrial College, 124,141,143.
Army Information School, Carlisle Barracks, Pennsylvania, 159.
Army Medical School, 6.
Army Military History Group, 175.
Army-Navy Cooperation, 37,46,102,108, 118.
Army-Navy Staff College, 140-141.
ARMY REGISTER, 46.
Army University, 148,149,154.
Army War College,
  Buildings
    Dedication, 60.
    22 Jackson Place, Washington, D.C., 22,23,45,54.
    Lemon Building, 45,54.
    New Academic, Carlisle Barracks, 271.
    See also: Washington Barracks; Carlisle Barracks, Pennsylvania; Root Hall; Bliss Hall
  Chief of Staff, 239.
  Coat of Arms, 68,70,127.
  Department of Military Planning, 237, 238.
  Department of Strategic Appraisal, 237, 238.
  Department of Strategy, 237,238.
  Director of Instruction and Research, 237,238,239,277,283.
  Doctrine and Studies Division, 210.
  Graduating Classes
    1st: 40,41.
    50th: 265-266
    Bronze Plaque: 127.

Marston, Anson Day, 149.
Marzke, Oscar T., 214.
Masland, John W., 182.
Medical Field Service School, Carlisle Barracks, Pennsylvania, 159.
Mershon Center for Education in National Security, Ohio State University, 229.
Mexican War, 77,78,83,105,283.
See also: Pancho Villa
Mexico, 37,48,129.
Michie, Robert E.L., 40.
Middleton, Troy H., 163.
Miles, Nelson, 18,283.
Military Education Coordination Conference, 211.
Military History, 53-55,75-76,79,85,98,125, 187-188,283.
See also: Comparative Military Strategy Seminar
Military History Research Collection, 272-274,277,283.
Military Information Committee, 57.
Military Information Division, 57.
Military planning, 50-51,81,94,101-102, 171,178.
MILITARY REVIEW, 213.
Military Strategy Seminar, 279,280.
See also: Comparative Military Strategy Seminar
Militia, 48.
Miller, Eugene H., 281.
Miller, Jessie A., 282.
Miller, Troup, 130.
Mills, Alfred L., 73-74.
Mitchell, William, 122.
Monographs, 49,52,57.
Moore, George D., 70.
Moore, James E., 176,177,179-181,186-187, 189,190.
Morgenthau, Henry, 106.
Morris, Thomas D., 262.
Morton, Charles G., 40,42,46.

N

Napoleon (Statue), 45.
National Archives, 132.
National Defense Act, 1916, 81-82, 83.
National Defense Act, 1920, 135.
National Guard, 99,113,131.
See also: Students, National Guard and Reserve Forces
National Security University, 142.

National Strategy Seminar, 175,176,185-186,191,194,199,201,223,252,270.
National War College, 143,144,145,146, 148,151,159,163,165,166,276.
Naval War College, 33,37,48,49,50,55, 66,77,78,80,108,116,118,140,143,256,276.
See also: Army-Navy Cooperation
Newport News, Virginia, 50.
Nimitz, Chester B., 137.
Nonresident Course, (See Correspondence Course)
North Atlantic Community, 222,249,266.
Nugent, George, 77.

O

O'Brien, Harold, 281,282.
OCCASIONAL PAPERS, 245.
Officers' Reserve Corps, 113.
Ohio State University (See Mershon Center for Education in National Security)
Oliver, Robert T., 281,282.
O'Ryan, John F., 76.

P

Pacific Division, 42.
Paley, George, 75.
Panama Canal Zone, 55,129.
Pancho Villa, 81.
Parker, Frank, 230.
Partisan Activities, 157.
Pass-a-Grillo, Florida, 149.
Patton, George S., 136,283.
Paymaster General, 5.
Peer Rating System (See Student Evaluation)
Pershing, John J., 40,46,87,104,119-121.
See also: General John J. Pershing Chair of Military Planning
Peyton, Philip B., 129,139.
Philippine Constabulary, 37.
Philippine Islands, 11,37,43,55,57,64,118, 129.
Philippine Scouts, 37.
Plattsburg Barracks, New York, 101.
Poland, 106.
Polk, James K., 174-176,179,185.
Pond, Dana, 119.
Powell, Ralph L., 274.
Preliminary Course, 58-60,63,71.
Princeton University (See Woodrow Wilson School of Public and International Affairs)

Index

LITHO BY WALSWORTH PUB. CO., INC., MARCELINE, MO.